Approaches to Teaching Blake's
Songs of Innocence and of Experience

Edited by

Robert F. Gleckner

and

Mark L. Greenberg

The Modern Language Association of America
New York   1989

©1989 by The Modern Language Association of America
All rights reserved. Printed in the United States of America
Fourth printing 2001

For information about obtaining permission to reprint material from
MLA book publications, send your request by mail (see address below),
e-mail (permissions@mla.org), or fax (646 458-0030).

Library of Congress Cataloging-in-Publication Data

Approaches to teaching Blake's Songs of innocence and of experience
edited by Robert F. Gleckner and Mark L. Greenberg.
p. cm. — (Approaches to teaching world literature ; 21)
Bibliography: p.
Includes index.
ISBN 0-87352-517-5   ISBN 0-87352-518-3 (pbk.)
1. Blake, William, 1757–1827.   Songs of innocence and of experience.
2. Blake, William, 1757–1827—Study and teaching.
I. Gleckner, Robert F.   II. Greenberg, Mark L., 1948–   . III. Series.
PR4144.S63A67   1989
821'.7 — dc19   88-7588

ISSN 1059-1133

Cover illustration of the paperback edition: William Blake, frontispiece,
Songs of Innocence, engraving, 1789.

Set in Caledonia and Bodoni. Printed on recycled paper

Published by The Modern Language Association of America
26 Broadway, New York, New York 10004-1789
www.mla.org

CONTENTS

PREFACE TO THE SERIES

In *The Art of Teaching* Gilbert Highet wrote, "Bad teaching wastes a great deal of effort, and spoils many lives which might have been full of energy and happiness." All too many teachers have failed in their work, Highet argued, simply "because they have not thought about it." We hope that the Approaches to Teaching World Literature series, sponsored by the Modern Language Association's Committee on Teaching and Related Professional Activities, will not only improve the craft—as well as the art—of teaching but also encourage serious and continuing discussion of the aims and methods of teaching literature.

The principal objective of the series is to collect within each volume different points of view on teaching a specific literary work, a literary tradition, or a writer widely taught at the undergraduate level. The preparation of each volume begins with a wide-ranging survey of instructors, thus enabling us to include in the volume the philosophies and approaches, thoughts and methods of scores of experienced teachers. The result is a sourcebook of material, information, and ideas on teaching the subject of the volume to undergraduates.

The series is intended to serve nonspecialists as well as specialists, inexperienced as well as experienced teachers, graduate students who wish to learn effective ways of teaching as well as senior professors who wish to compare their own approaches with the approaches of colleagues in other schools. Of course, no volume in the series can ever substitute for erudition, intelligence, creativity, and sensitivity in teaching. We hope merely that each book will point readers in useful directions; at most each will offer only a first step in the long journey to successful teaching.

Joseph Gibaldi
Series Editor

PREFACE TO THE VOLUME

We intend this volume to offer teachers and students of Blake's *Songs* useful information, challenging ideas, perhaps even inspiration for revising or redirecting current pedagogy. One of the Proverbs of Hell also reminds us that "The eagle never lost so much time. as when he submitted to learn of the crow" (E 37). Readers, we trust, will "submit" only to what they find compelling in this volume. Indeed, we delight in imagining fruitful class discussions emanating from significant disagreements with approaches offered here.

Despite most Blakeans' penchant for mental fight, this book's existence rests upon the extraordinary cooperation and selfless generosity that characterize Blake studies (especially at moments of mutually affirming intellectual engagement). In response to our request for detailed answers to the twenty-three questions of our questionnaire, seventy-one teachers from seven nations around the world offered us their classroom experiences, teaching materials, and ideas. Following our analysis of the questionnaires, we invited sixteen experienced teachers of the *Songs* to elaborate their pedagogical theories and practices in the essays that follow. In addition, Mary Lynn Johnson and John E. Grant fashioned a splendidly full essay on visual resources for teaching the *Songs*, augmented by Brian Wilkie's practical experiences using microfiches in the classroom. These generous contributions have made possible the production of this volume—a collaboration not only between editors but among members of the community of readers and scholars engendered by Blake's work.

The editors are especially indebted to Joseph Gibaldi, series editor, for his encouragement, shrewd guidance, and care with our ideas and manuscript, and also to his staff at the MLA. We are grateful to the members of the MLA's Committee on Teaching and Related Professional Activities for recognizing the importance of a volume devoted to Blake's *Songs* and for sponsoring the series in which it appears. We thank Gregory Forbes for making available to us his recorded musical settings for some of the *Songs* and the companion volume (available from Quarry Press, Kingston, ON K7L 4Y5) and also thank George Gopen for alerting us to other such settings. By kindly sharing with us the subscription list to *Blake: An Illustrated Quarterly*, Morris Eaves helped us reach many teachers of Blake. Paula Marantz Cohen, a colleague at Drexel University, offered valuable criticism during final preparation of the manuscript. Finally, we wish to record our deep thanks to Drexel University and especially to Dean Thomas L. Canavan of its College of Humanities and Social Sciences for recognizing the value of this project and supporting it generously throughout.

We cannot think and write about teaching without recalling the teachers who taught us how to think and, by the examples of their lives, how to live. To them and to generations of students, we dedicate this book.

RFG
MLG

INTRODUCTION:
TEACHING BLAKE'S *SONGS*

William Blake inscribed in his notebook a "Motto to the Songs of Innocence & of Experience," which he never incorporated into the work. In characteristically simple language, the first stanza traces a process of "education" that results in a fall into experience:

> The Good are attracted by Mens perceptions
> And Think not for themselves
> Till Experience teaches them to catch
> And to cage the Fairies & Elves   (E 499)

Passive, innocent minds (however "good" they are according to the prevailing criteria) become imaginatively imprisoned, Blake says, when they "Think not for themselves." Teaching his readers to think for themselves, to avoid or reverse the process sketched above, to free the "Fairies & Elves" of imagination, was a lifelong project to which he dedicated himself with extraordinary energy and devotion. Teaching Blake's teachings, however, challenges the best instructors. Although Blake "considered what is not too Explicit as the fittest for Instruction because it rouzes the faculties to act" and would not "Elucidate" his "Ideas," the form and substance of his work rouse, even demand, us to attempt such elucidation. In this book we aim to offer teachers of the *Songs* a range of options for responding to that work's powerful demands.

Ever since S. Foster Damon's pioneering *William Blake: His Philosophy and Symbols* (1924) and its extraordinary successor, Northrop Frye's *Fearful Symmetry* (1947), increasing numbers of teachers and students have taken up Blake's challenge; in the past quarter century that challenge has been interpreted even more widely to include Blake's unique "composite art" of verbal-visual form. As the responses to our survey of Blake instructors indicate, nearly everyone who studies Blake begins with the *Songs of Innocence and of Experience*; indeed, many students have no other acquaintance with Blake. Selections from it (occasionally the whole work) appear in virtually every anthology of English literature and are taught in a wide range of introductory and advanced courses. As a result, the *Songs* is Blake's best-known and most widely read work, and for most readers, with or without a substantial grasp of his entire career, it ranks somewhat ahead of Blake's other compositions as a "masterpiece" of world literature. Moreover, it has endured and reanimated itself, without becoming saturated or overwhelmed, through its extraordinary appeal to various critical approaches and interpretations.

For nearly two centuries, imaginative readers of the *Songs* have poured out readings of separate poems and of their graphic elements, even of isolated individual plates; analyses of the work's two main components and of specific companion poems in *Innocence* and *Experience*; and, of course, treatments of the whole as a unified, coherent book. The many current editions of the *Songs* and the abundant materials relating to it (detailed in the "Materials" section of this book) testify to the work's continuing importance in Blake studies and in the study of literature generally. Given such abundance, we believe that instructors will welcome a comprehensive—if not exhaustive—guide to the various editions and ancillary materials. In addition, the second part of this volume, a collection of diverse approaches to this rich work, may prove especially useful to those who hold with Blake that a single, privileged interpretation—"One Law for the Lion & Ox"—is "Oppression." Although these essays can hardly represent all possible ways of engaging the *Songs*, we believe they represent fruitful and provocative critical avenues that supplement and complement those available in the sources we cite in part 1 of this book, "Materials." We have also included approaches to teaching the work that are determined, at least in part, by departmental and institutional contexts; in certain types of institutions, for instance, one is more likely to find students who begin their study of an eighteenth-century visionary poet and engraver skeptically or antipathetically, though they may ultimately learn that "Opposition is true Friendship"—the "Friendship" produced by critical mental fight.

The design of this volume conforms, in part, to the experimental, provocative, highly original, and often playful spirit of Blake's art, even as it raises important theoretical problems and related pedagogical challenges in teaching not only Blake's *Songs* but all literature. Blake was himself a master teacher. He believed that teaching "man to think he's a free agent" (E 431) was perhaps the chief goal of art. That is, his art constitutes a verbal-graphic strategy that, imaginatively grasped, can liberate the reader from the tyranny of orthodoxies of various kinds. Blake teaches not by precept but by design, and his designs resonate through networks of associations. Consequently, critical and interpretive issues in the *Songs* virtually demand careful pedagogy, their verbal-graphic configurations insisting upon a *modus educandi* or form of class discussion in which scholarship and theory conspire with pedagogy. In ways that Blake would have found satisfying, the theoretical essays that follow ground their ideas in specific examples, and the more practical essays rest on theoretical foundations carefully articulated by their authors.

In every selection from Blake's works, in every anthology in which Blake appears, the *Songs* is the most fully represented of all Blake's compositions. In its own time and on into the nineteenth century, it was the only one of Blake's books to win public admiration, its fame preceding his posthumous acclaim by more than a generation. Yet Blake laboriously hand produced relatively few copies of the *Songs*. The history of its reception, in fact, offers an important lesson to students about how poetic works—and their authors— become canonized, bringing into focus the larger issue of canon formation. Blake printed and individually hand colored *Songs of Innocence* and *Songs of Innocence and of Experience* from 1789 to 1818. Twenty-one copies of *Innocence* and twenty-eight of the combined work are known to exist. No two are alike, Blake having altered his coloring more often than not, his arrangement, and even certain aspects of the plates' iconography from copy to copy. Wordsworth and his circle "admired individual poems which were occasionally reprinted in biographical notices and elsewhere" (Bentley, *Books* 383). Wordsworth copied three poems from the *Songs* into his commonplace book ("Holy Thursday" of *Innocence*, "Laughing Song," and "The Tyger") and said to Henry Crabb Robinson after reading a "number" of the *Songs*, "there is no doubt this poor man was mad, but there is something in the madness of this man which interests me more than the Sanity of Lord Byron & Walter Scott!" (Bentley, *Records* 536). Crabb Robinson transcribed portions of the *Songs* and read them to Hazlitt; Coleridge selected poems he especially liked and even ranked them according to his own responses; and Charles Lamb thought "The Tyger" was "glorious" when he heard it. Copies of the *Songs* were owned by important readers in nineteenth-century England, including Samuel Rogers, John Linnell, John Flaxman, T. F. Dibdin, Isaac D'Israeli, and Crabb Robinson. The work was first reprinted in letterpress in 1839—twenty-four years before Gilchrist's *Life of Blake* introduced the artist and his other works to a startled though generally appreciative Victorian audience. Bentley records twenty-eight reprintings of the *Songs* through 1977—far more than any other Blake book—in a variety of letterpress and illustrated editions, and the annual bibliographies in *Blake: An Illustrated Quarterly* add to that number each year. Currently, four illuminated editions are in print (one of *Innocence*, one of *Experience*, and two of the combined work), and of course the work appears whole or in part, occasionally with sample facsimiles (in color or black and white), in a wide variety of editions, selections, and anthologies.

It is hardly surprising, then, that the responses to our survey show that the *Songs* remains Blake's most widely taught work, included in courses from the most elementary introductions to literature or poetry to graduate seminars, as well as in religious studies courses, general humanities courses, even composition courses. How can we explain this book's continuing fascination? At the core of any answer to this question, we believe, is that despite the *Songs'* general familiarity to a wide range, and increasing number, of readers, it continually tests neophytes and experts alike. Manifold problems of interpretation, often emerging from classroom experience and treated in the voluminous and expanding scholarship on the poems, translate into specific teaching challenges, many of which are addressed in the approaches that follow. Pedagogical problems become possible issues of critical discourse in class; these problems range from the minute particulars of Blake's language and punctuation (and their relation to common eighteenth-century practice) to considerations of what, for Blake and other poets, constitutes "writing" and "the book." Apparently simple poems raise complex theoretical issues, a point underscored in recent discussions of "London" by Jonathan Culler ("Semiotics as a Theory of Reading," *Pursuit* 68–79) and of "The Tyger" by Stanley Fish (259–63, 339–42, 348–50).

Blake called his work *Songs*. What, some contributors to this volume ask, is Blake's "idea" of "song"? He introduced that deceptively simple title word in the 1783 *Poetical Sketches*, carried it over to *Song of Los* (1795), and used it to identify several sections of his major prophecies, perhaps most strikingly (and sweepingly) at the close of his magnum opus, *Jerusalem*: "The End of the Song of Jerusalem." If the *Songs* are songs in the conventional sense, why does the child in the "Introduction" to *Innocence* direct the piper to inscribe them "In a book that all may read"? Furthermore, this first song challenges us immediately to examine Blake's ideas of "reading" and "writing," since the piper concludes his "Introduction" with "I *wrote* my happy songs / Every child may joy to *hear*" (emphasis added).

Contributors also consider how to approach in class the evocativeness and deliberate ambiguity with which Blake endows each poem by his deliberate use of polysemous language and his revaluing of traditional symbols; how to express Blake's relation to contemporary theories of language and evaluate his response to the cultural effects of words' shifting definitions; and how to assess Blake's incorporation and transvaluation of the Bible. The essays also discuss how teachers may introduce their students to the poems' problematic points of view, their frequently unspecified speakers, and the psychological states these speakers embody. Such issues, of course, raise fundamental questions about interpretation, about the limits of interpretation, and about what constitutes a "good" or a "better" reading of a poem—questions that involve teachers and students in the consideration of aesthetic values and ideologies, as well as of the methodological problems inherent in any reading of a text.

Many poems in the *Songs* not only reflect but criticize aspects of eighteenth-century life—social, political, religious, economic, philosophical, sexual, and familial. By addressing the work's attitude—or its changing attitudes—toward particular issues and institutions, several contributors suggest ways of exploring relations among such socially constructed enterprises as literature, art, science, and technology. Indeed, a few contributors urge us to teach *Songs*, at least partially, by concentrating on the processes of its material production—to comprehend the work *as* a technological achievement.

Blake's art also prompts questions about art's relation to art—to traditional and contemporary practices—and about specific connections between *Songs* and other texts. Blake's first major effort at a new poetic-visual form, the *Songs* provokes us to explore the relation of each plate's graphic components to its writing, to probe Blake's composite art for its affinities with existing graphic art and illuminated manuscripts, its uniqueness, the craft involved in its production, and the values that inhere in technological choices. Because the *Songs* is Blake's first major composite artwork, its formal conditions deserve special study, a point worth keeping in mind, especially by students of Blake's prophecies, who are familiar with the development of his composite art. Furthermore, the *Songs* poses the problem of what, for Blake, constitutes a "book," as distinct from a collection of poems or an anthology (an especially pertinent question since so many students encounter the work in anthologies). Since Blake titled several of his engraved works "The Book of . . ." and divided even so late a work as *Jerusalem* into chapters, discussing the book as the unit of composition seems especially useful for students of Blake's prophecies; it should also aid students of the other Romantics (as Fraistat has demonstrated) and of Yeats, Pound, Stevens, Crane, Williams, and the modern long poem.

The subtitle of the *Songs*, *Shewing the Two Contrary States of the Human Soul*, which Blake added only after completing the *Songs of Experience* and yoking them with *Innocence* as an integral book, evokes in its seeming simplicity a host of problems that contributors to our volume consider as pedagogical possibilities and stimulants to critical thinking. What Blake means by a "state" or "states" is especially important in the light of his repeated references to these words and extensive comments on the ideas they embody, particularly in *Milton*, the prose work "A Vision of the Last Judgment," *Jerusalem*, and his letters. What is a "state of the human soul"? And what precisely can be said about the relation between "states" (or ideas) of innocence and of experience? In what ways, several essayists ask, do these categories accord with religious tradition and epistemology or call into question past assumptions?

Blake's shifting arrangements of the poems in his book show that he also wrestled not only with the interplay between Innocence and Experience but with the various interrelations among the songs that embody these states. Four of the *Songs of Experience* first appeared among *Songs of Innocence*, and Blake subsequently transferred them when he assembled the combined work. In no two copies of *Innocence* are the plates arranged in exactly the same order. In the twenty-eight extant copies of the combined volume, Blake offers nineteen different arrangements of poems. We cannot be certain of the order in which the copies were produced—though it may be crucial to interpretation—since the dates of many copies remain conjectural.

These varying arrangements pose for the reader a number of problems that involve the dynamics of poetic relations and the idea of context. A minimal shuffling of the order of, say, three poems creates a new "local" context, which, in turn, enforces a new larger context in each half book as well as in the whole of the *Songs*. The architectonics of Blake's book, then, powerfully affects what we can say about the relation of each song to poems adjoining or surrounding it, to poems in its respective half of the work, and to all the poems in the book that all "may joy to read." Important theoretical questions thus present themselves for class discussion: How does one determine the interpretive implications and relevance of such shifting contexts (especially in the light of our inability to determine the chronology of the *Songs*' various orders)? How do these changes affect our view of the counterpoint between the states of Innocence and Experience and among the poems that embody each state? What relations exist between poems in *Innocence* and their similarly or identically titled counterparts in *Experience*—or between those whose connection is less obvious? To what degree and in what perceivable ways do the two states interpenetrate? At the very minimum, Blake's reorderings open to question isolated interpretations of individual songs, readings across the work, and the kinds of relational networks a sensitive reader might discover or construct. Finally, Blake's constant experiment and play in the *Songs* (in addition to the abundant prior evidence of variation in his notebook drafts) also suggest something about not only his but any poet's process of composition. Virtually every respondent to our survey acknowledged some awareness of this problem, though many admitted that they merely mention it to students without fully elaborating its consequences or its applicability to other approaches to the *Songs*.

The fixed ordering of the poems imposed by currently available texts may depress or even forestall the critical freedom to reconstruct (and then discuss the effects rendered by) Blake's differing arrangements. This exigency of the publishing industry thus highlights the conjunction of bibliographic, interpretive, pedagogical, and perhaps even economic problems in the *Songs*. As Joseph Gibaldi points out in his *Approaches to Teaching Chaucer's* Canterbury Tales, "textbook selection determines in a number of different ways the nature and progress of a literature course" (3). The effects of choosing a text for the *Songs* are particularly far-reaching, because each choice partially determines the characteristics of the "Blake" as well as the "*Songs*" that students read and discuss, despite the poet's concerted efforts to overcome such determinacy. Even "complete" composite editions in color of one copy of the *Songs* present but one state of a work that Blake altered in color, visual design, and arrangement each time he printed and painted it; the instructor (constrained by the chosen edition of the work) thus fixes a text that was continually changing in its author's hands.

Blake began working on *Songs of Innocence* in 1784 or 1785; the earliest copies of the complete work bear the etched date 1789. The combined volume is dated 1794, though, as we have noted, Blake transferred four poems from *Innocence* to *Experience* and had been drafting songs for *Experience* in his notebook as early as 1790. While he was composing most of *Experience* he was also inventing, etching, printing, and selling *The Book of Thel, The Marriage of Heaven and Hell, Visions of the Daughters of Albion,* and *For Children: The Gates of Paradise*; in addition, he was composing *Tiriel*, a poetic text accompanied by sepia illustrations, and a symbolic epic entitled *The French Revolution* (only one "book" of its advertised seven is extant, in radical publisher Joseph Johnson's proof sheets). Consequently, students of the *Songs* confront the problems inherent in the passage of time between the completion of *Innocence* and that of the combined volume; the contemporaneous composition of other poems greatly expanded the context within which the *Songs*, when complete, falls. The question of context thus opens beyond the scope of this volume to considerations of the *Songs'* place in Blake's corpus, engendering thereby related problems about the legitimacy, in interpreting the *Songs*, of relying not only on Blake's contemporary works, letters, and notebook but on his later writings as well. Issues radiating from study of the *Songs*, furthermore, introduce students to the kinds of problems they will face in interpreting Blake's other compositions. Ultimately, the critical thinking stimulated by sophisticated study of this complex creation will heighten students' ability to question deeply, to probe intellectually and imaginatively, and to enjoy other works of literature and art.

To a remarkable degree, as the essays collected below affirm, Blake anticipated contemporary issues in the study and teaching of literature and art, and the speakers of his *Songs* embody and often confront conditions or ideas that seem eternally fresh and infinitely challenging. Taken together, the approaches in this volume (each articulating a distinct and fruitful way into the text) argue that the only avenues to Blake's *Songs* worth pursuing, like the aggregation of the songs themselves, are plural—and, we believe, interanimating.

Part One

MATERIALS

Robert F. Gleckner and
Mark L. Greenberg

Texts and Reference Works

The responses to our questionnaire indicate clearly that the text most frequently used in undergraduate survey courses that include some Blake is *The Norton Anthology of English Literature* (Abrams). Other wide-ranging anthologies used include, particularly, *The Oxford Anthology of English Literature* (Kermode and Hollander) and Brian Wilkie and James Hurt's massive *Literature of the Western World*, the latter of which includes all the *Songs*. Among anthologies of the Romantic period that contain generous selections of Blake, the most popular is David Perkins's *English Romantic Writers*; John L. Mahoney's *The English Romantics* and William Heath's *Major British Poets of the Romantic Period* are less frequently adopted.

For the complete poetry or the complete works of Blake, David V. Erdman's *The Complete Poetry and Prose of William Blake* and Geoffrey Keynes's *Blake: Complete Writings* are the texts most often employed, although instructors occasionally adopt Alicia Ostriker's *William Blake: The Complete Poems* and W. H. Stevenson's Longman edition of the complete poetry, the latter containing Erdman's text. Earlier editions of either the complete poetry or complete works that are still valuable include Edwin J. Ellis and William Butler Yeats's extraordinary, if eccentric and often inaccurate, *The Works of William Blake: Poetic, Symbolic, and Critical*, in three volumes titled *The System, The Meaning*, and *The Books*; John Sampson's *The Poetical Works*, the first modern scholarly edition; and G. E. Bentley, Jr.'s *William Blake's Writings*, in two volumes with many illustrations.

Editions of Blake's graphic works include David Bindman's *The Complete Graphic Works of William Blake* and Martin Butlin's *The Paintings and Drawings of William Blake*, with Butlin's textual commentary on the plates in volume 1 and the plates themselves in volume 2.

Since the 1860s an enormous number of selected editions have appeared, most of them now out of print. They represent the work of a distinguished group of scholars and critics, not all "Blakeans," whose introductions to and notes for the selected editions may still be read with profit. We list here some of the most prominent by editors' names in chronological order of the first editions: R. H. Shepherd, W. M. Rossetti, W. B. Yeats, John Sampson, Alice Meynell, Max Plowman, Basil de Selincourt, Laurence Binyon, Alfred Kazin, Ruthven Todd, Northrop Frye, F. W. Bateson, Jacob Bronowski, Ruthven Todd again, Stanley Gardner, Robert F. Gleckner, Hazard Adams, Kathleen Raine, R. B. Kennedy, Aileen Ward, David V. Erdman, and Peter H. Butter. Of these, in late 1988 the following are still in print: Bronowski, Butter, Frye, Kazin, Plowman, Raine, Rossetti,, and Yeats. Other editors include such recognizable names as John Adlard, Arthur Quiller-Couch,

Robert S. Hillyer, Laurence Housman, Vivian de Sola Pinto, and Denis Saurat. For a critical review of many of the above, see Mary Lynn Johnson's "Choosing Textbooks for Blake Courses: A Survey and Checklist." Her checklist includes anthologies of nineteenth-century British literature, eighteenth-century anthologies, complete editions of Blake, selected editions, "Guidebooks, Introductions, and Study Aids," facsimiles and reproductions "inexpensive enough for classroom use," casebooks and essay collections, guidebooks and essay collections on Romanticism, and visual aids.

Editions of the *Songs*, either selected or complete, are virtually as numerous as those previously mentioned; since many of these are selected editions, we shall not offer the same detailed chronicling as above, except to note that separate editions of *Innocence* and *Experience* date back at least to the 1880s. Among these earlier editions (listed under "Blake" in the Works Cited), a rather surprising number are photographic facsimiles—of *Songs of Experience* by Ernest Benn in color, by Joseph Patrick Trumble, Sophia Elizabeth Muir, and William Muir in color, and by Joseph H. Wicksteed in black and white; of *Songs of Innocence* in black and white (1883; editor unknown), by Frederick Hollyer in color, by Benn in color, by Trumble and Muir in color, and by Ruthven Todd in black and white. Earlier facsimiles of the combined sets of *Songs* include the 1947 "Albion Facsimile" (reprinted in 1973 in Folcroft, PA) and the 1973 black-and-white edition published in Norwood, PA.

Of the more modern or accomplished color facsimiles, the Blake Trust edition of 1955 and the Orion Press edition of 1967 (reissued by Oxford University Press in 1970) take clear precedence. The latter is the facsimile most often used in the classroom, its distant rival being the Dover Press color facsimiles of *Songs of Innocence* and *Songs of Experience*. Black-and-white facsimiles of the complete *Songs* are also available in Joseph H. Wicksteed's *Blake's Innocence and Experience*, Erdman's *The Illuminated Blake*, Werner Hofmann's *William Blake: Lieder der Unschuld und Erfarung*, and David Bindman's *Complete Graphic Works*. Eight sample color plates appear in Mary Lynn Johnson and John E. Grant's excellent *Blake's Poetry and Designs*; Bentley's two-volume Clarendon Press edition of the complete *Writings* contains numerous facsimiles; and the Huntington Library has published sixteen facsimiles (enlarged in color) from copies E and N in its collection. Two other facsimile editions are especially pertinent to the study and teaching of Blake's *Songs of Experience*: Erdman and Donald K. Moore's *The Notebook of William Blake: A Photographic and Typographic Facsimile* and Joseph Viscomi's striking handmade and hand-colored facsimile of the *Songs*. (In connection with the latter see also Viscomi, "Recreating.") For more specific comments on these and other facsimiles, see John E. Grant and Mary Lynn Johnson's essay in this volume.

Among the most pressing desiderata for teachers of Blake's *Songs*, according to our survey, are complete color facsimiles at a moderate price (with a generous sampling of plates of the same poem from various copies of the *Songs*). A number of respondents would also find useful a loose-leaf facsimile edition of the *Songs*, in color preferably, and a variorum critical edition, either in the Johnson-Grant Norton Critical Edition format or perhaps in an adaptation of Erdman's format in *The Illuminated Blake*.

The most complete and meticulous bibliography of primary and secondary works is G. E. Bentley, Jr.'s *Blake Books*, which incorporates and substantially adds to Keynes's 1921 *Bibliography* and Bentley and Martin K. Nurmi's *A Blake Bibliography*. Annual bibliographies of new editions, facsimiles, critical books, essays, and journal articles appear in *Blake: An Illustrated Quarterly*. The most recent bibliographical essay is Mary Lynn Johnson's chapter on Blake (for *Songs* especially, see the sections entitled "Facsimiles of Illustrated Books" and "Studies of Individual Works") in *The English Romantic Poets: A Review of Research and Criticism*, edited by Frank Jordan. Teachers and their students should also note the excellent two-volume *Concordance to the Writings of William Blake*, edited by Erdman et al.; its only disadvantage is that its basic text is Keynes's 1957 edition rather than Erdman's 1965–83 editions.

The first significant biography of Blake is Alexander Gilchrist's landmark *Life of William Blake, Pictor Ignotus* (1863; 2nd ed., 1880), since 1974 available in an Everyman edition. Although Gilchrist is still of value, the "standard" biography is Mona Wilson's *The Life of William Blake* (1927), which was reset with revisions and additional notes in 1948 and reedited by Keynes in 1971. Other biographies include Michael Davis's *William Blake: A New Kind of Man* and Jack Lindsay's *William Blake: His Life and Work*. Additional biographical material, reprints of documents related to Blake's life, and the like are to be found in Bentley's useful compilation, *Blake Records*. Overlapping *Blake Records* to some extent, but useful in their own right, are two compilations of early critical commentary on Blake: Bentley's *William Blake: The Critical Heritage* and Joseph A. Wittreich's *Nineteenth-Century Accounts of William Blake*. These works should be compared to Deborah Dorfman's *Blake in the Nineteenth Century*, mentioned below.

Critical Works on Blake's Poetry and Art

Although many books listed in the next section would fit with equal appropriateness under this heading, we will not duplicate that list here (with a few notable exceptions), concentrating rather on books, essays in collections, and articles that deal broadly and informatively with Blake as a whole or that focus on other topics or works yet pertain directly to the study and teaching of the *Songs*.

Although outdated and subsequently "corrected" in a variety of ways, S. Foster Damon's *William Blake: His Philosophy and Symbols* continues to be a valuable resource. Its critical approach to Blake as a mystic, however, should be compared with that of Helen White's *The Mysticism of William Blake*, which elaborates on the wide divergence between Blake's views and traditional mysticism in its various forms. Twenty-three years after Damon's pioneering work, Northrop Frye launched the modern era of Blake criticism with his magisterial study *Fearful Symmetry*. The next landmark in Blake studies is David V. Erdman's *Blake: Prophet against Empire*, which as a historical and political explication largely supersedes Mark Schorer's *William Blake: The Politics of Vision*, though Schorer is still valuable for other reasons. A much briefer study in the same vein as Erdman's and Schorer's is Jacob Bronowski's *William Blake, 1757–1827: A Man without a Mask*. No book since 1954 has assumed anything like the stature of Frye's and Erdman's, although in our judgment Leopold Damrosch's *Symbol and Truth in Blake's Myth* is noteworthy, as is W. J. T. Mitchell's earlier *Blake's Composite Art: A Study of the Illuminated Poetry*, a book that significantly advances the study of the interrelations between the verbal and graphic elements of Blake's works.

Other general studies of Blake that we would recommend include, in alphabetical order, John Beer's *Blake's Humanism* and *Blake's Visionary Universe*, Bernard Blackstone's *English Blake*, Harold Bloom's *Blake's Apocalypse* and *The Visionary Company* (which has a section of over one hundred pages on Blake), S. Foster Damon's *A Blake Dictionary*, J. G. Davies's *The Theology of William Blake*, Deborah Dorfman's *Blake in the Nineteenth Century* (a survey of criticism from Gilchrist to Yeats), David V. Erdman and John E. Grant's collection of essays *Blake's Visionary Forms Dramatic*, Peter Fisher's *The Valley of Vision*, Thomas R. Frosch's *The Awakening of Albion*, Stanley Gardner's *Infinity on the Anvil*, George Mills Harper's *The Neoplatonism of William Blake* (cf. Kathleen Raine's book below), Margaret R. Lowery's *Windows of the Morning: A Critical Study of William Blake's* Poetical Sketches (see also Robert F. Gleckner's *Blake's Prelude:* Poetical Sketches), Herschel M. Margoliouth's *William Blake*, Alicia

Ostriker's *Vision and Verse in William Blake* (the only sustained prosodic study), Morton D. Paley and Michael Phillips's *William Blake: Essays in Honour of Sir Geoffrey Keynes*, Milton O. Percival's *William Blake's Circle of Destiny*, Kathleen Raine's *Blake and Tradition*, and Denis Saurat's *Blake and Modern Thought*. Of these, the most frequently used by the respondents to our questionnaire (who include teachers from the junior-college to the graduate level) are, in descending order, Frye, Erdman, Bloom, Mitchell, Damon (both his books), and Raine.

We should note that our teachers were responding to the question, "Which five or so background, critical, or reference works do you consider essential reading for those teaching *Songs* to undergraduates?" Because of the specificity of that question, our respondents cited several books that we have placed in the next section. Again in descending order of frequency of mention, they are Robert F. Gleckner's *The Piper and the Bard*, E. D. Hirsch's *Innocence and Experience*, Hazard Adams's *William Blake: A Reading of the Shorter Poems*, Joseph H. Wicksteed's *Blake's Innocence and Experience*, Zachary Leader's *Reading Blake's Songs*, and D. G. Gillham's *Blake's Contrary States*.

To all the above works we should add these useful collections of essays: John E. Grant's *Discussions of William Blake*, Frye's *Blake: A Collection of Critical Essays*, Alvin H. Rosenfeld's *William Blake: Essays for S. Foster Damon*, Judith O'Neill's *Critics on Blake*, Harold Bloom's *Modern Critical Views: William Blake*, Nelson Hilton's *Essential Articles for the Study of William Blake, 1970–1984*, and Dan Miller et al., *Critical Paths: Blake and the Argument of Method*—in addition to Morton D. Paley's and Margaret Bottrall's collections of critical essays on the *Songs* alone, listed in the next section.

A number of journal articles and essays or chapters in books have special value in the teaching both of Blake in general and of the *Songs*. We list these as well in alphabetical order: Leslie Brisman's "Re: Generation in Blake"; T. S. Eliot's "Blake"; Northrop Frye's "Blake's Treatment of the Archetype," as well as his "Poetry and Design in William Blake" and "Blake after Two Centuries"; the section on Blake in Frederick C. Gill's *The Romantic Movement and Methodism*; Robert F. Gleckner's "Blake's *Tiriel* and the State of Experience" and "Blake and the Senses"; Jean H. Hagstrum's "William Blake Rejects the Enlightenment"; John Hollander's "Blake and the Metrical Contract"; Josephine A. Miles's "The Language of William Blake"; Martin Price's "Blake: Vision and Satire," in his *To the Palace of Wisdom* (390–445); E. J. Rose's "Blake's Human Insect: Symbol, Theory and Design" and his "Blake's Metaphorical States"; and Mona Wilson's "The Twilight of the Augustans."

On Blake as an artist, scholarship and criticism have developed considerably beyond Anthony Blunt's pioneering *The Art of William Blake*, but this book still remains useful in certain ways. More recent studies of Blake's art include David Bindman's *Blake as an Artist*; Morton D. Paley's *William Blake*; Robert Essick's *William Blake, Printmaker, The Visionary Hand*, and "William Blake, William Hamilton, and the Materials of Graphic Meaning"; Morris Eaves's *William Blake's Theory of Art*; and Janet Warner's *Blake and the Language of Art*. Also important on this aspect of Blake's work are a handful of articles and essays: Bindman's "Blake's Theory and Practice of Imitation," W. J. T. Mitchell's "Style as Epistemology: Blake and the Movement toward Abstraction in Art," Joseph Viscomi's "The Workshop," Hazard Adams's "Revisiting Reynolds's *Discourses* and Blake's Annotations," Eaves's "Blake and the Artistic Machine: An Essay in Decorum and Technology," Stephen Leo Carr's "William Blake's Print-Making Process in *Jerusalem*," Essick's "Blake and the Traditions of Reproductive Engraving," and John Wright's "Toward Recovering Blake's Relief-Etching Process" and "Blake's Relief-Etching Method." Works that provide helpful art-historical contexts for more specialized work on Blake are David Bland's *A History of Book Illustration*, Robert Rosenblum's *Transformations in Late Eighteenth-Century Art*, Walter Benjamin's "The Work of Art in an Age of Mechanical Reproduction," and William Ivins's *Prints and Visual Communication*. We should also note here Martin Butlin's two-volume *The Paintings and Drawings of William Blake*, which reproduces all the paintings and drawings, some in color, and Robert N. Essick's *The Separate Plates of William Blake: A Catalogue*, which has eighty-six pages of plates, some in color.

Teachers and students of Blake will find of great importance Henry Crabb Robinson's extraordinary firsthand accounts of his conversations with Blake, dating chiefly from 1825 to 1827. They constitute a recollective compilation of many of Blake's key ideas, referrable to both his poetry and his prose works—a sort of mental autobiography, to be read in conjunction with the biographies by Gilchrist, Wilson, and others. The most convenient edition of these conversations is Henry Crabb Robinson, *On Books and Their Writers*. For an earlier essay on Blake by Robinson, see Bentley, *Records*.

Critical Commentary on *Songs*

This section is intended to be generous rather than exhaustive, representing a wide range of views of, as well as approaches to, the *Songs* as a whole and individually. Needless to say, these critical commentaries vary considerably in quality, though none is without some value. While it is tempting for all editors of bibliographies to gloss each entry with at least brief critical comment, we have refrained in general from doing so, believing that the teacher and student of Blake's *Songs* should survey and evaluate on their own the critical materials available.

Although there are a few interesting nineteenth-century commentaries— notably Samuel Taylor Coleridge's letter of 12 February 1818, A. C. Swinburne's *William Blake: A Critical Essay*, and Edwin J. Ellis and William Butler Yeats's monumental three-volume *The Works of William Blake: Poetic, Symbolic, and Critical*—the major thrust of Blake scholarship and criticism dates from about the second decade of this century. The following selection of books, articles, and essays (or chapters) in books reflects this conviction. (For a discussion of Blake criticism prior to the twentieth century, see Deborah Dorfman's excellent *Blake in the Nineteenth Century*.) In selecting from the vast twentieth-century literature on *Songs*, we have largely excluded the brief notes and minianalyses of individual songs found in introduction-to-poetry and introduction-to-literature texts; in the pages of the *Explicator*, *Notes and Queries*, and similar publications; in most books that treat Blake more than casually; and in the many articles dealing primarily with other Blake works or with subjects and topics that do not impinge directly or centrally on *Songs*. We have included, however, under the heading "Background Materials and New Critical Approaches," a brief listing of other books on Blake that we regard as essential reading for any serious student and teacher of Blake.

Treatments of the Whole Work

Modern criticism of the *Songs of Innocence and of Experience* was inaugurated by Damon in *William Blake: His Philosophy and Symbols*, although Wicksteed's *Blake's Innocence and Experience* was the first book-length study of the *Songs* alone. Between the publication of these two books and that of Frye's *Fearful Symmetry* in 1947, two other book-length studies appeared that contain significant discussions of the *Songs*: Bronowski's *William Blake, 1757–1827: A Man without a Mask* and Schorer's *William Blake: The Politics of Vision*; for all their worth, these works do not approach the

achievement, along the same general socio-historical-critical lines, of Erdman's *Blake: Prophet against Empire* in 1954. Also in the 1940s we have
Blackstone's *English Blake* and Maurice Bowra's *The Romantic Imagination*,
both in 1949; the latter contains a substantial chapter on Innocence and Experience. In 1954 Stanley Gardner published his *Infinity on the Anvil*, a
book that frankly dismisses the longer poems in favor of the *Songs* and other
shorter pieces, but it was another ten years before a true successor to Wicksteed's study of the *Songs* appeared: Robert F. Gleckner's *The Piper and the
Bard*. Gleckner's book was followed in the early 1960s by Hazard Adams's
William Blake: A Reading of the Shorter Poems, which includes comment on
all the *Songs* as well as a checklist of explications of individual songs through
1959; Bloom's *Blake's Apocalypse*, a book-length expansion of the chapter on
Blake in *The Visionary Company*; E. D. Hirsch's *Innocence and Experience:
An Introduction to Blake*, which takes issue with previous critical ap-
proaches to *Songs*; Jean Hagstrum's *William Blake, Poet and Painter*; and
Martin Price's *To the Palace of Wisdom*, which includes a major chapter on
Blake. The later 1960s saw a flurry of British studies of Blake, with
significant attention to the *Songs*: D. G. Gillham's *Blake's Contrary States*,
Beer's *Blake's Humanism*, and John Holloway's *Blake: The Lyric Poetry*, all
in 1968, followed by Beer's *Blake's Visionary Universe* a year later. In 1965
Alicia Ostriker published what remains the only book-length study of Blake's
prosody, *Vision and Verse in William Blake*.

The decade and a half following 1970 gave us a number of critically varied
Blake books that contain substantial commentary on the *Songs*. Gillham's
William Blake and David Wagenknecht's *Blake's Night* were published in
1973, David V. Erdman's *The Illuminated Blake* (with black-and-white reproductions of and brief commentaries on the graphic aspects of all Blake's
engraved works) in 1974, Wallace Jackson's *The Probable and the Marvelous*
(with a section on Blake) in 1978. In 1980 there appeared more specialized
books by B. H. Fairchild (*Such Holy Song: Music as Idea, Form, and Image
in the Poetry of William Blake*) and Diana Hume George (*Blake and Freud*).
The first book since Gillham's *Blake's Contrary States* devoted entirely to
the *Songs* was Zachary Leader's *Reading Blake's* Songs (1981), and two years
later Heather Glen published *Vision and Disenchantment: Blake's* Songs
and Wordsworth's Lyrical Ballads, a contribution somewhat along the lines
of Erdman's *Prophet against Empire* and Bronowski. More recently, J. R.
Watson has included a useful section on the *Songs* in his essay on Blake in
English Poetry of the Romantic Period, 1789–1830, and Harvey F. Bellin
and Darrell Ruhl in their *Blake and Swedenborg* include comments by
Kathleen Raine (among others) on the *Songs*. An interesting book by a non-
Blakean, who nevertheless deals at some length with Blake's idea of inno-

cence, is Harvey Birenbaum's *Tragedy and Innocence*. Harold Pagliaro's *Selfhood and Redemption in Blake's "Songs"* explores in detail the psychological processes represented in the work's chief characters, and, by concentrating on the building and then the annihilating of selfhood—the passage from innocence to experience—it relates these psychological dynamics to Blake's attempt to redeem humanity.

Journal articles that deal with *Songs of Innocence, Songs of Experience,* the combined book of *Songs,* or with a substantial number of individual songs are scarce in the years before Frye's *Fearful Symmetry* in 1947. Indeed, the only one we shall cite in those early years is H. C. Beeching's interesting if conventional "Blake's Religious Lyrics." The next significant articles were published in the same year as Frye's book: S. F. Bolt's "William Blake: The *Songs of Innocence"* and Wolf Mankowitz's "William Blake: The *Songs of Experience."* In 1957, Robert F. Gleckner's often reprinted essay "Point of View and Context in Blake's *Songs"* appeared.

The sixties saw a distinct increase in journal publication of Blake essays, of which the most important are Donald Dike's "The Difficult Innocence: Blake's Songs and Pastoral," Martha W. England's "Wesley's *Hymns for Children* and Blake's *Songs of Innocence and of Experience,"* and John D. Howard's "Swedenborg's *Heaven and Hell* and Blake's *Songs of Innocence."* At the close of the decade, Morton D. Paley published the best of the essay collections on the *Songs, Twentieth Century Interpretations of* Songs of Innocence and of Experience, with excerpts from the books noted above by Adams, Bloom (*Blake's Apocalypse*), Damon, Gleckner, Hirsch, Ostriker, Price, Schorer, and Wicksteed, as well as three essays on individual songs (to be cited more fully below): Frye's on the "Introduction" to *Songs of Experience,* and Nurmi's and Paley's on "The Tyger."

In 1970, in an excellent collection of essays devoted almost entirely to Blake works other than the *Songs,* Eban Bass published his *"Songs of Innocence and of Experience*: The Thrust of Design." In the same year Margaret Bottrall edited *William Blake:* Songs of Innocence and Experience: *A Casebook,* which contains the essays by Bolt, Gleckner ("Point of View"), and Mankowitz noted above and excerpts from Bowra and Wicksteed. Also included is Martin K. Nurmi's *PMLA* article on "The Tyger," noted below. In 1972 Wallace Jackson published his dissent from the prevailing direction of criticism of the *Songs,* "William Blake in 1789: Unorganized *Innocence,"* an essay incorporated into his already noted *The Probable and the Marvelous* (89–121); and John Adlard's *The Sports of Cruelty* argued for Blake's use of folklore and folktales in *Songs.* In 1975 we have Brian Wilkie's "Blake's *Innocence and Experience*: An Approach" (in *Blake Studies,* a journal now lamentably defunct after more than a decade of important contributions to the

study of Blake's works); Nick Shrimpton's "Hell's Hymnbook: Blake's
Songs of Innocence and of Experience and Their Models"; and Clifford
Davidson's "Blake's *Songs of Experience* and 'Rebel Nature.' "

Useful essays later in the 1970s include Claudia Corti's "Acque natali e
acque lustrali nei *Songs of Innocence* di Blake," Geoffrey Keynes's introductory essay in the Oxford edition of *Songs of Innocence and of Experience*,
Michael L. Stepto's "Mothers and Fathers in Blake's *Songs of Innocence*,"
Heather Glen's "Blake's Criticism of Moral Thinking in *Songs of Innocence
and of Experience*," Dennis Welch's "Blake's Response to Wollstonecraft's
Original Stories," and Michael Phillips's "William Blake's *Songs of Innocence* and *Songs of Experience*: From Manuscript Draft to Illuminated
Plate."

The present decade was auspiciously launched in 1980 by Myra Glazer-
Schotz and Gerda Norvig's "Blake's Book of Changes: On Viewing Three
Copies of the *Songs of Innocence and of Experience*," Judith Wardle's
"William Blake's Iconography of Joy," and Porter Williams's "The Influence
of Mrs. Barbauld's *Hymns in Prose for Children* upon Blake's *Songs of Inno-
cence and of Experience*." The following year, Harold E. Pagliaro published
"Blake's 'Self-Annihilation': Aspects of Its Function in the *Songs*, with a
Glance at Its History." Since then, we have D. R. M. Wilkinson's "Blake's
Songs: Taking Stock, 1984"; Harriet Kramer Linkin's "The Language of
Speakers in *Songs of Innocence and of Experience*"; and Stanley Gardner's
Blake's Innocence *and* Experience *Retraced*, which grounds *Songs* in its so-
cial and historical contexts.

To conclude this section we note *The* Explicator *Cyclopedia*, edited by C.
C. Walcutt and J. E. Whitesell, the second volume of which includes notes
and queries on Blake's *Songs* printed in the *Explicator* from its inception up
to a year or so before this volume's publication in 1968. Specific Blake songs
addressed include "The Clod and the Pebble," the "Introduction" to *Innocence*, "The Little Black Boy," "My Pretty Rose Tree," and "The Tyger."
One would hope that a volume containing *Explicator* items since 1967–68
will be forthcoming shortly.

Treatments of Individual Songs

It is difficult to know how best to deal with the many essays, and sections of
books not primarily on Blake, that treat one or several of Blake's *Songs*; their
catholicity of focus, critical approach, thematic concern, sensitivity to the
composite art, and so on precludes any meaningful categorization. We have
elected, therefore, to gather the critical essays simply by subject matter—
that is, by the poem primarily addressed—with cross-references, when useful, to essays that touch on the song in question despite being primarily

devoted to other songs. We shall also note when a single essay deals substantially with more than one song. Within each of these essay clusters (organized alphabetically by song title), we list the bibliographical items in chronological order, since many of the later essays are precipitated by, are "responses" to, or represent significant differences from interpretations offered in earlier essays. The reader should also keep in mind the works already cited in "Critical Works on Blake's Poetry and Art." Although not all those publications deal with Blake's *Songs* in substantial or detailed fashion, our understanding of (and therefore our teaching of) any one of the *Songs* will be distinctly the poorer for ignoring such wide-ranging books and essays. One other preliminary note—perhaps a caution: as we indicated at the outset, the following is a generous sampling of articles and essays to date, not merely the best, certainly not only those with which we (or even the majority of Blake critics) agree. If, as Blake said, "Opposition is true Friendship," such friendship has informed our bibliographical summary of critical commentaries on individual songs.

"Ah! Sun-flower"

The earliest separate essay of any substance on "Ah! Sun-flower" is George M. Harper's "The Source of Blake's 'Ah, Sunflower' " (1953), although in 1948 Rosemary Freeman included an able interpretation of the poem in her *English Emblem Books*, a scholarly work with a number of important implications for the study of Blake's works. Not until 1962 did other analyses of the sunflower poem begin to appear, for example, Joan O. Simons's brief note "Teaching Symbolism in Poetry" and Hilton Landry's more important "The Symbolism of Blake's Sunflower." In 1965 William J. Keith contributed to an essay collection "The Complexities of Blake's 'Sunflower': An Archetypal Speculation," and in 1968 Kathleen Raine incorporated an analysis of the poem in her monumental, sometimes eccentric, and esoteric *Blake and Tradition*. In the following decade appeared Thomas R. Edwards's relatively brief but useful discussion of "Ah! Sun-flower" in his *Imagination and Power: A Study of Poetry on Public Themes* and Mary Lynn Johnson's "Emblem and Symbol in Blake," an essay that deals prominently with "The Lilly," which has received relatively little commentary, and with "My Pretty Rose Tree" in addition to "Ah! Sun-flower." John E. Grant's exhaustive, nearly monograph-length essay "The Fate of Blake's Sunflower: A Forecast and Some Conclusions" takes into account virtually all previous critical comments on the poem. At the end of the decade and the beginning of the eighties we have Marcella Quadri Iovine's "La presia del desiderio: 'Ah! Sunflower' di W. Blake" and Peter D. Juhl's commentary in his *Interpretation: An Essay in the Philosophy of Literary Criticism*, which also includes an interesting analysis of "London."

"The Blossom"

For "The Blossom," to which scholars and critics have been curiously indifferent, at least in journal essays (there is substantially more commentary in books on Blake), we list but two articles: Rodney M. Baine and Mary R. Baine's "Blake's 'Blossom' " and Jean Pauchard's less accessible " 'The Blossom': Une visualisation."

"The Chimney Sweeper": *Innocence* and *Experience*

Of the surprisingly few essays on these poems, at least one is of major importance: Martin K. Nurmi's "Fact and Symbol in 'The Chimney Sweeper' of Blake's *Songs of Innocence*." The following year, without benefit of Nurmi's essay, W. K. Wimsatt included some brief, provocative comments on both chimney-sweeper poems in his *Hateful Contraries: Studies in Literature and Criticism*, although his main critical concern is with "London." Two other essays are Jacques Blondel, "William Blake: 'The Chimney Sweeper': De l'innocence à la violence," and Porter Williams, " 'Duty' in Blake's 'The Chimney Sweeper' of *Songs of Innocence*."

"The Clod and the Pebble" and "A Cradle Song"

Jean Hagstrum's essay "William Blake's 'The Clod and the Pebble' " is perhaps the most balanced view we have of that troublesomely simple, apparently direct poem; but another essay of importance is Max Schulz's "Point of View in Blake's 'The Clod and the Pebble.' " Blake's beautifully intricate "A Cradle Song" has elicited but one substantial analysis outside of book-length studies of Blake, Vivian de Sola Pinto's "William Blake, Isaac Watts, and Mrs. Barbauld" (*Divine Vision* 65–87).

"The Divine Image," "A Divine Image," and "The Human Abstract"

Scholars have only recently recognized that Blake not only intended to include "A Divine Image" in *Songs of Experience* (as all had assumed) but did include it in at least one copy (E 32, 800). It thus should be regarded as an integral part of this three-poem cluster. In addition to David H. Rawlinson's comments on "The Human Abstract" in *The Practice of Criticism*, there are four essays that deal with the poems in this group: Robert F. Gleckner's "Blake and the Four Daughters of God," on "The Divine Image," and "William Blake and the Human Abstract"; Stephen A. Larrabee's "An Interpretation of Blake's 'A Divine Image' "; and Phillip Law's "Innocence Renewed," on both "Divine Image" poems.

"A Dream" and "Earth's Answer"

Virtually the only comments (outside of Blake books) of any substance on "A Dream" are Vivian de Sola Pinto's in his collection of essays *The Divine Vision*. Separate analyses of "Earth's Answer" are infrequent, perhaps because the poem is virtually inextricable from the "Introduction" to *Songs of Experience*. Such commentary as we have, then, tends to arise in discussions of that poem, which is seemingly more crucial to an understanding of what Blake means by the "state of the human soul" called "Innocence." Essays by Michael Ackland, Philip Hobsbaum, and Michael J. Tolley that touch upon "Earth's Answer" in important ways will therefore be noted below in the paragraphs on the two "Introduction" poems.

"The Ecchoing Green"

"The Ecchoing Green" receives a prominent analysis from E. M. W. Tillyard in his 1934 book *Poetry Direct and Oblique*, but not until 1979–80 do we find another substantial commentary in essay form, David Simpson's "Blake's Pastoral: A Genesis for 'The Ecchoing Green.' " Briefer comments on the poem may also be found in Michael J. Tolley's "Blake's Songs of Spring."

"The Fly"

In contrast to "The Ecchoing Green," which has inspired relative unanimity among critics, "The Fly" is one of the most vigorously contested of Blake's *Songs*. No fewer than nine articles or essays, plus rejoinders and rebuttals, have appeared since Gleckner, in *The Piper and the Bard*, indicated uncertainty about how to read the poem. The first effort was Leo Kirschbaum's "Blake's 'The Fly' " (1961), followed immediately in the same journal by John E. Grant's "Misreadings of 'The Fly.' " Two years later, Grant contributed another substantial essay to the critical dispute, "Interpreting Blake's 'The Fly,' " which seemed to settle matters for the moment. But late in the 1960s Warren Stevenson published his "Artful Irony in Blake's 'The Fly,' " and Jean Hagstrum an essay entitled simply " 'The Fly.' " Michael J. Tolley quickly responded to the latter with "Blake's Blind Man," Hagstrum wrote a "Rebuttal" to Tolley's essay, and Tolley countered with a "Reply" to Hagstrum's "Rebuttal." Although Robert Mikkelsen's "William Blake's Revisions of the *Songs of Innocence and of Experience*" contains brief comments on "The Fly," not until 1977 did the song resurface prominently in the periodical literature, in C. N. Manlove's "Engineered Innocence: Blake's 'The Little Black Boy' and 'The Fly' " and Robert F. Gleckner's "Blake, Gray, and the Illustrations." The most recent critical essay on the still-vexed issues raised by this remarkably provocative poem is Thomas E. Connolly's "Point of View in Interpreting 'The Fly' " (1984).

"The Garden of Love"

No such fiery debate enlivens discussions of "The Garden of Love," at least in the scholarly and critical journals. Indeed, the only substantive essay we have found that discusses "The Garden of Love" deals with a large number of Blake's other poems as well: Elaine M. Kauver's "Landscape of the Mind: Blake's Garden Symbolism." There are, however, two Freudian analyses of the poem: Morris Dickstein's in his wide-ranging essay "The Price of Experience: Blake's Reading of Freud" and Diana Hume George's in *Blake and Freud.*

"Holy Thursday": *Innocence* and *Experience*

The earliest periodical article of note on Blake's two "Holy Thursday" poems (with emphasis on that of *Innocence*) is Robert F. Gleckner's "Irony in Blake's 'Holy Thursday' " (1956). The following year saw briefer comments by Vivian de Sola Pinto in "William Blake, Isaac Watts, and Mrs. Barbauld" (*Divine Vision* 65–87). Somewhat more extensive commentary than Pinto's may be found in Robert Mikkelsen's essay cited above in connection with "The Fly," but other than these we have only Thomas E. Connolly's "The Real 'Holy Thursday' of William Blake," which corrects prevailing misconceptions by all earlier critics about what day "Holy Thursday" was (it was not Ascension Day or Maundy Thursday).

"Infant Joy" and "Infant Sorrow"

"Infant Joy" and "Infant Sorrow" have attracted a remarkable range of critical approaches in the journals, although the number of essays falls far short of the number devoted to "The Fly," not to mention "London" and "The Tyger." Norman Nathan published a fairly conventional note in 1960, entitled simply "Blake's 'Infant Sorrow,' " but it is another ten years before the first substantial essay on either poem appears: Roman Jakobson's "On the Verbal Art of William Blake and Other Poet-Painters," followed by Donald K. Moore's "Blake's Notebook Versions of 'Infant Sorrow.' " E. L. Epstein published a difficult but interesting essay, "Blake's 'Infant Sorrow'—An Essay in Discourse Analysis"; David Simpson has some brief comments on "Infant Joy" in his *Irony and Authority in Romantic Poetry*; and most recently John Bender and Anne K. Mellor produced their provocative "Liberating the Sister Arts: The Revolution of Blake's 'Infant Sorrow' " (1983).

The "Introduction" Poems

Appropriately, given their prominent positions in the two song series, the "Introduction" poems have received considerable attention, the "Introduction" to *Experience* usually being coupled, in critical analyses, with "Earth's Answer." Three early commentaries on this pair claim our attention first: Maud Bodkin's still useful pages (317–23) in *Archetypal Patterns in Poetry* (1934), F. R. Leavis's comments (140–42) in *Revaluation* (1936), and René Wellek's response to Leavis in *The Importance of Scrutiny* (1948). The last receives a counterresponse from Leavis in the same volume. Despite the continuing value of these pieces, however, the major phase of essay-type critical studies of the "Introduction" poems begins in 1957 with Northrop Frye's "Blake's Introduction to Experience" and Kathleen Raine's "The Little Girl Lost and Found and the Lapsed Soul," although this twofold gauntlet is not picked up in the journals for over ten years. In 1968 Karl H. Goller published "William Blake: 'Songs of Innocence, Introduction' "; in 1970 Philip Hobsbaum included an analysis of "Introduction" in his *Theory of Criticism*; and in 1972 Frank D. McConnell contributed "Romanticism, Language, Waste: A Reflection on Poetics and Disaster" (with substantial commentary on "Introduction"). Two other excellent essays are Michael J. Tolley's "Blake's Songs of Spring" (cited above under "The Ecchoing Green") and Michael Ackland's "Blake's Problematic Touchstones to Experience: 'Introduction,' 'Earth's Answer,' and the Lyca Poems."

"The Lamb," "Laughing Song," and "The Lilly"

"The Lamb," "Laughing Song," and "The Lilly" have not engendered significant controversy, no doubt because of the seeming obviousness of "The Lamb" (text and design) and the untranslatable simplicity of "Laughing Song" (which is, nevertheless, belied by a most problematic illustration), and despite the location of "The Lilly" in Blake's unique and complex triptych plate that also includes "My Pretty Rose Tree" and "Ah! Sun-flower." Aside from some attention paid in books devoted entirely to Blake (and even there commentary is minimal), the only major essay on "The Lamb" is Jean H. Hagstrum's " 'The Wrath of the Lamb': A Study of William Blake's Conversions"—though, properly speaking, this article is a discussion of Blake's *idea* of the lamb rather than a commentary on the poem itself. Harry Williams has some interesting observations on Blake's pairing of "The Lamb" and "The Tyger," as does T. Ford Sosnowski in "Meter and Form in Blake's 'The Lamb' and 'The Tyger' "; Jim S. Borck tackles the still-gnawing problem of Blake's eccentric punctuation in "Blake's 'The Lamb': The Punctuation of Innocence"; and Ronald Paulson deals briefly with "The Lamb" in a more substantial discussion of "The Tyger," in his *Representations of Revolution*. For "Laughing Song" we have only Thomas Dilworth's "Blake's Argument with Newberry [publisher of children's books] in 'Laughing Song.' " Mary Lynn Johnson provides some helpful comments on "The Lilly" in her essay cited above under "Ah! Sun-flower," and John E. Grant's "Two Flowers in the Garden of Experience," on both "The Lilly" and "My Pretty Rose Tree," is a meticulously detailed essay.

"The Little Black Boy"

Considerable dispute has arisen in critical analyses of "The Little Black Boy," perhaps predictably, going back to the fifties and Mark Van Doren's analysis in his *Introduction to Poetry*, Jacob H. Adler's "Symbol and Meaning in 'The Little Black Boy,' " and A. E. Dyson's " 'The Little Black Boy': Blake's Song of Innocence." No essays appear in the sixties, but in 1975 we have Howard H. Hinkel's "From Pivotal Idea to Poetic Ideal: Blake's Theory of Contraries and 'The Little Black Boy,' " and in 1977 C. N. Manlove's "Engineered Innocence," noted above under "The Fly." The most recent critical studies of the poem are Myra Glazer's "Blake's Little Black Boys: On the Dynamics of Blake's Composite Art" (1980) and Robert F. Gleckner's "Blake's 'Little Black Boy' and the Bible" (1982).

"A Little Boy Lost," "The Little Boy Lost," and "The Little Boy Found"

"A Little Boy Lost" of *Songs of Experience* is rarely discussed in extenso in books or journals, the only substantial essay we have found being Stephen D. Cox's "Adventures of 'A Little Boy Lost': Blake and the Process of Interpretation." Vivian de Sola Pinto has some useful brief comments in an essay in his *The Divine Vision* (65–87). The similarly titled *Songs of Innocence* poems, however, have provoked a sometimes ill-tempered and complicated controversy. Although there are a number of earlier commentaries on these two poems (all in books on Blake), the essay that triggered the critical dispute was published in 1967, Thomas E. Connolly and George R. Levine's "Pictorial and Poetic Design in Two Songs of Innocence." Later in the year, John E. Grant responded with "Recognizing Fathers"; Connolly and Levine rebutted with "Recognizing Mother"; and the debate between these participants continued into early 1968. The following year J. G. Keogh responded, in a letter, to the original Connolly-Levine essay, the authors of the essay responded to him, and there the matter rests to date, in the journals— though David Simpson in *Irony and Authority in Romantic Poetry* has a substantial analysis of both poems.

"The Little Girl Lost" and "The Little Girl Found"

More wide-ranging differences of critical opinion are apparent in the journal articles and other essays on "The Little Girl Lost" and "The Little Girl Found." One core controversy was touched off by Kathleen Raine's "The Little Girl Lost and Found and the Lapsed Soul," the debate occupying the letters to the editor section of the *Spectator* from December 1957 through January 1958, with (in addition to Raine herself) W. W. Robson, William Empson, Philip Sherrard, G. W. Digby, and John Wain participating. Irene Chayes even more vigorously responded to Raine's essay with "Blake and Tradition: 'The Little Girl Lost' and 'The Little Girl Found' " (1970), in which she develops further some aspects of her earlier article on the two poems, "Little Girls Lost: Problems of a Romantic Archetype." To Chayes's 1970 piece John Beer published "A Reply" and Chayes added "A Rejoinder to John Beer," and there that phase of the controversy seems to rest. Commentaries on the poems continue apace into the late sixties and early seventies, with Teut A. Riese's "William Blake: 'The Little Girl Lost' und 'The Little Girl Found,' " Reynold Siemens's "Borders in Blake's 'The Little Girl Lost-Found,' " Grevel Lindop's "Blake: 'The Little Girl Lost' and 'The Little Girl Found,' " and John Adlard's "Blake's 'The Little Girl Lost and Found.' " The last ten years have brought us Henry Trout's "A Reading of Blake's 'The Little Girl Lost' and 'The Little Girl Found,' " Michael Ackland's "Blake's Problematic Touchstones," cited above, and Norma A. Greco's "Blake's 'The Little Girl Lost': An Initiation into Womanhood."

"London"

We have collected no fewer than eighteen essays and substantive commentaries (outside of Blake books) on "London." Arranging them usefully is especially difficult since there is no "core controversy" to provide a convenient principle of presentation, aside from a steady quarreling, even bickering, about the last two lines. We shall proceed, then, in simple chronological order, clustering essays more or less by decades.

The two earliest analyses of especial use to teachers of the poem are Alfred Kazin's in the introduction to his *The Portable Blake* (1940) and the explication of "London" included in *An Approach to Literature* (ed. Cleanth Brooks et al., 1940). In the sixties we have W. K. Wimsatt's discussion in his book *Hateful Contraries* and a subsequent essay, "Genesis: An Argument Resumed," as well as Karl Kiralis's " 'London' in the Light of *Jerusalem*" and David H. Rawlinson's commentary in his *The Practice of Criticism*. Archibald Hill's somewhat off-beat analysis, "Imagery and Meaning: A Passage from Milton, and from Blake," closes out the decade.

The essays of the 1970s on "London" begin with Kenneth Johnston's "Blake's Cities," followed by Victor Doyno's "Blake's Revision of 'London' " and Horst Bodden and Herbert Kausser's "William Blake's 'London.' " In 1975 Raymond Williams included an important discussion of the poem in *The Country and the City*; 1976 saw equally important comments by Harold Bloom in his *Poetry and Repression*; and in 1977 Grant C. Roti and Donald L. Kent's note "The Last Stanza of Blake's 'London' " renewed an old debate. At the end of this decade there were two essays: E. P. Thompson's "London" and Gavin Edwards's "Mind Forg'd Manacles: A Contribution to the Discussion of Blake's 'London.' "

In the 1980s thus far three significant essays on "London" have appeared, in addition to P. D. Juhl's briefer comments in his book cited above under "Ah! Sun-flower": Jonathan Culler's semiotic reading in *The Pursuit of Signs* (68–79), Michael Ferber's " 'London' and Its Politics," and David Punter's "Blake and the Shapes of London."

"My Pretty Rose Tree"

Aside from a few discussions in books devoted entirely to Blake, commentary on "My Pretty Rose Tree" does not begin until the 1960s, although Robert F. Gleckner's 1955 note in the *Explicator* is worth looking at. In 1965 J. B. Thompson's "Blake's 'My Pretty Rose Tree'—An Interpretation" appeared, followed three years later by G. H. Durrant's "Blake's 'My Pretty Rose Tree' "; and, most important, John E. Grant published his "Two Flowers in the Garden of Experience" in 1969. Also in 1969 T. Olivier took issue with E. H. Patterson and G. K. Pechey (both cited below under "The Tyger"), as well as Durrant, on both "My Pretty Rose Tree" and "A Poison Tree." Finally, Mary Lynn Johnson has some useful comments on the poem in her 1974 essay "Emblem and Symbol in Blake."

"Night," the Two Nurse's Songs, "The School Boy," "The Shepherd," "Spring," and "To Tirzah"

Of the remainder of the songs, only "The Tyger" has generated an appreciable amount of criticism. In contrast, "The Angel," "The Little Vagabond," and "A Little Girl Lost" have attracted none in the journals or in sections of books not primarily on Blake. Before proceeding with bibliographical listings for "A Poison Tree," "The Sick Rose," "The Tyger," and "The Voice of the Ancient Bard," then, we gather together here some critical remnants, as it were, dealing with a few of the seven songs heading this paragraph. In alphabetical order by poem title, they include Rita Munson's "Blake's 'Night' "; Robert Mikkelsen's brief comments on "Nurse's Song" (*Innocence*) in "William Blake's Revisions," cited under "Holy Thursday"; Michael

Tolley's discussion of "The School Boy" and "Spring" in "Blake's Songs of Spring"; David Simpson's comments on "The Shepherd" in his *Irony and Authority in Romantic Poetry*; and Thomas F. Berninghausen's "The Marriage of Contraries in 'To Tirzah.' "

"A Poison Tree" and "The Sick Rose"

"A Poison Tree" has proved more worthy of comment, as has "The Sick Rose." Henry Coombes has some substantial comments on the former in his *Literature and Criticism*, and Robert Mikkelsen discusses it briefly in the essay cited above. Barbara F. Lefcowitz has contributed "Omnipotence of Thought and the Poetic Imagination," Philip J. Gallagher "The Word Made Flesh: Blake's 'A Poison Tree' and the Book of Genesis," and F. W. Bateson "Myth—A Dispensable Critical Term." John Brenkman's essay "The Concrete Utopia of Poetry: Blake's 'A Poison Tree' " appeared in 1985.

Despite this flurry over "A Poison Tree," more interesting critical arguments have arisen over "The Sick Rose" (which, not coincidentally, is a favorite poem for specimen explication in introduction-to-poetry texts), beginning with two radically different 1951 analyses: T. R. Henn's in *The Apple and the Spectroscope* and Reuben Brower's in *The Fields of Light*. A full twenty years elapses after these comments, though, before the poem begins to receive its critical due in essay form. In 1972 two distinct critical approaches are employed by Doris Jakubec in " 'La rose malade' de William Blake" and by John Neubauer in "The Sick Rose as an Aesthetic Idea." The following year saw the appearance of still another approach, Michael Riffaterre's "The Self-Sufficient Text," and in 1976 F. J. Berwick published his " 'The Sick Rose': A Second Opinion." The newest interpretation is that of Elizabeth Langland, "Blake's Feminist Revision of Literary Tradition in 'The Sick Rose' " (1987).

"The Tyger"

We come now to by far the most frequently and extensively interpreted poem Blake wrote, "The Tyger." As with "London," the earliest reading of note is Alfred Kazin's in the introduction to his *The Portable Blake* in 1946, followed by Roy P. Basler's comments in his *Sex, Symbolism, and Psychology in Literature* (1948), and Jesse Bier's "A Study of Blake's 'The Tyger' " (1949). In the 1950s only two essays, both influential in subsequent study of "The Tyger," need detain us: Kathleen Raine's "Who Made the Tyger?"— included, in much revised and expanded form, in her two-volume *Blake and Tradition*—and Martin K. Nurmi's "Blake's Revisions of *The Tyger*."

In the 1960s there are no fewer than seventeen separate essays or parts of books not primarily on Blake devoted to "The Tyger," beginning with two discussions of first importance: Hazard Adams's "Reading Blake's Lyrics: 'The Tyger' " and John E. Grant's "The Art and Argument of 'The Tyger.' " In 1962 Paul Miner published " 'The Tyger': Genesis and Evolution in the Poetry of William Blake," and in 1964 two essays appeared: Philip Hobsbaum's "A Rhetorical Question Answered: Blake's 'Tyger' and Its Critics" and Fred C. Robinson's "Verb Tense in Blake's 'The Tyger.' " Two years later Grant and Robinson collaborated in "Tense and the Sense of Blake's 'The Tyger,' " an essay preceded by Morton D. Paley's " 'Tygers of Wrath,' "—which Paley revised and greatly expanded for inclusion in his book *Energy and the Imagination*. (In response to Paley's essay, Michael J. Tolley published "Remarks on 'The Tyger.' ") Other 1966 analyses of the poem include G. K. Pechey's "Blake's Tyger" (discussed the following year by E. H. Paterson) and Charles B. Wheeler's briefer commentary in his *The Design of Poetry*. Rodney M. Baine published "Blake's 'Tyger': The Nature of the Beast" in 1967, and in the same year Fred Kaplan contributed his " 'The Tyger' and Its Maker: Blake's Vision of the Artist."

The last years of the 1960s witnessed little abatement in "Tyger" studies. Coleman O. Parsons published two essays on the poem in 1968, "Tygers before Blake" and "Blake's 'Tyger' and Eighteenth-Century Animal Pictures," and three additional analyses appeared in 1969: Robert Graves's in his *"The Crane Bag" and Other Disputed Subjects*, L. J. Swingle's "Answers to Blake's 'Tyger': A Matter of Reason or of Choice?" and Kay Parkhurst Long's "William Blake and the Smiling Tyger," the only essay especially written for Winston Weathers's collection of essays *William Blake: "The Tyger."* Other than Long's essay, Weathers includes all or part of the essays cited above by Adams, Baine, Basler, Bier, Hobsbaum, Nurmi, and Paley, as well as excerpts from Damon's *William Blake: His Philosophy and Symbols*, Gardner's *Infinity on the Anvil*, and Hirsch's *Innocence and Experience*.

The decade of the 1970s produced nine substantial interpretations of "The Tyger," two of them in 1970: Warren Stevenson's " 'The Tyger' as Artefact" and Eli Pfefferkorn's "The Question of the Leviathan and the Tiger." In 1971 James Hazen published "Blake's Tyger and Milton's Beasts," and in 1972 two commentaries appeared: Harry Williams's "The Tyger and the Lamb" and Fred Kaplan's in his book *Miracles of Rare Device*. Three notably different critical approaches are exemplified in the 1975 essays by Mary R. Baine and Rodney M. Baine ("Blake's Other Tygers, and 'The Tyger' "), Winston Weathers ("The Construction of William Blake's 'The Tyger' "), and E. L. Epstein ("The Self-Reflexive Artefact: The Function of Mimesis in an Approach to a Theory of Value for Literature"). Also in the 1970s are Harold Bloom's analysis in his *Poetry and Repression* and Andrew Welsh's in his *Roots of Lyric*.

To date, the decade of the 1980s seems fair to produce more essays and sections of books devoted to "The Tyger" than has any previous ten-year span. In 1980 alone there are four commentaries: Stewart Crehan's "Blake's 'Tyger' and the 'Tygerish Multitude,' " Nelson Hilton's "Spears, Spheres, and Spiritual Tears: Blake's Poetry as 'The Tyger,' " Shaun McCarthy's "Riddle Patterns and William Blake's 'The Tyger,' " and Stanley Fish's unsettling comments in his *Is There a Text in This Class?* (esp. 259–63, 339–42, 384–50). In 1982 R. L. Rumsby published "Trinities in 'The Tyger,' " and Steven Shaviro comments on the poem in his " 'Striving with Systems.' " Ronald Paulson includes a provocative analysis of the poem in his *Representations of Revolution* (1983), in 1984 David Punter published "Blake/Hegel/Derrida" (which includes comment on "The Tyger"), and in 1987–88 Robert F. Gleckner contributed "Blake's 'The Tyger' and Edward Young's Book of Job."

"The Voice of the Ancient Bard"

The last poem to be accounted for is "The Voice of the Ancient Bard." In addition to David Simpson's brief comments in *Irony and Authority in Romantic Poetry*, there is but one substantial essay on the poem, Robert F. Gleckner's "The Strange Odyssey of Blake's 'The Voice of the Ancient Bard.' "

Background Materials and New Critical Approaches

In addition to Erdman's indispensable *Blake: Prophet against Empire* and Bronowski's briefer, though still useful, similar work, *William Blake 1757–1827: A Man without a Mask*, some more recently published books, articles, and essays deal with the sociopolitical background of Blake's works or with Blake as a self-conscious artist working in that sociopolitical milieu. Of these, the most prominent (in book form) are Raymond Williams's *Culture and Society 1780–1950*, E. P. Thompson's *The Making of the English Working Class*, Marilyn Butler's *Romantics, Rebels, and Reactionaries*, Paulson's *Representations of Revolution (1789–1820)*, Glen's *Vision and Disenchantment*, and Ferber's *The Social Vision of William Blake*.

More sharply focused on ideology and literary criticism than the works above are David Aers, Jonathan Cook, and David Punter's *Romanticism and Ideology*, Jerome J. McGann's *The Romantic Ideology*, and two essays: Peter Middleton's "The Revolutionary Poetics of William Blake" and Edward Larrissy's "A Description of Blake: Ideology, Form, Influence." Related to both groupings above are Kurt Heinzelman's "William Blake and the Economics of the Imagination" and Paul Mann's "Apocalypse and Recuperation: Blake and the Maw of Commerce." More specifically Marxian approaches to Blake, which seem to be increasing in number, include Eleanor Wilner's *Gathering the Winds: Visionary Imagination and Radical Transformation of Self and Society*; Fred Whitehead's "William Blake and the Radical Tradition"; David Punter's *Blake, Hegel, and Dialectic*, as well as his earlier essays "Blake, Marxism and Dialectic" and "Blake: Creative and Uncreative Labor"; Jackie DiSalvo's *War of Titans: Blake's Critique of Milton and the Politics of Religion*; and Stewart Crehan's *Blake in Context*, which contains a useful chapter on "The Tyger" and eighteenth-century revolutionary politics.

An increasing number of articles have been appearing on Blake and women, or, more sharply, on Blake's sexist attitude toward women in his works. Some challenging studies include David Aers's "William Blake and the Dialectics of Sex," Susan Fox's "The Female as Metaphor in William Blake's Poetry," Diana Hume George's "Is She Also the Divine Image? Feminine Form in the Art of William Blake" (a position she expands on in *Blake and Freud*), Margaret Storch's "Blake and Women: Nature's Cruel Holiness," and four articles that make up the Winter 1982–83 issue of *Blake: An Illustrated Quarterly*: Anne K. Mellor's "Blake's Portrayal of Women," Alicia Ostriker's "Desire Gratified: William Blake and Sexuality," Nelson Hilton's "Some Sexual Connotations," and Michael Ackland's "The Embattled Sexes: Blake's Debt to Wollstonecraft in *The Four Zoas*." The last should be compared to Jackie DiSalvo's book noted above, which is devoted largely to *The Four Zoas*. On Blake's use of Wollstonecraft, see also Dennis M. Welch's "Blake's Response to Wollstonecraft's *Original Stories*," Henry H. Wasser's "Notes on the *Visions of the Daughters of Albion* by William Blake," E. B. Murray's "Thel, *Thelophthera* and the Visions," and Norma A. Greco's "Mother Figures in Blake's *Songs of Innocence* and the Female Will."

Most psychological and psychoanalytical approaches to Blake have been either Freudian or Jungian. The former school is represented by Daniel Majdiak and Brian Wilkie's "Blake and Freud: Poetry and Depth Psychology," Morris Dickstein's "The Price of Experience: Blake's Reading of Freud," George's *Blake and Freud*, and Brenda S. Webster's *Blake's Prophetic Psychology*. The Jungians include W. P. Witcutt in *Blake: A Psychological Study*, June K. Singer in *The Unholy Bible: A Psychological Interpretation of William Blake*, and Christine Gallant in *Blake and the Assimilation of Chaos*.

On Blake and science, the fullest study to date is Donald D. Ault's *Visionary Physics: Blake's Response to Newton*, though Ault himself takes issue with portions of that book in *Narrative Unbound*. Many books ostensibly on other aspects of Blake's work also treat Blake's relation to the scientific ideas—and "scientists"—of his day. There are, as well, a number of useful articles: Martin K. Nurmi's "Negative Sources in Blake," F. B. Curtis's "Blake and the 'Moment of Time': An Eighteenth-Century Controversy in Mathematics" and "William Blake and Eighteenth-Century Medicine," Ault's "Incommensurability and Interconnection in Blake's Anti-Newtonian Text," Mark L. Greenberg's "Blake's 'Vortex,' " Stuart Peterfreund's "Blake and Newton: Argument as Art, Argument as Science," Bryce J. Christensen's "The Apple in the Vortex: Newton, Blake, and Descartes,"and Greenberg's "Blake's 'Science.' "

Several books and articles dealing with the relations between Blake's *Songs* and eighteenth-century children's literature appear in the previous section of this essay, but a more capacious examination of this background may be found in Geoffrey Summerfield's *Fantasy and Reason: Children's Literature in the Eighteenth Century*. In a somewhat similar vein are several articles and a book on the relation between Blake's "composite art" and emblem literature: Piloo Nanavutty's "Blake and Emblem Literature," Mary Lynn Johnson's "Emblem and Symbol in Blake," Joseph S. Salemi's "Emblematic Tradition in Blake's *The Gates of Paradise*," and Judith Wardle's " 'For Hatching Ripe': Blake and the Educational Uses of Emblem and Illustrated Literature." The sole book is Aquilino Sánchez Pérez's *Blake's Graphic Work and the Emblem Tradition*.

Among the more interesting and illuminating recent critical approaches to

Blake, we offer a number that are representative. A symposium on the directions "new" Blake criticism should go, according to a dozen or so Blake scholar-critics, appeared in the Fall 1982 issue of *Studies in Romanticism*. More concerted efforts at such new directions are Jonathan Culler's "Prolegomenon to a Theory of Reading," Lawrence Lipking's "Blake and the Book" in his *The Ordering of the Arts in Eighteenth-Century England*, Nelson Hilton's provocative semiotic analysis *Literal Imagination: Blake's Vision of Words*, and two collections of essays: *Blake and Criticism*, edited by Thomas A. Vogler, and *Unnam'd Forms: Blake and Textuality*, edited by Vogler and Nelson Hilton. Edward Larrissy devotes the first three chapters of his *William Blake* to the *Songs*. Although not on Blake, Maureen Quilligan's *The Language of Allegory* is also most suggestive for Blake study, and Robert F. Gleckner's *Blake and Spenser* also addresses in extenso the much-vexed issue of Blake's attitude toward allegory.

A mode of criticism that Blake himself would particularly have appreciated is that represented by the designs an extraordinary range of illustrators have created for some of Blake's poems, more often than not for the *Songs*. These works (usually small, handsomely produced books) are far too numerous to list, but many of them may be found in Bentley's indispensable *Blake Books* and in the annual checklist of Blake scholarship and criticism published in *Blake: An Illustrated Quarterly*. To this "Blakean" kind of criticism, however, there is a complement from another art: the setting of Blake's *Songs* (and, less frequently, others of his short poems) to music. In Bentley and his *A Blake Bibliography*, Martin K. Nurmi described a number of these musical settings, and ten years later Peter Roberts published another compilation entitled "On Tame High Finishers of Paltry Harmonies: A Blake Music Review and Checklist." Most of these settings are available in published scores, and many have been recorded. We list here a sampling of the latter. Probably the most famous are Benjamin Britten's *Songs and Proverbs of William Blake* (available on London Records OS-26099) and Allen Ginsberg's recording of his chanted-sung versions of twenty of the *Songs* (MGM Records, Verve series, FTS-3083). Morris Eaves reviewed the Ginsberg recording, and Ginsberg wrote a song-by-song commentary on it, in the *Blake Newsletter* of 1971. Available on several different records is Ralph Vaughan Williams's *Ten Blake Songs*, which was written for the film *The Vision of William Blake*. Three recordings of this song series are Desto DC-6482, Argo ZRG-732 (Decca), and EMI (Odeon) HQS-1236.

Other recordings include George Rochberg's "Blake's Songs" (setting to music "Ah! Sun-flower," "Nurse's Song," "The Fly," and "The Sick Rose") on Nonesuch H-71302; "A Poison Tree," set by Richard Wernick, Smithsonian Collection, N 027; Gordon Crosse's "Nurse's Song" on Argo ZRG 656; "The Ecchoing Green" and "The Shepherd," set by William Busch on Argo

ZRG 5439; Michael Berkeley's settings of "A Divine Image" and "The Tyger" on EMI ASD 2700 581; Walter Kemp's *Five Poems of William Blake* on RCI 491 (sung by the Tudor Singers of Montreal); David Axelrod's *Songs of Innocence* on Capitol ST-2982 and Capitol Stereo SKAO-338; John Harbison's *Five Songs of Experience* sung by the Cantata Singers and Ensemble on CRI-SD313; Gregory Forbes's *Musical Settings* to selected *Songs* on Ecchoing Green Records (Kingston, ON); and (newly recorded at McGill University, though we have no other information) David Patriquin's *Songs of Innocence* for women's voices, harp, and flute, which premiered in Montreal in 1984. A striking jazz version of four of the *Songs of Experience* was recorded by Mike Westbrook on Europa Records JP2006.

Finally, we note the performance of William Bolcom's vast choral cantata Songs of Innocence and of Experience: *A Musical Illumination of the Poems of William Blake (1757–1827)*, presented in January 1987 at the Brooklyn Academy of Music by nine vocal soloists, a full-sized chorus, a children's choir, and a symphony orchestra augmented by a rock band. As of this writing, Bolcom's work is not available in commercially recorded form; the performance, however, was widely and well received.

Visual Resources for Teaching *Songs*

John E. Grant and Mary Lynn Johnson

During the past twenty-five years it has become increasingly evident that the best way to study Blake's *Songs of Innocence and of Experience* is to read the poems in a form that comes as close to the original as possible—that is, with text and design together. The trouble is that Blake's *Songs* "in the original" is actually in twenty-four originals—twenty-four different versions of the same work, executed over thirty-two years in an astonishing variety of individual copies that are now dispersed in museums and private collections around the world. In addition, there are at least twenty-two copies of *Songs of Innocence* alone, as well as four more or less complete copies of *Songs of Experience* alone, so that for any single poem there are dozens of variations to consider, some of which may affect interpretation. Few complete copies of *Songs* have been reproduced at all; still fewer are widely available in a format well suited for frequent use in the classroom.

Despite formidable bibliographical, interpretive, and logistical problems, despite whatever uneasiness literary scholars may feel in stepping outside their discipline, teachers of *Songs* owe their students the opportunity to explore the pictorial side of Blake's work, in as many different versions as can be managed. This obligation entails using inexpensive reproductions as supplementary texts or arranging showings of slides and rare facsimiles—whether by borrowing from the art department, negotiating with the rare-book room, commissioning the audiovisual service to make slides from books, or building a collection of slides ordered directly from museums. The more energy one puts into sorting and loading slides and fretting over the handling of valuable facsimiles, however, the more fervently one longs for the day when technological advances will make a complete color archive of Blake's images conveniently accessible. In the meantime, a brief guide to the best facsimiles and sources of slides will be a time-saver.

The finest facsimiles of Blake's illuminated books were published from 1951 to 1977 in limited editions, usually of only several hundred copies, by the Blake Trust, a British endowment organized by Geoffrey Keynes. Blake Trust facsimiles were executed by the Trianon Press of Paris, under the direction of Arnold Fawcus, usually by hand coloring through stencils over a collotype base, on paper especially made to match that used by Blake. On the infrequent occasions when books in this magnificent series now come on the rare-book dealers' market, they usually fetch prices in the hundreds or even thousands of dollars. These stunningly beautiful works of art offer an experience as close to Blake's originals as any method of replication can provide.

To show something of the range of Blake's styles of coloring, the Blake

Trust chose an early and simply colored copy for its 1954 facsimile of *Songs of Innocence* and a late, elaborately finished copy for its 1955 facsimile of the combined *Songs of Innocence and of Experience*, one with deep, rich colors and gold embellishments. The originals of both copies are in the Rosenwald Collection of the Library of Congress: *Songs of Innocence*, copy B, and *Songs of Innocence and of Experience*, copy Z (according to the identifying code used by Keynes and Wolf and by Bentley, *Blake Books*). With six- and eight-color offset photography, Oxford University Press reproduced the Blake Trust facsimile of *Songs of Innocence and of Experience* in 1970, from plates used for the Orion Press reproduction of 1967. Dover Press has also published inexpensive color reproductions based on Blake Trust facsimiles: in 1971, the *Songs of Innocence*, and in 1984, the *Experience* part of the *Songs of Innocence and of Experience* volume.

In 1983 the Manchester Etching Workshop published a limited edition of sixteen plates from *Songs*, using handmade ink and paper, a rolling press similar to Blake's, and colors mixed according to eighteenth-century recipes; the prints were hand colored without the aid of stencils on the model of copy B of the complete *Songs* (British Museum). Werner Hofmann's *William Blake: Lieder der Unschuld und Erfahrung* (1975) is a photographic reproduction in color of copy T, a composite copy in the British Museum. The Huntington Library has published an inexpensive pamphlet of sixteen pages selected by James Thorpe from the two copies of *Songs* in that library's collection (copies E and N), in color enlargements. For a sample page from copy W (King's College, Cambridge), see Keynes, " 'Blake's Own' Copy." Mary Lynn Johnson and John E. Grant's *Blake's Poetry and Designs* contains eight color plates from the Blake Trust facsimiles of *Songs* and from copies U (Princeton) and V (Pierpont Morgan Library), as well as numerous black-and-white illustrations.

Advanced students who become interested in matters of technique or iconography will wish to compare colored copies with unadorned prints of *Songs*. Sixteen uncolored pages printed from electrotypes—that is, mechanically duplicated copies of Blake's plates—appear as illustrations in Alexander Gilchrist's standard biography. (One of the sixteen, however, the title page for *Songs of Experience*, is based on a crude forgery.) Prints made from a replica of the Gilchrist electrotypes appear in the two editions of Geoffrey Keynes's *Blake Studies* (1949, 1971)—half in the first edition, half in the second. An uncolored posthumous copy at Harvard (copy b), erroneously retouched in places, was issued by Ruthven Todd in 1947 and reprinted in Folcroft, Pennsylvania, in 1969 (no publisher, place, or date is given). Bentley's edition *William Blake's Writings* reproduces many plates from a privately owned posthumous copy (copy c). Complete monochrome reproductions of *Songs*, many based on uncolored or lightly colored originals, appear in the following books: David V. Erdman's *The Illuminated Blake*, taken from copy I (Widener Library, Harvard) and from the Gilchrist electrotypes; David Bindman's *The Complete Graphic Works of William Blake*, taken from copy B (British Library) and copy B of *Innocence* alone (Library of Congress); Joseph Wicksteed's *Blake's Innocence and Experience*, intermingling plates from all three copies in the British Library (A, B, and T) and from copy AA in the Fitzwilliam Museum, Cambridge.

Although Blake's page designs for *Songs* were intended for close-range viewing by individual readers, they adapt well to slide projection for large audiences. Indeed, because some of Blake's effects are most easily appreciated under magnification, the enlargement gained through projection is a distinct asset, as is the opportunity for an entire class to see the same detail at the same time. On the negative side, students may approach a slide show as if they were going to the movies, expecting passively to receive impressions of larger-than-life figures in a darkened room, and the teacher must take care not to flash too many images without sufficient time for absorption. But a well-managed slide presentation stimulates lively discussions of text-design relationships and amply repays the bother of obtaining slides and the heavy investment in set-up and take-down time.

Most institutions will provide satisfactory slides of copies in their collections for $2.50 to $10.00 apiece (although some years ago the Cincinnati Art Museum charged $28.00!); the per-slide price is usually less for slides sold in sets by slide dealers. A few individual slides of sample pages of *Songs* can be purchased inexpensively at the sales desks of the Bodleian Library, Oxford (*Innocence*, copy L), and the Fitzwilliam Museum, Cambridge (*Songs*, copy R). Charges and currency values are so variable that it is pointless to include prices with comments on slide sources.

By far the most convenient single source of slides for the illuminated books, and for many other Blake works as well, is the E. P. Group of Companies (formerly Micromethods), Main St., East Ardsley, Wakefield, West Yorkshire WF3 2AT, Eng. (According to *Slide Buyers Guide*, 4th ed., ed. Nancy DeLaurier [Kansas City: Mid-America College Art Assn., 1980], the American distributor is Prothmann Associates, 650 Thomas Ave., Baldwin, NY 11510; we have not dealt with Prothmann.) E. P. sells reasonably priced color microfilm strips for library use; for a small additional charge, this company will mount the frames in sets of slides (no individual slides are available). E. P. offers two copies of *Songs*: copy B from the British Library, with *Innocence* and *Experience* in separate sets, and copy AA from the Fitzwilliam Museum, Cambridge, in one large set. These slide or microfilm sets, together with the Oxford University Press and Dover facsimiles mentioned above, provide enough examples of *Songs* to meet the needs of most teachers and classes.

If additional slides are desired, they must be specially ordered from museums. The waiting time can be very long indeed. Of the great public repositories holding more than one copy of *Songs*, the following should head the list of anyone setting out to build an extended slide collection for research and teaching:

Photographic Services Dept., British Museum, Great Russell St., London WC1B 3DG, Eng.: *Songs* copies A, B (a copy also available from E. P.), and T (a composite made primarily from two different originals by Blake, one color printed, one watercolored; this is reproduced in the German facsimile edited by Hofmann, mentioned earlier).

Henry E. Huntington Library and Art Gallery, San Marino, CA 91108: *Songs* copy E and *Experience* copy N (sample pages from both copies are reproduced in the Huntington facsimile mentioned earlier); also *Innocence* only, copy I. (Unusually full verbal descriptions, together with a black-and-white reproduction of the title page of *Songs* copy E and a list of reproductions elsewhere, are contained in Essick's catalog of the Huntington Blakes.)

Library of Congress, Washington, DC 20540 (Rosenwald Collection): *Innocence* only, copy B (the copy used for the Blake Trust facsimile); *Songs* copies C and Z (the copy used for the Blake Trust facsimile and photographically reproduced in facsimiles published by Oxford University Press and—the *Experience* portion only—by Dover Press).

Other institutions having more than one copy of *Songs* include the Fitzwilliam Museum, Cambridge (copies G, from the Keynes collection, R, and AA—the copy reproduced by E. P.—as well as *Innocence* only, copy R); Cincinnati Art Museum (copy S, as well as copy S of *Innocence* alone); the Houghton Library, Harvard (copies I and O, as well as copies F and U of *Innocence* alone); the library of Princeton University (copy U, as well as copy T of *Innocence* only); the Pierpont Morgan Library, New York (copies K and V, as well as *Innocence* only, copy D); and, within Yale University, the Beinecke Rare Book Library (copy M) and the Yale Center for British Art (copies F and L, as well as *Innocence* only, copy G).

Two commercial companies sell assorted slide packages of Blake's work that may be useful in teaching:

Budek Films and Slides, 73 Pelham St., Newport, RI 02840 (tel. 401 846-6580): ten-slide set, with three plates from copy Y (Metropolitan Museum of Art)—the general title page, "The Lamb," and "The Tyger."

Miniature Gallery, 60 Rushett Close, Long Dutton, Surrey KT7 OUT, Eng.: seventy-two–slide set based on the 1978 exhibition at the Tate Gallery.

A fifty-slide pack, SP008, including several frames from copy Z (Library of Congress—the same copy available from Oxford University Press), was issued by British Council Literary Study Aids, 65 Davies St., London W1Y 2AA, and sold at the 1978 Tate Gallery exhibition.

Once the slides are in hand, selections made, and the carousel tray loaded, the teacher still faces the problem of getting the images onto the screen. If the art department's projection room is available, there are no worries with equipment (including side-by-side projectors, if needed for comparisons between differing copies). But if the audiovisual department is to deliver equipment to a classroom in the English building, finicky adjustments will be necessary to ensure a smooth-running presentation; the teacher must have access to the room well before class time and must allow time to disassemble equipment afterward. For small classes, the teacher might prefer to use a magnifying slide viewer, now available with a seven-and-a-half-inch-square screen and three different levels of magnification; this device is easy to set up and is particularly convenient for study and previewing.

One frustration of working with a large collection of slides, in addition to the time required for labeling, filing, sorting, and refiling, is the inflexibility of the sequence of slides in a presentation. Videodisc technology has the potential to end these frustrations. A videodisc makes a large archive of images truly accessible—instantly retrievable in any order, with no filing required. Each image has a five-digit "address," a frame number; to see any picture, one need only punch in its number on a hand-held keypad. A laser-reflective videodisc the size of a phonograph record can store up to fifty thousand images, more than enough space for all six thousand pictures in Blake's oeuvre, counting all versions of the illuminated books, along with paintings, drawings, illustrations of other poets, commercial engravings, and miscellaneous works and allowing plenty of additional room for detailed close-ups.

At the University of Iowa, we have developed a prototype of a computer-driven videodisc archive of Blake's work, based on the 2,700 Blake slides in our collection. Our computer program, which runs on the Prime computer at the university's Weeg Computing Center, allows us to search our archive by title, subject, motif, and other categories. Our partial archive is successful enough to make us eager to develop a larger archive suitable for distribution off campus.

The quality of videodisc images, especially when shown on a first-rate color television monitor, has improved greatly over the past ten years. The quality of the videodisc, however, can never be better than the quality of the slides used as its foundation. The Iowa videodisc was made from slides that were acquired over a twenty-year period for study and teaching purposes, not for reproduction. They are uneven in quality: some are excellent, but many have faded; others were taken under poor lighting conditions or at bad angles; still others seriously distort the colors of the originals. A publishable videodisc would have to begin with fresh slides.

Because of copyright restrictions, we can show our pilot videodisc system outside the University of Iowa only in lecture-demonstrations; we cannot distribute copies of the disc. Our project shares space on a single videodisc with six other departments in an experimental program organized by Joan Sustik Huntley of the Computer-Assisted Instruction Laboratory at the Weeg Computing Center. Images on the Iowa videodisc range from thousands of pictorial subjects used in art-history courses, to maps for the geography department, to all manner of oral abnormalities studied in the College of Dentistry; our computer program addresses only the Blake portion of the disc.

Another way to make images of *Songs* more widely available would be to reproduce the illuminated books in microfiche. G. E. Bentley, Jr., laid the groundwork for a complete archive of Blake's works on color microfiche but could not secure foundation support for color photography. Brian Wilkie developed on two microfiches a color collection of illuminated books in the Huntington Library for his students at the University of Illinois (he details his experiences using the collection in the note following this essay).

Nonbook forms of reproduction will one day help make *Songs* more accessible, but they can never take the place of facsimiles on paper. Blake was a book designer, graphic artist, and printmaker, not a video artist. If his works were known only through microfiche, videodisc, or slides, readers would miss some of the effects he had in mind when he chose his paper, inks, and colors. Blake's readers will continue to want books they can touch—beautiful facsimiles that re-create his works of art in a form as close to the original as possible.

Blake on Microfiche

Brian Wilkie

In 1975 I had been teaching Blake regularly for some years, frequently showing in the classroom color slides of his work that had been expertly prepared by the Office of Instructional Resources at the University of Illinois, where I then taught. It goes without saying that students' seeing these slides was better than their merely reading the words Blake wrote. It goes equally without saying, I imagine, that the procedure was enormously inefficient and frustrating: students were getting their first look at the designs, and it was as if, in a Shakespeare course, one had to read aloud in the classroom a whole scene from *Hamlet* before discussing it. Students had had no time to peruse and ponder Blake's plates before class sessions, nor could they return to the plates thereafter to review for exams, write papers, or just study Blake more thoroughly on their own. Facsimiles in book form were no answer; even those facsimiles that were both available and inexpensive enough for the university library to purchase in plentiful duplicate would have worn out after two or three semesters of use by whole classes of students.

Our solution was to put Blake's works on color microfiches. Each of these little four-by-six-inch transparency cards can hold ninety-eight tiny frames (seven rows, fourteen frames to a row), so we could easily accommodate on two microfiche cards the complete *Thel, Visions of the Daughters of Albion, Innocence* and *Experience, The Marriage of Heaven and Hell, Urizen, America,* and *Europe.* New photography was required for those works we did not already have on slides. The photography was based on good facsimiles in the public domain; to these we added, with the permission of the Huntington Library, a smattering of alternative versions of certain plates, colored and uncolored, from the Huntington's collection. When all the slides were prepared, we shipped them off to a commercial photo-processing company and had fifty sets made of the two microfiches, for what I believe was under two hundred dollars. (This figure does not include, of course, the cost of the original photography.) The instructional audiovisual department of the library at Illinois possessed at that time only eleven microfiche-reader machines, but we wanted to have enough duplicates of the microfiches to provide the people who taught Blake with "desk copies" and also to have a back-up supply in case any of the eleven copies placed at the library reserve desk were lost or mutilated.

Our worries about durability were idle, however. Microfiche cards seem almost indestructible, short of deliberate violence, even after years of heavy use. The microfiche-reader machines, which are not mechanically intricate or inordinately expensive, are easy to use (they have the feel of a Ouija board with its planchette). One can move from any frame to any other frame on the same microfiche card in a few seconds, and to substitute a different card is almost as fast. (Such mobility is important for tracking the innumerable cross-references, from one plate or work to another, in Blake's graphic art.) Images projected from such works as *America* are approximately their actual size on the screen; smaller designs such as those in the *Songs* are significantly magnified. Detail emerges with pretty fair definition, and color fidelity is good, since transparencies introduce less distortion of color than do most opaque reproductions, such as plates in a book.

I'll add that the usefulness of the microfiches was much enhanced by a commentary designed to accompany them. The commentary provided students with a kind of lexicon of Blake's mythology and visual iconography, focusing (literally) their attention on significant visual images in the individual plates and (since this package was designed not merely to inform but to stimulate thought and class discussion) mixing explanations with questions posed but left unanswered.

The microfiches package has worked even better than we hoped, and I have installed a version of it at the University of Arkansas, to which I recently moved from Illinois. Students have found it indispensable, and so have I. Its main value, put simply, is that it has solved the problems I outlined at the beginning of this note. It also allows students to do course assignments on their schedules and at their own speeds. Finally, in combination with the commentary, it makes a do-it-yourself study guide to Blake available to faculty members in all departments and to general library users.

Part Two

APPROACHES

INTRODUCTION

Perhaps more than the work of any other artist, Blake's illuminated books raise questions of theory that are inseparable from questions of practice. In addition to the manifold challenges to interpretation and analysis generated by words and images "on" the plates, there are also questions of interpretation involving the minute particulars of a symbolic act or system executed deliberately by hand upon a chosen material (the copper plate) in a specific historical context. Composite art demands that we attend in class not only to the nuances and polyvalent references and echoes of language but to the very design of the words on the plate, along with the network of visual associations formed with surrounding words and the relation of this network to the plate's purely graphic elements. The contributors to this volume are aware of these interacting modes and of the essential complexity that represents perhaps the greatest challenge to teachers and students of Blake's art. As a result, most of the following essays move deftly between ideas and practice. While the essays thus remain true to the complexity of Blake's art and the pedagogical problems it engenders, their necessary comprehensiveness presented a challenge for us as we sought to group the approaches in some useful arrangement.

The four divisions into which we have collected the essays may seem arbitrary. To be sure, other arrangements suggested themselves to us, and in a few cases only by emphasizing one aspect over others in a given essay did we become satisfied with its "fit." Nevertheless, we believe that *an* arrangement may be useful to readers of this book, and we offer *this* arrangement while making no absolute claims for it.

Essays in the first group stress theory. For the most part, they insist either that we emphasize theory in our teaching of the *Songs* or that we bring theoretical issues to bear on particular poems. Mitchell's piece focuses on the interconnections among images, texts, and history in teaching the *Songs*. Simpson argues that "ideology is innate to language" and that it represents a dimension of the *Songs* that teachers and students should struggle to recover—even as they acknowledge that not all of this dimension may be recoverable until we learn more about Blake and his time. And Johnson, drawing on literary and cultural history along with close readings of the poems, suggests ways of teaching the *Songs* from a feminist perspective. As if to illustrate the connection between theory and practice we have been emphasizing in this introduction, the final essay in this group (Viscomi's) progresses from Blake's theory of seeing to a detailed description of how one might guide a class through his actual practices as an engraver.

The second group of approaches addresses problems that emerge, principally, from particular institutional or departmental teaching situations and illustrates their authors' fashioning of successful classroom strategies and practices. The essay by Frosch, for example, presents an approach that has worked well in a large, urban university (though it by no means suggests that this method's usefulness is limited to that context). Tayler and La Belle sketch entertainingly a variety of tactics they have used in teaching Blake to students at technological institutes—students who, for the most part, have elected not to study literature in any depth. Their experiences, we believe, characterize the problems many teachers face in presenting Blake's *Songs* to nonmajors or to students in required classes. Focusing on the relation among instructor, student, and canonical text, Stephen Cox advocates taking risks in discussing Blake. He argues that by asking difficult, even provocative questions about the text, teachers may cultivate in their students independent thought and judgment.

The third group of essays advocates classroom approaches that center upon intertextuality and the idea of context. Robert Essick stresses the manifold variations among different copies of the *Songs* that Blake produced over time and sketches a practical way of addressing these issues with a class. Blake called the Bible "the Great Code of Art," and from it he derived words, images, ideas, cadences, and a "mythic" paradigm that informs the shape of his art and is especially important in understanding the *Songs*. Taken together, the essays by Tannenbaum and Gallagher illustrate not only how fruitful class discussion can emerge out of attention to biblical contexts but also how approaches emphasizing similar texts may be substantially different. Exploring the relations between Blake's *Songs* and other mid-eighteenth-century poetry, Wallace Jackson's piece is especially useful for teachers of period or survey courses. Like the other essays in this section, Jackson's highlights the idea of historical and thematic context.

The final group of essays, concentrating on individual poems from a variety of perspectives, also suggests connections between particular works and larger categories of thought. Brian Wilkie and Harold Pagliaro are chiefly concerned with teaching students to explore the minds of the poems' speakers. Wilkie maps in detail the essential implication of the speaker with the world that speaker "describes," and he suggests ways of introducing students to this idea; Pagliaro traces the dynamics between speakers' psychologies dramatized in the *Songs* and those of students engaged with the drama, arguing that full involvement with such dynamics redeems, in effect, students' minds. Essays by Vogler and Ault demonstrate how sophisticated theory may inform the teaching of particular poems, especially "London." Vogler sensitizes us to the sounds in the *Songs* and how we "hear" them. Ault teaches his students that Blake's art subverts perceivers' expectations about reading and thus spurs within the reader a perceptual and ontological reorganization.

Readers of this introduction must have perceived by now the insufficiency of the organization we have chosen. Fortunately, the essays easily overcome the limitations we impose by our categories.

APPROACHES EMPHASIZING THEORY

Image and Text in *Songs*

W. J. T. Mitchell

How can we get students to *see* Blake's *Songs*? What is it that we want them to see? Beauty? Semantic complexity? Skill? My aim is to make them see a specific symbolic act in a historical context. I begin by asking them to see the dates (in some copies erased) inscribed on the title pages of *Innocence* and *Experience*: what can they see in "1789" and "1794"? What could it mean to erase these dates? What does it say about the *Songs'* relation to history? What other strategies for erasing history can be found in the *Songs*? (Some answers that one gets: the "unrealistic" or "childlike" character of the designs and texts; the tendency toward fanciful, visionary, religious, pastoral, and allegorical imagery.)

I find this sort of question more useful than the usual supplying of "historical background" as something to be "reflected" in the text. It helps the students see that the expression of meanings in a text or image may be as much a function of repression as of intention, that "innocence" (like the sunrise) is a code word for that "dawn" (as Wordsworth later puts it) in which it was "bliss to be alive" and "experience" a code word for postrevolutionary consciousness—awareness of terror, guilt, alienation, apostasy, unrelenting tyranny, irony, and a kind of sober wisdom coupled with unrelenting utopian hopes. I don't think it's a bad idea to let the students see the *Songs* as polem-

ical tracts against determinate social injustices, as long as they can also see
the acts of displacement, erasure, and repression that accompany the representation of 1789 as a "state of the soul" called "innocence." If the students
can supply the "information" (really a kind of cultural myth or pseudonarra-
tive) about what happened between 1789 and 1794, so much the better. One
way or another, you put into the record the story of the French Revolution
(best of all, have them read the Burke-Paine debate), stressing its presence
in this text as a subtext already being written and rewritten, even as it happens. Then bring them back to the presence and absence of these dates in
Blake's text. What is the meaning of the placement of dates in graphic space?
("1789" glimmers on the horizon of the pastoral landscape, or hangs like a
fruit from the lowest branch of the tree of life, or stands free of pictorial
space altogether, as a date on a title page. "1794" is inscribed unambiguously
in stone; it stays locked in the pictorial space, an epitaph that is part of the
scene.)

Somewhere in this discussion the issue of "seeing" versus "reading into"
will come up. I like to convert this topic from a question about the "rules" or
limits of reading (when are you going too far, "reading into" a text or image)
into the substantive issue of Blake's composite art: the relation of seeing and
reading, picturing and writing (or speaking). One can pursue this subject as a
thematic issue in the *Songs*—the scenes of writing, reading, speaking, and
picturing (in dreams, in set-piece descriptions, in figures, in graphic images)—
the paradigm being the "Introduction" to *Innocence*, with its cyclical narrative of the fall from music to vision ("I saw a child") to song to writing to
reading to reproduction (and rebirth) as aural performance. Why does the
frontispiece that "illustrates" this narrative pick out for its *punktum* the moment of seeing the child? Why does the title page to *Innocence* take us to a
scene of instruction, where children pore over a book not to "hear" the voice
encrypted in it, but to immerse themselves in a silent, tutored reading of the
open text in their nurse or mother's lap? Is it "reading into" this scene to
wonder whether this person is the mother or the nurse and to ask what difference it makes? What is the relation of tutor and pupils? (The relation of
the tree and serpentine vine as emblems of forbidden knowledge will not be
long in coming to the surface.) Are the children looking at pictures or reading words, or doing one as a way of preparing for or interpreting the other?

It will be objected that these questions are unanswerable. True enough,
but this is a good opening for a discussion of the poetics of unanswerable
questions in image and text ("The Tyger" and its enigmatic pussycat design).
The "unanswerability" trope leads us back to ourselves as questioning readers: How do we get from Blake's images to his texts? What are the routes
(not roots) of reference between visual and verbal signs? I generally ask each
class member to present a five-minute explanation of some text-design con-

junction, either a song and its accompanying design(s) or a piece of framing matter (title pages, frontispieces). Their responsibility is to identify the minute particulars of textual and pictorial iconography (Erdman's *Illuminated Blake* should be on reserve or on their reading list), to make observations about the meaning of those particulars, and to map out the routes of image-text reference in both directions. Their terminology can emerge spontaneously and can be theorized as it comes: literal transcription or illustration ("The Little Black Boy," "The Lamb," "The Shepherd"), ornament and allegory ("Introduction" to *Innocence*), translation or transposition (textual "blossom" to pictorial flame-flower or angel-mother; human infancy to fairy's nativity scene in "Infant Joy"), independent invention (frontispiece to *Experience*; design of "The Divine Image").

One can readily deconstruct these ad hoc classifications to make the main point that should be emerging in the discussion: text and design in Blake's books do not have univocal functions regulated by the predictable binary oppositions we associate with visual and verbal communication. Categories like time and space, "natural" signification and "convention," narrative and depiction, the ear and the eye, lose their reified character in the dialectical matrix of Blake's plates. The relation of text and design is as likely to be subversive, repressive, ironic, or (in general) "contrarious" as supplemental, cooperative, or parasitical. And the parasite has a way of turning itself into a host: the visual form of "The Divine Image" swallows the textual abstractions of "Mercy Pity Peace and Love" in a whirlwind of line and color. At one level, this point is as simple as getting the students to notice that pictures have as much meaning—as much power to narrate, describe, signify, and argue—as the words do. At a more complex level, the task is to reveal the relations of text and design as what Fredric Jameson (87) has called an "ideologeme"—a basic unit of polarized, dialectical thought that echoes all the contraries of Innocence and Experience, male and female, good and evil that are being deconstructed by Blake's "text," now understood as a composite visual-verbal structure. The students' initial assumption (which critics share) that the pictures are the more primitive, childish, "direct," or "natural" mode of producing meaning can now be reread for what it is: a piece of semiotic ideology, a prejudice about signs that reproduces distinctions of class, race, and gender (a relation I treat in *Iconology: Image, Text, Ideology*).

When these connections are in place, we need to take two further steps: a re-formalization of Blake's text around categories other than the binary opposition of word and image, and a return to the initial project of historicizing this text in the context of the French Revolution. To encourage the first ("re-formalization") step, I have developed a fourfold system of textual protocols for the description of Blake's illuminated books (and for any other text as well) that turns attention from semiotic to discursive difference. These protocols—Narrative, Image, Argument, and Dialectic (acronym: NaIAD)—cut directly across the apparent divide between pictures and words. I first ask the students to analyze Blake's composite·text for stories, plots, sequences, "histories," genealogies, and other temporal patterns. This enables them to break down the image-text divide, to see designs as moments or extensions of verbal narratives, and to see verbal narratives as consisting of determinate strings of pictorial "narremes" (like scenes in drama, or "takes" in film). This sort of analysis leads to the consideration of both designs and texts as "Images": that is, (1) as depictions of determinate "states of affairs," as scenes populated by figures, features, and identifiable (nameable, picturable) forms; (2) as likenesses, analogies, isomorphisms in which features of form and content map onto a parallel system in terms of some code (the religious imagery of children, lambs, and Christ; the analogy of religious, psychological, and political falls into experience); (3) as determinate formal gestalten that unite graphic and typographic expression (the calligraphy of Innocence and Experience, for example, a feature I treat in "Visible Language").

The account of Narrative and Image quickly leads to the question of "point" or "meaning," to issues of rhetoric and "designs on the reader." I ask the students at this stage to treat Image and Narrative as constituent features in an argument and invite them to formulate the "moral" of Blake's stories and scenes in the most definite possible terms. It seems to me crucial that we not shrink from the determinacy of Blake's moral outrage in the *Songs*, the fact that his text has definite historical objectives not to be wished away by "eternizing" or psychologizing maneuvers. The risk of vulgarity and oversimplification cannot be circumvented; my experience is that the students and the texts will resist reification if the instructor allows them to interrogate one another (not just what questions we pose of the text but what it poses for us). This interrogation will invariably bring them to the fourth protocol of a discursive mapping of the *Songs*: the rituals of dialectic. These rituals will be familiar to them at a formal and thematic level in the dialectics of image and text and the play of ideational contraries. Now we may give the dialectic a human face in staging dialogue poems and images, telling contrary stories, depicting antithetical scenes, mustering antagonistic arguments. The examples ("Clod and the Pebble," "Infant Joy," "Introduction" to *Experience*, and "Earth's Answer") may proliferate if we add in the paired poems from *Innocence* and *Experience* and count poems with implied listeners (the father of "A Little Boy Lost," the mother of "The Little Vagabond") or narrative poems and images that frame dialogues or moments of interaction. The four protocols at this point become interchangeable as framing devices (dialogue inside of narrative and vice versa, images of dialogues in narratives that make arguments, etc.).

But it quickly becomes evident that the dialogue and dialectic of contraries constitute the master code in Blake's text, the one that prevents it from settling into the simple allegorical codes we fret over at the level of argument. What is difficult is the return to our initial problem, the meaning of all these strategies as parts of a specific symbolic act in a historical context. Blake's text is so rich in itself, so full of timeless evocations for the students, that we are tempted to monumentalize it as the object of endless formal inquiry. I would suggest that our current challenge is to read the textual strategies of Blake's *Songs* not as part of his emerging monomyth but in the context of writers like Rousseau (especially the discussion of education and children's books in *Emile* and Rousseau's lifelong obsession with innocence), Wollstonecraft, and Godwin (the critique of marriage, sexuality, and political education elaborated by the Joseph Johnson circle in the 1790s). Most important of all is the "contrary" that haunts the discourse of Blakean radicalism in the 1790s, the voice of Edmund Burke, whose writings on the Revolution provide all the basic tropes (the seditious "pastoral"; ambiguities of gender; revolutionary "tygers," "devils," "furies," and "savages"; religions of nature, dissent, and established order; the "wild gas," or ignis fatuus, with its "wandering light") in Blake's political subtext. When this subtext is in place, we can see that Blake's *Songs* deploy a specific array of formal ideologies, not at all congruent or homogeneous: they are "illuminated" texts at a moment when the "illuminati" of France and the "conquering empire of light and reason" and European Enlightenment are the most fearsome objects on the English political horizon; yet they are updated relics from a feudal mode of production, a compromise between new printing technology and archaic manuscript illumination. They are dissenters' emblem books that resemble Catholic prayer missals, made at a time when Burke was identifying left-wing Puritan dissent as a new kind of revolutionary popish plot. They are children's books that Coleridge would recognize as too dangerous for adults, books about a radical innocence that fly in the face of Rousseau's imperative to keep books away from children, putative instruments in a utopian scheme of mass education ("every child may joy to hear") that instantly achieved the status of esoteric marginality and a durable, but highly mystified, cult value. It may be well to conclude your students' introduction to Blake's *Songs* with the admission that we do not yet have a way of saying what they are. What they will do with this information is beyond your control. One can hope that it will challenge them to write interesting papers.

Teaching Ideology in *Songs*

David Simpson

Blake's *Songs* always provide, for me, some of the most exciting classroom experiences of the teaching year. Seldom has the collective effort of two or three dozen pairs of eyes focused on a poem of ten to twenty lines failed to produce something that I have never thought for myself or heard from other students or professional critics. We like to think that this exhilaration is possible in all teaching, but Blake elicits such responsive engagements more often than anything else I teach. Students seem to feel that he grants them an unusual permission to suggest things that other texts might inhibit or complicate. Some occasionally freeze up, at least temporarily, protesting that "these poems could mean anything," or even that "Blake doesn't know what he means." Not all get beyond this point of anxiety, but when the thaw does come, the doors of perception open almost explosively, and all sorts of things come tumbling out.

The most frequent task I face, then, is to explain that there are constraints upon what can responsibly be said about Blake's poems—no mean task with a writer who constantly barrages us with memorable aphorisms about the infinitude of imaginative vision. This problem brings us to "ideology," a term all too often, and with some justice, associated with fixed vision, rigidity, and a denial of the joys of reading and the roads of interpretive excess. At first glance, Blake seems to espouse beliefs that counter ideology thus conceived. So we find ourselves wondering whether an aesthetics of openness and cocreation is really an escape from ideology or just an ideology of escapism. Moreover, does such an approach explain all of Blake's writings, or just some of them, the ones we understand most readily?

The elucidation of these questions in the classroom is largely determined, for me, by the minute particularity of Blake's poems. To an extraordinary degree they resist being talked about as a whole before they have been carefully examined as separate identities. Even when we think we have a fix on the verbal dimensions—a rare enough achievement in itself—the visual information in the plates is likely to set us back where we began. We may offer neat analogies, for example, about the ambiguously opening-closing flower in "Infant Joy," or the purposively meek tiger in Blake's most famous poem, but all too often we are adrift in a sea of possibilities. Who is the figure to the right of the text of "The Little Boy Found"? Why is the tree in the first plate of "The Ecchoing Green" altered in the later copies? Is it a polled liberty tree? If so, what does it say about the poem? Does its changed shape make the poem in 1824 different from the poem in 1789? The harder one looks at any one poem, the more we lose hope of ever encoding all such details into hard-and-fast meanings or arriving at a view of Blake "as a whole."

These features of Blake's poems might seem to make them almost uniquely resistant to sociopolitical or ideological specification. Those who have written about Blake's ideology have often felt safest in pitching their arguments at a sanitary distance from the minute details of text and design. Symptomatically, the most recent account, by Michael Ferber, stays well away from close readings, although it promises future restorations (*Social Vision* xi). Ferber's description of Blake's ideology as emerging from contact with English Dissent and radical Christian sects, among others, is unexceptionable in itself but serves to brand ideology once again as a general set of convictions or priorities never really seen at work in the dark corners of Blake's poems. Ferber finds that "the particulars demand a multiplanar organizing interpretation to situate them properly" (5), but I suspect here that he is searching for a vision of woods before having identified any trees. There are so many woods in Blake's landscape, moreover, that one risks producing yet another history of ideas rather than an analysis of the workings of writing. For classroom purposes especially, such an approach is of limited use, since it confines the student to the passive reception of contexts that only the superior reading experience of the professional scholar can authenticate as relevant. Reading and debate are replaced by yawning and note taking.

If our talk of ideology is to convince the students (and ourselves), we cannot simply bring up the names and systems of Brothers, Southcott, Swedenborg, or Marx. We must respect the literalism of the poems and make those words live. There are not many published examples of such intensely localized specifications of ideology. David Erdman's *Blake: Prophet against Empire* was and still is a foundational book, one of the two or three that all students should read and ponder, but it is often casual or over brief in its comments on individual poems. By contrast, Heather Glen's *Vision and Disenchantment* tries to provide a closer focus on the politics of Blake's language, but it is hampered by a naive thesis about both Innocence and Experience, by a trenchant Leavisite approach to the relation of Blake to Wordsworth, and by a remarkably incomplete (given its exclusive focus on the *Songs*) coverage of the very poems it promises to discuss. Glen's book is useful for the classroom but only if we invoke the above reservations, and others besides. We cannot, once again, avoid involving the student in the political dramas of the contemporary academy—a healthy thing in itself, but not appropriate to some classrooms, least of all when the dramas, like Glen's, are peculiarly British rather than international.

It is time for some examples: I begin with *Songs of Innocence*. Some of these poems express an apparently straightforward ideology. "The Lamb," once we have deciphered its cannily synthetic syntax and its nonexclusive logic of identity (students are always impressed by the function of the absence of a comma in the last line), seems a fairly clear exposition of how Christ's coming to earth illuminates the divine oneness of all forms of life. "The Divine Image," "Night," and "On Another's Sorrow" seem similarly explicit in their argument that there is, properly understood, no "other." Though these notions were not exactly orthodox Christianity as espoused in the eighteenth century, Blake seems comfortable in his explicit publicizing of his doctrine of love. Of all the *Songs* these poems are the ones that might be read to children without too much knitting of the adult brows, and we may suggest that they represent a high degree of ideological clarity or self-confidence. What Blake wants to say here does not seem to involve any ambivalence or retraction. There is no irony—at least none that I am yet convinced of.

Given Blake's reputation as always on the admirable side of the political fence—a reputation subscribed to both in the academy and outside it—it is very strange to suggest, as I do, that the ideologically complex poems in *Innocence* are exactly those that address urgent, well-known, and generally well-delineated debates in late eighteenth-century England. It is with these poems that students are puzzled and unsure. "Holy Thursday" is too runic to allow its readers to feel sure that Blake is merely decrying the current condition of England. By attending to detail I can usually lead them to entertain the ironic interpretation. The disruptive imperative of the last line, the observation that the children's radiance is "all their own" (E 13) and that they sit above their guardians, as if nearer to heaven, all persuade most students that Blake is not just celebrating the benevolence of the state in looking after its pauper children. But it is an elusive irony, and some find themselves wondering why, if the poem means to expose the hypocrisy of charity, it does not speak more clearly, more directly. How do we know, unless we already know a good deal about Blake, that the sexual segregation imaged in the design of the plate is a repressive tactic? And what kind of "innocence" is this, the divine simplicity of the children or the self-deceiving ignorance of the middle-class reader?

Having established this uneasy consensus over "Holy Thursday," I move on to two other poems of *Innocence* where the problem of irony emerges in clear ideological terms: "The Chimney Sweeper" and "The Little Black Boy." These poems have worked well for me in the classroom because the choices are unusually obvious; that is, the poems *can* be read (though perhaps should not be read) in either of two ways with more or less equal credibility. They are not at all vague in their social messages, but they can be interpreted convincingly as offering either of two different messages.

We know, for example, that "The Chimney Sweeper" made it into James Montgomery's 1824 anthology the *Chimney Sweeper's Friend and Climbing*

Boy's Album. But I at least wonder what the editor thought he was including, for the poem does not work as an unambiguous expression of outrage at the horrifying conditions of child labor. Nonetheless, it was written and published at a high point in the public consciousness of the question: a bill, although an inefficient one, was passed in 1788, and was accompanied by widespread public debate (Erdman, *Prophet* 132). The ideological crux of this much-discussed poem inheres in the status and effect of Tom Dacre's vision. We can base a coherent reading on the assumption that the speaker (presumably an experienced child sweep, but why not an adult supervisor or employer?) and/or Tom himself are complete victims, dupes of the establishment Christian rhetoric that counsels patience in this life and concentration on the life to come. The cast of the speaker's address is certainly "kind," but it may also be seen to have a repressive function. Tom's dream of a paradisal world in which all suffering and exploitation have disappeared is what gives him the strength to get up in the morning and go to work. The whole poem can be understood as an expression of "false consciousness," as it explores the function of the conventional Christian mythology in keeping the slaves of society in their places. The vision is not a relief or compensation: it is the means of coercing an alienated (and potentially dissident) little child into being "a good boy" (E 10). The last line is then disjunctive and sardonic, and the "want joy" of the penultimate stanza punningly reflects on the deadening results of the Christian doctrine: thinking about the rewards of the afterlife renders one indifferent to this one and unable to "want" (desire) joy. Tom will never "want" (lack) joy because he will never know what it is, having "God for his father."

This reading of the poem makes excellent sense of its language and is compatible with a great deal of evidence on the same ideological points that we might draw from the rest of Blake's writings. But there are always students who are uncomfortable with such a negative view of the effects of Christian doctrine. They would prefer to interpret Tom's vision as valid and sustaining, and the transformation of his spirit as authentic and admirable. Assiduous users of the library can find support for their case. Heather Glen, for example, tells them that the dream is an example of the positive imagination's survival in hostile surroundings, of a subversive faculty that "the established official religion and morality of late eighteenth-century England sought to contain" (*Vision* 102). Following this lead, why is the poem not an injunction to exploited children to cultivate the inner light and the world beyond, ignoring as best they can the (theologically inevitable) suffering here on earth? We are all in chains, all fallen, and perhaps those who suffer now are actually the lucky ones, since they will have less to atone for afterwards. The "lesson" seems unassailable.

One can point out that the first, ironic reading makes the poem seem more sophisticated (as well as more sympathetic) but no such reliance upon the old New Critical standards of complexity should convince the recalcitrant reader that this reading is therefore correct. Although Blake was not generally in favor of deferred gratification, is there anything intrinsic to the poem that prevents us from taking the vision in complete good faith, from reading its last line as a ringing affirmation of the way in which "duty" to imagination protects us from ultimate "harm"? Such an interpretation is not only quite credible in itself, it may well have been more popular in 1790 than its ironizing rival. It does not question the establishment, since recommending spiritual consolations (in the imagination or the afterlife) is exactly what the establishment would have done. Given the general propensity of student readers (not to say those more experienced) to find in a poem exactly what they want and either to ignore ambiguity or to resolve it in the direction most comfortable to themselves, why should any author who really wished to expose hypocrisy have left his poem so open to an antithetical construction?

The question only becomes the more tortured when we produce the evidence for the Swedenborgian allegory that Kathleen Raine (*Blake and Tradition* 1: 20–26) has brought forward. What does the cogent reading of the child sweeps as emblems of semen burning to escape from a compressed place say about the ideological affiliation of the poet? The reader of 1790 who was primed to discover this code would, presumably, have forgotten or passed over the empirical woes of these wretched children even more completely than would the "establishment" Christian.

Our class is now visibly scratching its collective head, an imaginative response that becomes almost audible when we look at "The Little Black Boy." Here again we have an urgent contemporary occasion for the poem—the slave trade—and here again we have a muddle. To assume with Erdman that the poem was meant to "assist" those working for abolition in the 1780s (*Prophet* 132) involves, once again, reading the poem as ironic. The little boy repeats the platitudes that he has heard from his mother, who has heard them from the missionaries, and thus articulates the ideology that supports and maintains his own repression. He can be interpreted as reminding us of his ultimate spiritual equality (even superiority) as a means of asking for justice here and now, in the fallen world, but what he finally looks to is a reward in heaven rather than an earthly revolution.

The poem makes sense as a savagely ironic exposure of the quietistic effects of Christian doctrine, but again, it can be read in good faith by anyone who believes that the next life really does make up for the shortcomings of this one. Many well-intentioned abolitionists could have believed this, even if they did not push the idea so far as to proclaim that there was no point in meddling with earthly inequities, since all would come right in heaven. Which is the way, the right or the left?

Those of us who take ideology seriously had best be on our toes at this point. Here are two poems that can mean two different things to two kinds of readers, and both kinds of readers may well be competent. We cannot turn to the sacred "text" to prove one reading against the other. How can we know whether Blake himself is indecisive, unable to make up his mind, or merely an "establishment" voice? Is the ironic reading a function of our knowledge of his later and more radical work? Or third, is he a cunning craftsman seeking to produce in a select band of readers an awareness of the availability of a choice? It is hard, perhaps impossible, to come up with a definitive answer. And we must add into the equation some notice of Blake's medium as itself an ideological quantity: we have looked hard at words, but the visual-verbal complex that Blake produced, with its cultural analogue in children's books, may have distracted from rather than focused on the verbal dimension as the primary bearer of significance. The design of "The Chimney Sweeper," at least, does not seem to "read" ironically. And the *Songs* was an expensive book, not at all akin to relatively cheap childrens' books or the six-penny sheets of *The Rights of Man* that were being sold on the streets of London. Blake was a complex elitist: he seems to have hoped for a wide circulation for his books, but he did not compromise his visions for the sake of the sales figures.

The possibility (raised by some students) that Blake might have designed his ambiguities to confuse the censors does not carry much weight in view of the facts of the market: few people read them, and Godwin, for example, got away with far more because the *Inquiry* was so expensive. Moreover, there was no censorship on expressing outrage at the slave trade or the conditions of chimney sweeps. Looking at the poems in the context of contemporary book production and the market, then, does not solve our problems so much as compound them.

So far we have limited our attentions to the *Songs of Innocence* (and have generated the sort of skepticism that must reflect on other seemingly one-dimensional poems, such as "Laughing Song" and "The Shepherd"). Does an inspection of the *Songs of Experience* help us out? These poems generally seem to be at least as difficult to construe as those of *Innocence*, although local certitudes may once again emerge. We are often—as in "The Tyger"— faced with the intuition that we need to involve some allegorical (or quasi-allegorical) code to make sense of the poem, without being exactly sure what that code might be. For "The Chimney Sweeper" of *Experience*, we at least here have a companion poem. Does the later one reflect authoritatively on the questions raised by its predecessor? In the *Experience* sweeper poem, the child was and is happy, maintaining his good spirits against great odds, almost as if he had shared Tom Dacre's dream. But here we find no mention of Christian mythology: his energies seem to be entirely natural and spontaneous, not stimulated by visions of angels. His career seems almost a parental punishment for his happy disposition ("Because I was happy," E 22). The adverse commentary on the Christian establishment seems clear. The state—priest and king—is a direct cause of the boy's sufferings, and his parents may well belong among those who believe that it is good to suffer on earth for the sake of one's eternal soul. The irony of this poem is relatively clear: the boy seems to know exactly what is going on and is unsparing in his exposure of cruelty and hypocrisy. Does this reading tell us how to read the earlier poem?

Not really. First, the *Songs of Innocence* was published earlier and separately; though Blake never published it on its own after 1794, his letter to Turner of June 1818 suggests that he would have been prepared to if the buyer so wished (E 771). We cannot assume that the poem of 1794 is a rewriting of that of 1789, and even if it were we should already have learned from our reading of *Songs of Innocence* not to trust it. Although the relation between Innocence and Experience is one of the most familiar cruxes in Blake criticism, one on which every class should be invited to pronounce, we still do not have a dogmatic conclusion. At this stage I have found it most convincing to propose a *range* of relations: contradiction, dialectical identity, irony, and so forth (a range similar to that which can appear *within* the *Songs of Innocence* and the *Songs of Experience* taken separately). Looking at *Experience*—which I can do only briefly here—what overall frame of interpretation can make sense of "The Sick Rose" and "The Little Girl Lost" without abandoning unitary (or at least consistent ideological) thinking?

After all this close reading, it is tempting to pronounce that Blake's ideology is that of progression by contraries, as defined in *The Marriage of Heaven and Hell*. The true misunderstanding would then be precisely a fixed interpretation of anything, the poison of "standing water" referred to in the "Proverbs of Hell." But I am not sure that the contrary readings of, for example, "The Little Black Boy" amount to a progression for any but the most astute and detached readers, those who are able to restrain their endorsement of either reading in order to perceive the availability of both. Is this openness an ideology of radical Protestant self-election, whereby we must choose between God and the Devil and decide for ourselves which is which? Regardless of how one characterizes such flexibility, it represents good news for the classroom, since it instigates the Bakhtinian debate that always makes the teacher glow with the pleasure of a job well done. Does Blake finally ask to be defined as a writer who dramatizes the inevitable clash of ideologies in the social evolution of "meaning"?

If so, we must lodge one very firm caveat: he is emphatically not licensing the sorts of conclusions that repose comfortably in beliefs about the relativity of everything. Reading poems, especially those that are about contemporary social conditions, in two different ways makes us aware that ways of reading have consequences, both for ourselves and for how we act. We cannot simply abandon ourselves to a reading of Blake that explores the uses to which his poems can be put, however historically unjustifiable, by invoking the ethic of progression by contraries. For it remains clear that some readings carry more weight than others. I do not agree, then, with Stanley Fish, whose now famous account of the criticism of "The Tyger" leads him to affirm that "the text as it is variously characterized is a *consequence* of the interpretation for which it is supposedly evidence" (340). Fish thinks that all constraints on interpretation are imposed by "the literary institution which at any one time will authorize only a finite number of interpretative strategies" (342), and never by textual-historical evidence. This case, which has received a good deal of attention in pedagogic circles, needs answering if a notion of ideology that belongs to language in history, and not just to its latter-day readers, is to have any serious credibility.

Fish is right to say that "canons of acceptability can change" (349). I would guess, for example, that Harold Bloom's now influential theory of the anxiety of influence will prove ephemeral as a theory. After a number of years, we will cease to see this tragical-Freudian paradigm trotted out every time influence is to be explained. At the same time, I would also guess that some readings that Bloom and others have carried out under the influence of this theory will remain unignorable. They will survive because of a demonstrated fit between the model and the evidence it uncovers, one whose credibility does not depend on the continuity of the "literary institution" but on the sheer weight and detail of the proved relation between, say, a Wordsworth poem and a Miltonic prototype. Should bourgeois individuality ever cease to be the obsession of the American critical mind and the tenure system the means of its reproduction, the machine that is Bloom's theory will rust away, for it will no longer be validated by the literary institution. But bits and pieces of the structure will continue to shine brightly, not because they appeal to our uncritically projected selves but because they have been verified against a historical archive that is, despite widespread assumptions to the contrary, able to remain as "other" to ourselves.

There are, then, readings that cannot be ignored by any serious reader who comes after them (I do not, of course, mean to say that they are absolute or exclusive). Many will pass away, as Fish projects, but they will simply be the bad ones—and it is not merely contingent institutions that will judge them so. Hence Fish chooses to describe not the best readings of "The Tyger," but only those he feels fairly confident in pronouncing ephemeral.

He does not, for example, mention Kathleen Raine's second account of the poem (*Blake and Tradition* 2: 3–31), wherein she adduces the analogues provided by Paracelsus and the Gnostic tradition, as well as a literal paradigm for the poem's images in *The Divine Pymander of Hermes Trismegistus.* This context is so persuasive, I suggest, that it must be figured into any subsequent account of the poem and its ideology. It must be accepted, adapted, or disproved. Similarly, Ronald Paulson's documentation of the ubiquity of the imagery of wild beasts, and of tigers in particular, in the rhetoric surrounding the outbreak of the French Revolution (88–110) brings forth the sort of evidence whose relevance to Blake's poem would be extremely difficult to deny. To do so, we would have to posit that he spent the years 1789–94 in some private bedlam with no access to newspapers or to a public.

Raine and Paulson taken together do not tell us what to make of "The Tyger," but they give us a good start by bringing forth evidence that we cannot responsibly ignore (even as there will continue to be plenty of irresponsible criticism). We must, for example, ponder the connection between these two readings. Can the poem be both a lament for the negative creation of a demiurge who should not be considered the true God, as well as a commentary on the political rhetoric (and the events behind it) of the times? If so, how? Is Blake in some sense rewriting Milton's relation between political turmoil and the Fall of humanity as set forth in *Paradise Lost*? And if so, to what end?

I seem to be asking as often as answering questions. In so doing, I would not hide behind some Socratic legitimation of the teacher's role: I would simply say that we do not yet know enough to provide many firm answers. I usually end my Blake classes by looking at a poem I cannot begin to explain with conviction: say, "The Sick Rose." Of course I can offer a reading, as we all can, but I am sensible that I offer it with minimum conviction, aware that a Raine or a Paulson might discover a precise occasion for the poem, with which we might then begin an interpretation. My hunch is that when we do know more, Blake will seem less and less the canny, perspectively ironic Derridean that classroom convenience and the limits of our historical knowledge make him out to be. Considering the sheer amount of Blake criticism, very little of this kind of work has been done: we have all been too busy with our interpretations.

I come now to my final point. I have had to confess the incompleteness of my understanding of Blake's ideological personality, even as I have been able to toss out a good many possibilities (some of which work well in some poems and not so well in others)—and also, I hope, some sense of the forms of evidence that cannot be ignored. I see by glimpses Blake the forthright radical, Blake the confused Christian, Blake the private visionary, and sometimes I do not see at all. Do I not stand uncomfortably exposed as the teacher who does not have all the answers? Do I not undermine Blake's appeal by presenting him as difficult or confused? Worst of all (for me), does not the ideological approach appear useless, because always incomplete, demanding even for its inception the kinds of dogged research that even graduate students, let alone undergraduates, seldom have the time and energy to carry through?

No to all such intimations! The credo of this ideologically minded teacher runs as follows:

Say first: Ideology is innate to language. It is not an "approach to" or an "aspect of" that we can ignore if we choose. Good scholarship always convinces us that it was there from the start, however deflected, impacted, or written over. There indeed lies the fascination.

Say second: Trying to recover the ideological dimensions of poetry can be difficult and inconclusive. There are often no clear answers. The teacher may have to stick out a neck that never quite gets back to where it came from.

Say third: No educative purpose is served by pretending that we know more than we do. The New Critical and related formalist traditions had the effect of placing the teacher in control. Godlike, the instructor knew in advance all the puns and ironies, and how to adjust them one to another. This practice was based in part on a misunderstanding of what the humanist had to do to meet the challenge of the scientists, but all serious scientists I have known are driven by what they do not know and are very clear about how and why it is difficult to know some things. Thus they often do come up with worthwhile, even objective knowledge.

Say fourth, and last: The ideological explanation of Blake's poems is not just a specialist pursuit, an important but regrettably unteachable approach, a failure in its own terms. Handled closely and carefully, it is an exciting experience for both teacher and student. Both learn that language matters, that some meanings make more sense than others, that authors and teachers need not be authorities, that it is hard to separate the conscious and the unconscious in language, and that the past is not the same as the present. They learn above all that there is much still to do, indeed that we have hardly begun. And that too is an ideology—ours.

Feminist Approaches to
Teaching *Songs*

Mary Lynn Johnson

While working through the tangle of ideas on sexual difference that Blake eexpressed in his life, poetry, paintings, and theoretical manifestoes, a teacher who wishes to explore feminist approaches to *Songs of Innocence and of Experience* must also keep in mind the rich multiplicity of views represented in the various schools of feminist criticism. Feminist studies of Blake—which generally focus on works other than *Songs*—have abounded in recent years (for a sampling, excluding dissertations, see Johnson, "William Blake" 172–73), but these writings have been less closely identified with feminist criticism as such than with more traditional approaches to Romantic or eighteenth-century literature. That is, most Blake critics who have addressed issues of concern to feminists have concentrated on Blake's women characters and the androcentric bias of his key metaphors, employing critical procedures developed at a relatively early point in the fifteen-year development of contemporary feminist criticism.

In the meantime, the leading edge of Anglo-American feminist criticism, which is literary-historical in orientation, has increasingly shifted its emphasis from woman as sign to woman as artist (Showalter, "Women's Time" and "Introduction"; Greene and Kahn; Moi), a focus that obviously precludes investigation of Blake (or any male writer). The exponents of the other main branch of feminist criticism, the more psychoanalytically, philosophically, and linguistically oriented "new French feminisms" (Marks and de Courtivron), are less concerned with analyzing literary works than with subverting dualistic systems of logic and structures of symbolism. Although some insights drawn from these French feminisms may be suggestive for study of a poem like *The Four Zoas*, their pedagogical usefulness in relation to *Songs* seems remote indeed. For the present, it appears that a continuation of work in the wide range of interpretive traditions embraced by Anglo-American feminist studies of Blake holds the greatest promise for teaching *Songs*: liberal-humanist (Tayler; Ferber, "Blake's Idea"; Hagstrum, *Romantic Body*), empirical-philosophical (Damrosch), Freudian-biographical (Webster, Storch), neo-Freudian literary-critical (George, *Blake and Freud*), Jungian-mythic (Sanzo), Marxist or Marxist-feminist (DiSalvo; Aers, "Blake: Sex" and "William Blake"; Punter, "Blake, Trauma"), and mainline Anglo-American feminist (Fox, Ostriker, Mellor, Langland). In addition, feminist art-historical studies (Gouma-Peterson and Mathews), investigations of Blake from black, lesbian, or third-world perspectives, and analyses more directly concerned with feminist theory might be fruitful areas to explore.

Like other contrarian critical initiatives of the past twenty years—and like Blake's own readings of the Bible and Milton—Anglo-American feminist critiques tend to be calculatedly outrageous, running counter to the writer's overt intentions, disrupting habitual modes of thought, defamiliarizing received meanings, and undermining the intuitive certainties of the audience. One widely adopted practice is to scrutinize literary works for culturally ingrained systems of value, frames of reference, and concepts of human nature in order to bring to consciousness any bias originating in gender—that is, those differences between the sexes that are socially rather than biologically ordained. For most Anglo-American feminists, the aim of criticism is necessarily political: it is part of a comprehensive effort to overthrow male-dominated or "phallocentric" power structures—legal, economic, or cultural—that exclude or undervalue women.

Blake held different views of woman, the "feminine," and human sexuality at different times and sometimes held inconsistent and incompatible views at the same time; all these should be examined in their cultural and historical contexts. In a century when no one—not even feminists—fully escaped the fourfold grip of father, priest, king, and God, Blake stands out as one of the few writers who understood the pervasiveness of this patriarchal power alignment and resisted its influence. But feminist readers of Blake must perform a double twist, working against the grain of the poet's underclass sympathies to uncover traces of his complicity with the value system he opposed, in order to determine the extent to which his work perpetuates mind-forged linkages of power, value, and gender. A further complication arises from the notion that the English Romantic movement is itself a "femininization" of literature—or "colonization" of the feminine (Richardson)—in that it reclaimed for the "human" certain aspects of consciousness that had traditionally been identified with nature, the extra-rational, and the feminine.

Of the major English Romantic poets—who held fiercely antiauthoritarian views, spoke out against oppression, criticized abuses of power, championed the causes of the downtrodden, rejected traditional hierarchical structures (whether religious, political, or literary), and envisioned a better world—only Blake and Shelley perceived what we now call patriarchy to be a root of social evil (Blake may actually have been the first writer to use the word *patriarchal* pejoratively). When Blake's indignant social criticism in *Songs* is augmented by memorable passages on sexuality from his other works of the same period, 1789–94, his ideas can appear strongly in accord with the most advanced feminist thought of his day. What other contemporary of Mary

Wollstonecraft, for example, within a year of the publication of *A Vindication of the Rights of Woman* (1792), excoriated the legal, social, and theological oppression of women in an independent work of art—as Blake did in *Visions of the Daughters of Albion* (1793)? Who but Wollstonecraft and Blake thought of placing primary blame for the catastrophe of sexual abuse on ideology rather than on the behavior of perpetrator or victim? Who but Wollstonecraft and Blake saw in women's internalization of men's values a primary source of their oppression? Who apart from Wollstonecraft and Godwin understood as clearly as Blake the internal and external politics of marriage, both as the institution chiefly responsible for socializing the young and as a model for the hierarchical structures of human and divine governance?

But these antipatriarchal elements in Blake's thought are countered everywhere by antifeminist elements of equal or greater force, especially in his later work. The Female Will, for example, is more than just a pernicious human trait that Blake happens to describe in imagery of the feminine; in this figure, he condemns any woman's refusal to defer to men's authority, any independent exercise of the power of choice by a woman, all manifestations of women's power over men (men are described as "Woman-born / And Woman-nourished & Woman-educated & Woman-scorn'd" [*Jerusalem* 27.77–78; E 173]). Blake created no female Zoas to be counterparts for the few token male Emanations in his myth; he allows no female character to enter the ideal androgynous state by absorbing a masculine element; the feminine side of the supposed androgyne Albion actually disappears when it unites with the masculine. Blake invariably personifies the creative genius as male, his creation as female. He always represents the ideal fourfold human state in masculine terms (although it is hypothetically androgynous) and the threefold sexual state in feminine terms. With all this and more in mind, Anne K. Mellor rightly objects to Blake's being hailed "as an advocate of androgyny or sexual equality to whom contemporary feminists might look for guidance" (154). As Susan Fox observes, "No woman in any Blake poem has both the will and the power to initiate her own salvation, not even the strongest and most independent of his women, Oothoon"; indeed, "females are not only represented as weak or power-hungry, they come to represent weakness . . . and power-hunger" (507). Alicia Ostriker has discerned no fewer than four Blakes: one who celebrates sexuality; one who depicts a "complex web of gender complementarities and interdependencies"; one who views woman's love, whether maternal or erotic, as entrapment; and one who places the female principle in subordination to the male (Ostriker, "Desire" 156). Ostriker sees Blake as both ahead of his time and imprisoned within it; in his work a "richly developed anti-patriarchal and proto-feminist sensibility" exists side by side (and in irreconcilable tension with) a "homo-centric gynophobia" (164). That tension will be strongly felt in the class-room.

A class exploring feminist approaches to *Songs of Innocence and of Experience* might begin by asking why Blake chooses a form for which the primary analogues are children's books—nursery rhymes, primers, picture books. Although both men and women wrote such books, at a time of widespread debate on proper reading for children (Leader, Summerfield) the adult presiding over the reading, as in Blake's title page for *Innocence*, would ordinarily be a woman (or Mother Goose). Is Blake's development and elaboration of this marginal genre the elevation of an undervalued art form (undervalued because of its association with women and children)? Or is it the appropriation by a male artist of the art of the nursery, a man's intrusion into a sphere properly dominated by women? Does it make a difference that the execution of the designs requires the hand of a miniaturist or that coloring of etchings and engravings was a skill associated with women? What if Blake had chosen the patchwork quilt rather than the children's book as his medium: would that be elevation of a folk art into high art, or would it be appropriation? Such questions about a man's use of art forms associated with women lead into controversial and perhaps yet unformulated aspects of feminist theory that may be especially appropriate for classroom discussion.

Moving closer to the words and pictures of separate poems and plates in *Songs*, a class approaching the work from any feminist perspective will find it extraordinarily difficult to get a fix on the fast-moving and chameleonlike target of its conflicting ideologies of gender. The separate songs—voiced by individual speakers caught up in their own ways in the "two states" of the "human soul"—resonate differently in the various reorderings of the poems that Blake devised as he worked on other projects, while constantly criticizing and reinterpreting *Songs*. The most problematic poem is "To Tirzah," with its vehement rejection, by a universalized human voice, of a mother-goddess who embodies sexuality, nature, mortality, and the flesh. Because Blake added this poem to the volume after he had developed his mature mythologies, it is often read outside the context of *Songs* (but see Hirsch and Berninghausen) as an offshoot of *Jerusalem*, in conjunction with other stories of Tirzah and her nymphomaniac, sexually manipulative, castrating confederates. But the link between early and late mythologies works both ways. By inserting "To Tirzah" in *Songs*, Blake changes its meaning and invites readers to reexamine the earlier poems for embryonic forms of the bitches and whores who plague Albion. Knowledge of "To Tirzah" makes us look differently at the benighted world mother in "Earth's Answer," the neurotic tease who comes to well-deserved grief in "The Angel," the envious nurse in "Nurses Song" (*Experience*), and all the nubile maidens and delicate victims in human or flower form that populate the pages of *Songs of Experience*. Feminist readers cannot dismiss the extreme hostility and contempt for the feminine and the maternal in "To Tirzah," emphasized in the bitter evocation of Jesus's rebuke to Mary (John 2.4), as dramatic license or as an innocuous allusion to the biblical association of woman with fallen nature and corruptible flesh. Instead, the poem prompts us to ask from what deep source flows this fear and hatred of women (Webster 144–53)—and of all that Blake, swept along in the mainstream of his cultural tradition and ours, makes woman to symbolize.

Yet *Songs of Innocence and of Experience* cannot be called "phallocentric" in any sense in which feminist critics have employed that term. In searing vignettes of injuries done in the name of "God & his Priest & King," most poems of *Songs of Experience* present an unsparing critique of a male-dominated world order and an androcentric value system. Moreover, the world of *Songs of Innocence* is manifestly uterocentric—a world of nests, valleys, bowers, enclosed spaces. It takes seriously the nursery, the mother-child relationship, the domestic or private sphere—the traditional realm of women's experience—almost as if anticipating the program of cultural transvaluation that some twentieth-century feminists have seen as part of the exclusive mission of women writers. In *Innocence*, men are quiet, gentle, nonaggressive; they pipe, watch sheep, laugh at children's games, sit in the shade. Children of both sexes play together without self-consciousness, in outdoor romps, and without dividing into the girl/doll and boy/soldier camps that Wollstonecraft deplores (43). In both *Innocence* and *Experience* many poems work against gender stereotyping: men care for children; women welcome sexual advances or make advances of their own.

Blake takes special care to free "innocence" of its traditional associations with sexual immaturity and with the sexual inexperience of women. The merriment in the text of "Laughing Song," for example, has the innocent ring of a children's tea party; only from the design can we tell that the participants are unchaperoned male and female adolescents at an outdoor wine party, conversing in an atmosphere that allows their sexuality to blossom naturally, without restraint, in all innocence. In a transitional poem to *Experience*, "A Little Girl Lost," the state of Innocence continues to mean sexual innocence for both lovers, but not the absence of sexual contact: Innocence here is freedom to make love and freedom from a degrading idea of sexuality. Ona is "lost" not because she has had sexual experience but because she cannot resist her father's interpretation of the experience (George, *Blake and Freud* 109–10). And on the three-flower-poem plate, the lily who delights in love seems on the verge of escaping from the state of Experience altogether; she is free from "stain" not because she has preserved her virginity but because she eschews sexual defenses. From a feminist perspective,

however, what is most notable about this glorification of the lily is the unconscious androcentrism revealed in Blake's linkage of his new and freer conception of purity with the traditionally "feminine" attributes of passivity and
vulnerability.

In his probing of both states of the "human soul," Blake makes a special
point of including both sexes, especially through the illustrations. Given the
binary structure of the paired volumes contrasting the two states, however,
the activities of male and female characters are egregiously out of balance.
The overarching vision of both Innocence and Experience is reserved for
male characters—not only the piper and the bard but also their sources of
inspiration, cloud child and Holy Word. And throughout the collection, as
Wicksteed observed as long ago as 1928, the sexes are assigned roles along
stereotypical lines:

> The difference between boys and girls in Blake's symbolical mind lies
> in the Miltonic principle that woman worships Man as man worships
> God. "Little boys" in the "Songs" are concerned with theological or
> philosophical ideas and "little girls" with the affections. If it is indepen-
> dence in love which leads the latter into trouble (and joy), it is inde-
> pendence in thought which leads the former into trouble, and
> sometimes to truth. (*Blake's Innocence* 39)

Nowhere in *Songs* does a girl or a woman appear in a context that isn't somehow related to her sexuality or her responsibilities as a guardian of children.
Even Earth, the strongest female presence in *Songs of Experience*, sees her
bondage in terms of the sexual possessiveness of the heavenly father. Although she expresses the rebellious fighting spirit that is the saving attribute
of the most perceptive souls in *Experience*, her earthbound protest—
however much our own antiauthoritarian impulses may leap up in response
to it—is represented as far inferior to the cosmic vision presented by the
all-seeing bard. The wisest female character in *Songs* is the nurse of *Innocence*, but her ability to see into the future is related only to her role as
guardian of the children. The most daring female character in *Songs* is Ona
in "A Little Girl Lost," but one look from her father silences her utterly.
More poems are in the male voice than the female; all in all, male characters
are more adventuresome, more inquisitive, and more spirited than female
characters.

Blake's treatment of the sexes is somewhat more evenhanded in the designs, and occasionally he even seems to enhance the position of women in
subtle ways. The two sexes are given what amounts to equal space in the
general title page. Although Adam is placed in a superior position above
Eve, in some copies Blake has mitigated this depiction of masculine power

by reversing the position of Eve's head and representing her with open eyes and mouth—in a scream, probably, although it just might be an expression of defiance against the expelling angel, a sign of hope. At any rate, in these copies Eve appears to be more active, alert, and aware than Adam. In the title page for *Innocence*, the dominant figure is a woman, mother or nurse, but Blake softens her position of authority by turning her book toward the children, who are the ones doing the reading; the presence of the small figure of the piper in the *I* of "Innocence" also lightens the effect of her power. In the severely symmetrical title page for *Experience*, the two sexes are perfectly balanced in three pairs: the dead parental figures, the boy and girl mourners, and the boy and girl dancers above.

Although all textual presentations of women in *Songs* are conditioned by the women's relations to men or to children in their care, in the illustrations Blake does not limit every aspect of their performance in these roles by gender. Twice in *Innocence* women caring for children are shown with books rather than, for example, the gender-specific needlework that might have been expected. And Blake seems to go out of his way to include girls and women in designs for poems in which they are not specifically noted in the text ("The Garden of Love," for example, and "The Divine Image"—a poem in which, unfortunately, he glosses the gender-neutral word "all" as "Every Man of every clime"). Occasionally Blake softens the lines of male figures enough so that some viewers have taken them to be female (e.g., Christ in "The Little Boy Found"); in others, the sex is indeterminate (is the reclining figure floating on a cloud in the design for "Introduction" to *Experience* supposed to be the bard, since he is the speaker of the poem, or Earth, since the pose is that of an odalisque?). Significantly, Cruelty, theoretically a gender-neutral human trait, is personified as a male in "The Human Abstract" and this squat, crouched, brain-entangled Urizenic figure is the most negatively portrayed personage in the entire set of designs.

The impression that lingers after many readings of *Songs of Innocence* is that the world is a home held together by the love of parents and children, with all relationships being an idealized extension of the family unit. But as the title page of *Innocence* prepares us to see, fathers are notable by their absence—not in the separately published *Songs of Innocence* but in the *Innocence* section of the combined volume. It would seem that the absence of a figure of paternal authority is a necessary condition for the existence of the state of Innocence. The only human fathers mentioned in Blake's final grouping for *Songs of Innocence* are the father who apparently abandons his son in "Little Boy Lost" (Stepto), the father who sells his motherless son into virtual slavery in "The Chimney Sweeper," and the generalized father who weeps over his child's distress in "On Another's Sorrow." The only earthly father who actively cares for his children is a fantasy figure twice over: he is the head of an emmet family as fantasized by a prodigal mother-ant who is herself a figure in a child's dream. What does it mean that in the nursery world of *Innocence*, the only family unambiguously headed by two parents is a family not of people but of ants, the dreamwork of a child who is unaware that ants live in colonies?

In the womblike environment of Innocence, protective figures can be either male or female, so long as the male guardians do not take on the authority of fathers. The close-knit communitarian social unit in "The Ecchoing Green" is an expansion of the harmonious mother-child relationship depicted in "Infant Joy." No father intrudes on either scene: the fairy blessing the mother and child in the design is female; the group of villagers consists of old people, mothers, sisters, and brothers (but no fathers), with Old John presiding as a kind of shepherd or nurse. Christ the Son, who is associated with fatherly roles in the texts of "The Little Boy Found" and "The Little Black Boy," is depicted visually only as the Good Shepherd, comforter of children, finder of the lost. The ideal caretaker of either sex is exquisitely attuned to the expressed and unexpressed needs of those under his or her protection, particularly as conveyed by the sound of their voices: the shepherd's willingness to follow his sheep and the nurse's willingness to let the children play a little longer are parallel in their assured permissiveness. Various feminist schools may view this situation positively or negatively, but in *Songs of Innocence* Blake has made a long step toward a gender-free division of the responsibilities of caregiving.

It should not be claimed, however, that all mothers in *Innocence* appear in a positive light (for an emphasis on subtle indications to the contrary, see Greco, "Mother Figures"). In an effort to preserve her child's dignity and loving spirit in a world in which racial conflict and slavery are ever-present threats, the African mother in "The Little Black Boy" has taught her son a comforting myth of black superiority in matters of the soul. Blake critics (Leader is an exception) view the mother's story as false doctrine because it separates physical from spiritual spheres and defers gratification for the afterlife; thus it has the effect of deflecting the black boy's indignation and inuring him to his condition of servitude in this life. But a black feminist reading of this poem in its historical context might give us a different work entirely—as would a lesbian feminist reading of "The Sick Rose." Even if the black boy's mother deserves all that Blake critics have said against her, she is exactly like the other mothers of *Innocence* in that she does her best to nurture, guide, and protect her child (Leader).

In *Experience*, by contrast, the influence of the mother or nurse becomes sinister and oppressive (Stepto). As foreshadowed in the design for the second plate of "Cradle Song" of *Innocence*, what we now call mother-child bonding becomes one of many forms of binding, the ultimate form being imprisonment in mother nature's bonds of flesh and sexuality. Mothers become silent allies of fathers in schemes to blight or destroy the lives of children (e.g., "The Chimney Sweeper," "The Little Boy Lost"). An exception is the little vagabond's mother, who apparently lacks the support of a male authority to enforce church attendance and so by default has reared the freest spirit in the whole of *Experience*. Another possible exception to the pattern of maternal complicity with paternal oppression is expressed in the clod's song in "The Clod and the Pebble": many readers will see in this creed a form of neurotic and manipulatively self-martyring love that is often caricatured as maternal. A good test of assumptions about gender, by the way, is to ask students whether they imagine the clod and the pebble to be the same sex, different sexes, or truly inanimate beings without sexual identity.

Consideration of gender roles in *Songs* is sure to arouse curiosity about the relation of the poems to women's real-life experiences within the range of Blake's observation. As the dates of the title pages of *Innocence* (1789) and *Experience* (1794) indicate, *Songs* spans the most turbulent years of the French Revolution, when no political, social, economic, artistic, or religious structure—the family included—was immune from questioning. Students might well consider the situation of the "youthful Harlot" of "London" in relation to changes brought about in the lives of prostitutes by the sudden increase in their numbers as displaced farm workers doubled and tripled the population of London in Blake's time (Stone 615–20). Or they might look at parent-child relations in *Songs* in the context of eighteenth-century disputes on methods of child rearing, debates that soon led in England to decreased swaddling, increased permissiveness, and milder and less frequent punishments (Gardner, *Blake's* 123–28; Stone 424, 437–39). Grim statistics on infant mortality and the resulting tendency of mothers to withhold affection also cast a disturbing light on "Infant Joy," "Infant Sorrow," and "Cradle Song," as do beliefs about infant baptism, original sin, and the necessity of "breaking" a child's spirit (Trumbach 188–91, 244–47; Gardner 52–54). At a time of great controversy about the best way to feed infants (maternal nursing, wet-nursing, or "by hand" feeding [Trumbach 197–208]), a time when enlightened aristocratic women were beginning to breast-feed while many women even of the middle class sent their infants out to nurse—a practice deplored by both Blake (*Tiriel*; E 285) and Wollstonecraft (176, 190–91)—would the nursing mothers of *Songs* have been regarded as old-fashioned, lower-class, or avant-garde? And if mothers and nurses dress alike, what are the codes of class distinctions among women? And what of differences in the education of boys and girls, from the children on the title page of *Innocence*, to "The School-Boy," to the charity-school procession? (Note that the aproned girls at the bottom of the "Holy Thursday" plate of *Innocence* are destined for domestic servitude, while the boys at the top of the page—like Coleridge, Lamb, and Leigh Hunt at Christ's Hospital—are marching toward a more open future.)

A class working with feminist approaches to *Songs* may also wish to discuss gender and class bias, subtle or blatant, in biographical, bibliographical, and critical references to Blake's marriage, whether written by men or women. Blake's biographers, for example, invariably mention that Catherine signed the marriage register with an *X* (as did fifty-five percent of Englishwomen of all classes in 1800 [Stone 353]) and state that Blake "supported" his wife. But they rarely take into account the value of her services in the labor-intensive family enterprise of making beautiful books, in her forty-five years as assistant colorist, general factotum, and (in later years) press operator. Standard bibliographical descriptions all too readily attach the label "perhaps by Mrs. Blake" to crude or garish coloring, lavish ornamental borders, or other features deemed displeasing—despite the lack of internal or external evidence that the details in question even have a common origin (sometimes owners added their own coloring). Catherine Blake's few known independent works, such as her painting *Agnes*, though entirely in Blake's idiom, are no mean accomplishments. It seems unfair that Blake's brother Robert, who at nineteen died before producing anything except juvenilia derived from Blake, is recognized as his star pupil, while Catherine remains as much a shadow for biographers, critics, and bibliographers as for Blake himself. Of his mother and sister, also named Catherine, there is even less to say.

In the end, the best reason for teaching *Songs* from a feminist perspective is not to expose one person's failings to the glare of hindsight; instead, it is to alert students to a broad range of contemporary androcentric and gynocentric cultural biases, including their own. Blake's gender stereotyping and his antifeminist tirades, occurring as they do in the face of the remarkable clarity and prescience with which he identified the most secret workings of patriarchal oppression, achieve their highest pedagogical use as a sort of memento mori on the insidiousness of gender-based ideologies. In contemplating the irony of a great soul's entrapment within the very systems from which it strove to liberate itself, students will draw their own lessons.

Reading, Drawing, Seeing Illuminated Books

Joseph Viscomi

As a man is, So he Sees. As the Eye is formed, such
are its Powers.

(Letter to Trusler; E 677)

Perception, according to cognitive psychology, depends on the "skill and experience of the perceiver" (Neisser 13). If so, what is true of cognition is also true of the study of art: one can see only what one knows how to look for. Consequently, our "anticipatory schemata (together with the information actually available) . . . determine what will be perceived" (Neisser 20). Or, as Blake put it: "As the Eye is formed, such are its Powers." Reflecting on the formation of his own eyes—or schemata—Blake could say that "the only School to the Language of Art" was "Copying Correctly" the drawings and prints of the masters (E 628; Bentley, *Records* 423). By copying Blake meant drawing, which is a most effective way to become visually literate, technically proficient, and historically informed. More than a grounding for painting and engraving, drawing could transform looking into seeing; as Kandinsky points out, it was "a training towards perception, exact observation and exact presentation not of the outward appearances of an object, but of its constructive elements, its lawful forces . . ." (Lambert 75). Blake seems intensely aware of this complementary relation between hand and eye, between making and seeing, as exemplified by Los but negated by Urizen, who writes his book on the laws of unity with his eyes closed.

Concern for my students' powers of observation has led me to develop an exercise in which students make drawings of illuminated prints. They use a method analogous to illuminated printing, which entails drawing, and thus learn about Blake's composing and printing processes as well as about his prints. They learn to see his particular use of line and gesture, mass and negative space, composition and color. In this light, their reading of Blake's illuminated books becomes literally a "hands-on" experience, analogous to the complementary relation between hand and eyes, making and seeing, embodied in Blake's Los and enacted in Blake's graphic-verbal art.

In 1788, Blake began to experiment with relief etching, the innovative printmaking process he used to create *Songs of Innocence* (1789) and *Songs of Experience* (1794) and most of his other beautiful illuminated books. In *The Marriage of Heaven and Hell* (ca. 1790), he referred to it as the "infernal method" and described it as "melting apparent surfaces away" to display "the infinite which was hid" (E 38). In practical terms, the method involves four basic stages: drawing a design on a copper plate with an acid-resistant varnish, etching away the unprotected metal in acid to bring the design in relief, printing the plates on an etching press, and coloring the impressions by hand in watercolors.

It is inviting to think of Blake, the visionary artist, as having cunningly contrived all manner of innovative techniques instead of intelligently adapting the current printmaking technology to his own needs. But the truth is that the four stages of illuminated printing are not difficult and the tools and materials of each stage commonplace. The difficulty is making illuminated prints that look like Blake's. The purpose of any class exercise, however, is not to make printmakers or facsimilists out of students but to demonstrate how technique gives rise to different kinds of images, how the materiality of Blake's execution affected what he said and saw, and, perhaps most important, to enable the student to gain access to a way of thinking and seeing like Blake's.

Some scholars have suggested that Blake used illuminated printing because it enabled him either to combine text and illustration on one plate or to escape the division of labor inherent in reproductive engraving. That the medium appealed to Blake technically and aesthetically is no doubt true, but text and illustration can be combined, and complete control of production secured, in intaglio printing also, as the etched plates to *The Gates of Paradise* and *The Book of Ahania* demonstrate. Only in relief etching, however, could Blake write and draw autographically and reproduce certain book conventions, such as facing pages.

Blake's basic tools were pens and brushes, and his main material, besides copper plates and acid, a liquid medium. Together these implements exert far less dictatorial control over the hand and eye of an artist than do burins (or any other metal tool heavy with convention, technique, and translation), making possible spontaneous looking and calligraphic lines. Indeed, the execution of the design in illuminated printing is drawing in a literal sense: one produces rather than reproduces the appearance of drawing and writing because the acts one engages in are writing and drawing. With no resistance to the hand, the execution of the design is autographic, and, formed by a dark "impervious liquid" on a copper plate, the design is positive and direct. That is, the marks made by the tool are dark on a light background, unlike those in etching, which are light against the smoked ground, and they are the marks that directly print—unlike those in woodcuts, which do not print but delineate a shape that does. But like woodcuts, relief etchings are essentially two-dimensional, boldly contrasting black-and-white forms because, unlike intaglio lines, relief lines are all on the same level, receiving equal amounts of ink, and thus are incapable of producing tonal gradations.

But the way the design is put on the plate is entirely different from wood-cutting in tools, technique, and materials. If illuminated printing has a graphic-art analogue, it is lithography, which was called polyauthography when first invented (1796–98) and is neither intaglio nor relief but plano-graphic. Although the marks made in lithography have tone, they too are made autographically (with either a greasy ink [tusche] or crayon), and, more important, they print as they appear on the stone, instead of being translated into another kind of line. The lines Blake drew on the copper plate in asphaltum varnish would have retained their character in the print: fluid mono-chrome pen and brush lines on a metal plate. The main difference between the design on the plate and the print is due not to the slight thinning of the lines caused by acid but to the whiteness of the paper, which throws the design into much bolder contrast, revealing the purity of the forms and ac-centing its lack of detail.

To the untrained eye Blake's design looks very detailed, but the nib of a pen and the tip of a brush cannot make lines as fine as etching needles or burins. Given the basic materials of brushes, pens, and a liquid stop-out var-nish, firm and simple outlines are inherent in the medium, making line, not detail or tone, the medium's natural language. That Blake should use this kind of line in relief etching is due in large measure to the tools, the medi-um's inability to define tone, and the small plate size, all of which subordi-nated detail to outline. Given these tools and materials, Blake could freely conceive, compose, and execute in the same medium and at the same time—the essential aspects of drawing on which illuminated printing is grounded.

Because of the central role of drawing in illuminated printing, the facsim-ile exercise I use concentrates on executing the design, the first stage of Blake's process. We draw and write with fine quill brushes and real quill pens, though metal nibs are permitted. Instead of Blake's impervious liquid, copper plates, and acid, we use materials, analogous in appearance, feel, and method, that even the untrained can easily manipulate. In place of copper plates, we use four-ply copper-colored mat board; in place of asphaltum var-nish, we use a dark-brown water-soluble drawing ink, the color of the var-nish. For printing and coloring, we use a relief etched plate I have already made and we color the impressions. I show slides of those stages of the pro-cess that cannot be done in class or the studio, like preparing the copper plate to accept the varnish, biting the plate in nitric acid, and making ink and watercolors. Since my slides are unique, I suggest using photographs in readily available manuals like Chamberlain's *Etching and Engraving*. In this way, we experience Blake's process in all its stages.

Blake would start with a hand-hammered piece of copper, which he would plane and polish with oil, and then degrease with whiting to remove the oil so the design would adhere to the metal and not the oily film. Since mat board is analogous to polished, degreased plates, we skip this laborious but important step. The board, however, is already cut into roughly equal-sized plates. Consequently, the size of the plate, or "support," affects what the student can and cannot do, as I believe was true for Blake. Although eighteenth-century etchings and engravings began with copper plates that were usually bought from coppersmiths already cut to size, Blake seems to have cut his small plates out of larger sheets of copper himself (Viscomi, *Art* 2–3). If the *Innocence* plates were cut out of larger sheets, then the number of desired parts into which a larger sheet could be cut—and not the design, letter size, length of text, and shape of the illustrations—would have determined the size of the plates. Even for *Innocence*, then, and not just for *Experience* and other illuminated books executed on the versos of earlier plates, Blake would have had to design within fixed shapes and sizes rather than cut and shape plates to fit existing designs.

The next step is to draw and write on the plate. But because a print is the mirror image of its plate, letters print in reverse unless they are written backward. It has long been suggested that Blake wrote his text on specially treated paper and counterproofed it on the plate, but Robert Essick, the leading expert on Blake's printing processes, and I have independently come to the conclusion that Blake did not use this method (Essick, *Printmaker* 89; Essick, "Review" 49, 49n; Viscomi, *Art* 4–8). Instead, Blake worked directly on the plate, writing his text backward, a skill neither difficult for, nor uncommon among, engravers, and one that we know he had mastered (Bentley, *Records* 212n1, 460n1). He would have drawn the illustration directly also, which explains why illustrations in the illuminated prints are the reverse of their sketches.

Working without a transfer means working without an original copy or, since we are really talking about pages in a book, without a makeup of the page design. In this method, therefore, the relation of text and illustration is not determined before the design is drawn on the plate. Unlike the copy engraver, Blake was not reproducing already existing designs, and unlike the chalk engraver or other facsimilists, he was not imitating the media of original designs, since these designs per se had not yet been invented. The few pencil sketches of illustrations that exist are studies and ideas; poems, whether written in pen or pencil, are manuscripts. Independent of each other they are only raw materials and do not constitute designs or copy to be reproduced. The image drawn on the plate, then, was the original invention, because it was the first time that these raw materials came together and were actually composed and set as designs and pages. In illuminated printing, as in drawing, execution and invention were inseparable.

Since the size and shape of the plate preceded the design, and since Blake executed the design directly on the plate without a makeup or transfer, the relation and proportion of text and illustration are variable and not predetermined, invented only during the execution of the plate image. This method of composing meant that Blake, unlike letterpress printers, could not cast off copy. In a narrative poem, he did not know what stanza would go on what particular plate, or how many plates the poem would need. Working without model or copy forced him to compose his pages seriatim rather than in forms. Such a composing process allowed each illuminated print and book to evolve organically.

To reproduce Blake's composing process, then, and not merely the appearance of his prints, students need first to learn reverse writing. Aside from simple practice letter by letter, one especially effective technique is to place a mirror next to Blake's design and to copy the image reflected in the mirror, text and illustration, as one integrated form. As with upside-down drawings, the left side of the brain doesn't recognize the patterns and allows the subordinate right side, which is designed to process visual information spatially, to take over. Writing backward a text already known is drawing words: words cease to be symbols or names and become forms, marks, lines, things. Students need also to copy a few songs in different sizes, copying the design—not the coloring just yet—as closely as possible, first as seen, which forces attention to the minute events taking place in the composition, and then in the mirror, which forces them to see the design holistically as a composition. With this preparation, the student is ready to compose designs in Blake's style for the in-class exercise.

Students bring to class a short poem or song, with, preferably, a thumbnail sketch separate from the poem. They also bring a fine brush (.000), a quill pen, and a board on which the plates can be placed. The board is slanted at about forty-five degrees, like a scriptorium, and the pen kept horizontal to the desk. This position facilitates writing the text (especially if one were to use real asphaltum varnish). The teacher supplies the plates, which have already been cut to the size of the *Songs*, and the brown ink, which can be dispensed into shells, the traditional vessel for ink and watercolors.

The students begin by writing the text. The main technical difficulty they will encounter is not in writing backward but in giving the letters the proper slant. Blake wrote Roman and pseudoitalic scripts, both of which we see in *Songs*; probably for technical as well as aesthetic reasons, the latter came to dominate. Italic script looks more difficult to execute, but to connect letters and to give them a slant in the direction the pen is moving is actually easier than to write one letter at a time with a vertical axis while moving from right to left. Because there are fewer letter ends to coordinate, an italic script makes it easier to keep lines straight and words the same size. Besides simplifying the writing of the text, italic script also simplifies biting the plate: words are better protected against foulbiting and undercutting when fewer letter ends are exposed to acid.

Whether writing an italic or a roman script, students must keep the space between lines tight or break it up with ascenders, descenders, and interlinear decorations. As they are composing text and illustration, they need to imagine how their design will be affected by the second and third stages, biting the plate in acid and printing it in ink. A tightly composed design need not be etched as deeply as one with open areas, which further reduces the chances of the design's lifting off of the plate in the acid bath. By filling out lines, interlinear decorations become part of the relief line system, and by decreasing the number of open areas, or shallows, they help to keep the ink dabber on the surface, thus preventing ink from touching those areas bitten below the surface that are to print white. (Blake himself did not seem to follow any set rules to determine which he executed first, text or illustration.) Note too that in the *Songs*, the illustration is usually placed at the bottom of the print, unless the poem is very short or very long; the long poem's need for a second plate makes it possible to start with an illustration without crowding the text.

The objective of this exercise is to give students a clear idea of Blake's composing process, not of how the design is put in relief. Consequently, we use no acid and produce no printable plate. Extending the exercise to include printing plates and coloring impressions requires a relief plate, a rolling press, oil-based relief inks, and printing papers. I use a facsimile plate I made according to Blake's technique; for nonprintmakers, I recommend having an unmounted line block made of an uncolored *Songs* impression in *The Illuminated Blake*. A commercial printer can do this from a photocopy for a nominal fee.

One can print a relief plate by burnishing the paper from the back. Blake, though, used a rolling press, and you may want your students to experience the "machinery" of printmaking. Such a press may be found in the college or university's printroom. Use commercially made relief inks, which are easier to handle than intaglio inks, the kind Blake seems to have used, and spread a thin, even film on a marble slab. Apply the ink with hard rollers rather than with the cumbersome but traditional linen ink dabbers. The paper should be pure rag (such as Arches Heavyweight or Rives BFK), cut to quarto and folio sizes, and printed damp, which produces better impressions and was standard practice in Blake's day (Viscomi, *Art* 24n30). The paper should be soaked in a tub or tray of water for a few minutes before printing and the excess water blotted off.

Inking the plate, preparing and registering the paper, and pulling the plate and paper through the press are jobs that can be divided and rotated among three students. Each group of students should print impressions in either Blake's early or late printing style. In the former, the plate, with its borders wiped of ink, is printed in a cool color (like brown) on both sides of the sheet. In the latter, the plate with borders is printed in a warm color (like orange) on one side of the sheet. These impressions can then be painted at home in imitation of Blake's early or late coloring styles (as reproduced in the Trianon, or more accessible Dover, facsimiles of *Innocence*, copy B, and *Songs*, copy Z). The palette should consist of the following watercolors: Prussian blue, gamboge, yellow ochre, Indian red, umber, black, vermillion, rose madder, and alizarin crimson. Note that, in the early style, colors are applied thinly and sparingly and not at all to the texts and that, in the later style, the palette is fuller, the colors more layered, the texts washed, and the designs given frame lines. The final step is to gather the impressions and bind them between two sheets of laid paper by tying string through three or more stab holes, the binding Blake used, knowing his buyers would have the books bound professionally. When bound, the impressions printed and colored in the early styles will face one another and function more like pages in a conventional, text-centered book; the impressions printed and colored in the later styles will function more like individual paintings and effect a different kind of relation with the reader.

"The activities necessary for producing a facsimile can themselves lead to insights about the originals" (Essick, "Review" 49). Indeed, they help us understand Blake as a printmaker and artist by forcing us to see more in the art and see more *like* an artist. Seeing "behind" the surface reveals what is not apparent, the alternatives and choices Blake had and made in his own compositions. To know how and why this or that mark was made, to understand its relation to all the marks around it, to begin to grasp the orchestration of all the minute events taking place, the relation (sometimes interdependence) between text and illustration (and their equality as *markings*), is to see the work as opposed to merely looking at it. Such an exercise in making also provides the opportunity to move from seeing to vision, from altered perception to altered state of awareness.

APPROACHES ADDRESSING SPECIFIC TEACHING CONTEXTS

The Borderline of Innocence and Experience

Thomas R. Frosch

I teach the *Songs* at the beginning of a one-semester undergraduate course on English Romanticism and am able to devote about a week to it. My students, at a large urban university, vary widely in ability; many of them would be overwhelmed by much background reading or much attention to theoretical and historical issues. In this situation I find it best to pursue intensively a single idea about the *Songs*. Consequently, I begin my classes on the *Songs* by analyzing the "Introduction" to *Innocence* as a poem of passage. The child's successive orders to the piper—to pipe the song, sing it, and write it down—embody a process of maturation from music, to which an infant can respond, to words and then to books. Writing takes the piper beyond the child's capacity, so the child now vanishes. To write his songs, the piper "plucks" a reed and, with this "rural pen," "stains" the "water clear," acts tinged with destructiveness. To celebrate Innocence, the piper must leave it; indeed, as soon as he has an objective vision of Innocence, seeing the child on the cloud, he is outside it. I stress the ambivalence of this process of maturation: something within us—something within the child himself, since he gives the orders that result in his own disappearance—impels us out of an idyllic childhood world toward new forms of expression and experience. And I particularly stress that the poem focuses on a crisis of Innocence, its moment of transition into something else.

I go on to present the *Songs* as dealing primarily with not Innocence or Experience but the borderline between them. First, however, I discuss "The Lamb," which, instead of being on the borderline, seems firmly established within the world of Innocence and thus offers us the chance to define the salient features of that world: in its form (a stanza of questions followed by a stanza of answers), the poem expresses a confidence that all questions can be answered; in its treatment of child and lamb as symbols of the infant Jesus, it expresses a sense of mildness and benevolence at the center of existence and also a lack of separation between humanity, nature, and divinity. Innocence is a world of connections, or echoes. I also suggest that it is exactly in such songs as "The Lamb," in which Innocence seems most firm and positive, that Blake uses an emphatic nursery-rhyme style to distance the poem from the adult reader, as if to say that here is an ideal world for children, not adults.

I then examine a series of songs in which the state of Innocence is threatened or even breaks down. I suggest that in each case Innocence is put back together with some little fiction or myth, and, to illustrate this process, I tell the students of Freud's description of the dream as a response to a threat to sleep. In Blake, however, although the healing fiction may be charming and even necessary to preserve emotional stability, it is ultimately delusory or destructive.

Starting with the songs in which the threat is slight, I work up to those in which it is severe. Several poems on the subject of darkness make a good sequence. Ideally, the world of Innocence is guarded during the day by protective and permissive nurses and shepherds, and later, as in "A Cradle Song," the mother, with her lullabies and smiles, "All the livelong night beguiles." But in "A Dream" an emmet searches helplessly in the dark for her lost children until a glow-worm appears and lights her home. What would happen without such a magic helper? "Night" answers that question: here, when darkness descends on the green fields, the shepherds are replaced by "angels bright," who protect the sheep from wolves and tigers; if the angels should fail—and the mere acknowledgment of such a possibility moves us to the borders of Innocence—they will receive the spirits of the slaughtered innocents into heaven, where even the predators become angelic. In "Night," Innocence must leave the world to preserve its paradise, a paradoxical situation given the Blakean child's love of the earth and its creatures and his absorption in the present, physical moment. In "The Little Boy Lost" and "The Little Boy Found," the child does return to Innocence in this world but requires the magic help of God to do so. Under the pressure of the child's nightmare of separation from his father, divinity assumes a new form, like his father rather than, as in "The Lamb," like himself.

In "The Chimney Sweeper" and "The Little Black Boy," the threats to Innocence are particularly harsh, and the myths needed to restore it are proportionally desperate. For the chimney sweeper, the world is always dark, as he and his companions are "lock'd up in coffins of black"—their chimneys, their soot-covered bodies, and the dark and deadly worlds of their experience. Merely to survive, they have to accept pathetic rationalizations, and in Tom's dream of the angel who releases the sweeps from those coffins to play in the sun, Innocence is, as in "Night," projected to a life after death. I ask my students to whose advantage it would be to take the poem's moral—"So if all do their duty, they need not fear harm"—at face value. In this poem, Innocence has become a necessary evil: it both preserves the child from emotional fragmentation and sends him back to his work, allowing his exploitation to continue. This situation recurs in "The Little Black Boy." I suggest to my students that unless they can think of some other possibility, this poem must be either a work of racism or a work of irony. Here, the unsettling darkness is the color of the speaker's skin. Innocence is imperiled for him by his recognition that, because of his color, the English boy doesn't love him, a condition inconceivable in a world of connections and echoes; it is restored through his mother's well-intentioned little myth that his blackness helps him bear God's "beams of love" and that in heaven he will be released from his blackness; and it is restored as well through his own confused conclusion that in heaven he will serve the white boy, shading him from the heat—even though he no longer has his blackness—until finally he will be like the white boy "and he will then love me." I stress in this case the helplessness of the vision of Innocence and the devastating price that its preservation exacts on the child's sense of himself and of life. "The Chimney Sweeper" and "The Little Black Boy" are songs of Innocence that primarily make us hope that Innocence is not our highest possibility.

In conclusion, I suggest to the students that in the *Songs of Innocence* as a whole Blake gives us the sense that the age of echoes is for the most part over, although a dreamlike myth can extend its sweet sleep. But we must be careful to note the point at which Innocence ceases to be a sensuous participation in present divinity and becomes a stopgap. At the same time, the mental and physical freedom of Innocence at its best and its sense of moral and perceptual connections should be valued as prophetic of a human liberation as yet unavailable.

If the ruling impulse in Innocence is to stay there at all costs, the ruling impulse in Experience is to get out. Here the threat is uncontrollable: the sleeper does wake up, and Blake examines the various fictions or myths with which speakers respond to their unpleasant awakenings. These songs dramatize a moment just beyond the borderline, as each focuses on a particular kind of recognition that forces us out of Innocence once and for all.

In the "Introduction" this recognition is a sense of time and loss. While Innocence at its best is a world of the present, the bard in this poem sees "Present, Past, & Future" and has a sense of living in a fallen world: even the light is fallen. In response, the bard asks the Earth to arise from its physical being; expecting nature to institute any renewal, the bard asks for a transcendence rather than a transformation of the world. That this thinking needs critical evaluation is clear from the companion poem, in which Earth contradicts the bard, claiming that her well-being depends on humanity, not the reverse: she is imprisoned because an oppressive concept of authority, "Starry Jealousy," has bound "free Love," and it is up to human beings to "break this heavy chain."

The act of recognition that this second poem studies is sexual: when we become aware not of sexual desire but of restricted sexual desire, we are in the world of Experience. I then go through the songs that continue the theme of sexual restriction, showing that each focuses on a different aspect of the problem: in "The Garden of Love" sexual restriction is imposed from without by religion; in "The Angel" it comes from inner fear; in "The Lilly" it results from a hypocritical modesty that conceals aggression; in "My Pretty Rose Tree" it comes from jealousy, the tormented masochistic pleasures of possessing and being possessed. In "The Sick Rose" sexual intercourse does take place, but it is so entangled in feelings of guilt and in fantasies of sex as a kind of violence that it becomes a destructive rather than a gratifying experience. And in "A Little Girl Lost," even when our desires find a happy fulfillment, we still eventually have to face the crackdown of "Starry Jealousy," here in the surrogate form of an earthly father.

But the awareness of sexual restriction is only one way across the borderline. We find another in "The Clod and the Pebble," in which the former argues that "Love seeketh not itself to please" and the latter that "Love seeketh only Self to please." I ask the students which position Blake supports and then suggest that the whole debate could never take place in Innocence, where children conceive of themselves as connected with otherness. Once they are aware of themselves as separate and thus have to wonder whether to please themselves or the other, they are out of Innocence.

"The Fly" records a first recognition of death: the speaker, still talking in the nursery-rhyme style of Innocence, has just been jolted out of the innocent world by his "thoughtless" killing of a fly. He tries to reassert the old connections, which he himself has shattered, by trying to identify with the fly, but this at first intensifies his problem, for he too in that case could be brushed away by "some blind hand." At last he seizes on his feeling of thoughtlessness to develop a saving myth: if thought is life and thoughtlessness is death, then if he has thought he is "A happy fly, / If I live, / Or if I die." He responds to his recognition of death by dividing himself into a part that dies, the body, and a part that survives, the mind or soul, and identifying so thoroughly with the soul that it doesn't even seem to matter whether the body is alive or dead.

This myth affords the speaker an escape not only from his fear of death but also from his fear of his own aggression. Other songs, "A Poison Tree" and "Infant Sorrow," focus on an awareness of uncontrollable anger as the entrance into Experience. Still others focus on righteous indignation, the sudden, unmitigated recognition of social injustice. Yet while Experience can recognize tyranny and hypocrisy, seeing its way through them is another matter. The chimney sweeper of Experience tells us that he was sent to work "Because I was happy upon the heath," and now "because I am happy, & dance & sing, / They think they have done me no injury." I ask the students to question his logic. If the authority figures of Experience oppress children out of vindictiveness or envy of their Innocence, then why would they be relieved to see them still happy? The child may be correctly reading a wish to hurt that is unconscious. Still, his own fatalistic belief in a sadistic God limits his potentiality to see that social conditions can be changed.

Several of the songs explore the kinds of general reaction people may have to the new world. One kind is cynicism or dead-end despair: for the speaker of "Nurses Song" no possibilities exist for us beyond hypocrisy and repression, and in retrospect innocent play seems a sheer waste. Another kind is a longing for some indefinite future paradise or afterlife: for the Sunflower, the present is a weary journey or a grave of frustrated desire; fulfillment is postponed to a "sweet golden clime" at the journey's end, which when we reach it seems only the beginning of a new weary journey. In "The Tyger" we see still another kind of reaction. If we read the questions of this poem as rhetorical, then "The Tyger" presents an image of an awesome and sadistic God, exactly the kind of authority Blake attacks elsewhere in the Songs. But if the questions represent a dramatic speaker's genuine lack of knowledge, then the poem gives us a picture of a person trying to reason out a new and awesome phenomenon and never reaching any solution. The questions of Experience seem unanswerable. I suggest to the students that we think of this speaker as one who has passed through the states of mind expressed in the other songs of Experience, who has become aware of such feelings as sexual passion and righteous anger, but, unable to accept these feelings, experiences them in projected form. At the same time, the poem embodies a beautiful image and pulsates with a thrilling and fiery energy. We might think of the speaker as aware of desires and dissatisfactions that call for the fires of liberation but as not yet able to identify with them or act on them.

The speaker of "London" seems able to observe Experience lucidly and without being emotionally overwhelmed by it. In contrast to those who see some external power as responsible for both our suffering and our redemption, this speaker sees our manacles as "mind-forg'd." I particularly stress the doubleness in this poem: the punning association of "chartered" and "charted" and that of proscriptive bans and marriage banns; the double association of charters with permission and exploitation; the oxymoron of "marriage hearse"; the punning oxymoron of the church that is both blackening and appalled; the synesthetic transformations of sound into sight; the ironic unification of Innocence and Experience, both equally crying. Here is a world of astonishing and disturbing connections that parody the echoes of Innocence. In London, eros turns into disease, and marriage into death; a sight turns into blood, and blackness into pallor; the opening of an infant's eyes turns into blindness, and permission or freedom into enslavement. The pivotal connection in the poem, however, is the use of *mark* as both verb and object of the same sentence: when the speaker marks "in every face I meet / Marks of weakness, marks of woe," the seen and the seer are linked; what we see depends on our powers of vision. I suggest that while the speaker observes London, we must observe the speaker and wonder where these observations will lead. As in "Nurses Song," Blake would consider it a mark of weakness and woe not to be able to mark possibilities other than weakness and woe. Indeed, the ability to see problems without the ability to see solutions is a common characteristic of the state of Experience. The wanderer of "London" is poised at a crossroads.

At the end of our discussion, I suggest that the *Songs* pose questions that they do not resolve, that they point to undefined possibilities beyond themselves. In this way I use them as introductions to future Blake readings: in Oothoon's ideals in *Visions of the Daughters of Albion*, for example, the spirit of Innocent freedom and connection returns in the mature form of sexual love; in *The Marriage of Heaven and Hell* the artistic imagination is the true divine power within us, capable of consuming the given world and leading us to a new one. The *Songs* dramatize phases that we must pass through before these possibilities become fully apparent and show how we can misinterpret the signs of such potential along the way. I thus stress an elusive, ironic, negative element in the *Songs*, to give the students, in contrast to a common association of Romanticism with fantasy and wish fulfillment, a sense of Blake as at once visionary and analytical. But I close by emphasizing the former. According to the *Songs*, it is a signal feature of our condition to be able to sense paradise but to misconstrue it; I tell the students that the rest of the course will now go on to study Blake and the other Romantics as they attempt to develop visions of paradise that are beyond the capacities of the dramatic speakers of either group of the *Songs*. As Blake examines failed or destructive products of the mythmaking faculty, he calls attention to the centrality of the imagination, which he and the other Romantics will develop in a positive way.

Blake at MIT

Irene Tayler

Among the kind of bright, highly disciplined, and intellectually engaged young scientists and engineers who choose to study Blake at MIT, the best way to teach his work is in effect to open the door and get out of the way. Many of them will admire his art and love his poems, but those who can read him at all will recognize almost at once that he offers a profound and disturbing challenge to their whole mind-set as technologists. They see him as offering a new perspective not into literature or art, but into the heart of their own disciplines.

Let me begin by describing our teaching situation here at MIT. There is no graduate program in literature, nor is there ever more than a scattering of majors in any field of humanities. Even these few are usually joint majors whose principal fields lie elsewhere. The students who come here are not widely read, and they have absolutely no sense of literary history. Nor is there much point in trying to provide it, except perhaps in the most broad-gauged and introductory way. Those who choose to take courses in literature generally do so because they like to read but fear they will never take time to do it unless they are formally registered and therefore "morally" obliged. My goal as a teacher of our introductory courses is to alter this attitude, to help them discover that what they like, in liking to read, might well give meaning to everything else they do.

Our curriculum in literature is designed to provide an exposure to the humanities for students early committed to careers in engineering or science. Some of the best of those students find here an occasion to convert their doubts and vulnerabilities into moments of self-inquiry: What am I doing here? or, Technology for what? or, Am I missing out on something important? We have tiered the curriculum in literature so that students who have completed an introductory course can continue to a slightly more advanced level if they wish. Among the courses offered at this second level is one entitled Romantic Poetry, and of course Blake is included. For the student who wishes to advance still further we offer a third tier, composed of a selection of seminars whose topics change every year. About every two or three years I offer a seminar on Blake.

In the course on Romantic poetry we spend about two weeks on Blake, and I usually limit the reading to the *Songs of Innocence and of Experience* and one of the short prophecies. I rarely assign secondary readings, unless to show how varied are the critical responses to a given poem. We focus all our attention on Blake's plates, as seen in the color reproductions in the Oxford paperback edition, which I amplify with alternative versions of my own (e.g., the facsimile of the British Library version of the *Songs*, published in

1927 by Ernest Benn) and with individual slides. My concern in this course is by no means to prepare the students for graduate school, or even to give them more than a rudimentary sense of the world out of which Romanticism arose. Rather, my goal is to get these gifted young people close enough to the major Romantic poets that at least one poet will become important to each student, will be a resource to which he or she will later return, for pleasure and personal enrichment. Most often it is Blake who winds up filling this role for them; I have found that he holds a special fascination for students of science and technology.

This fascination is what fuels the seminars, which are often dizzying experiences for the students and me alike. Seminars are limited to twelve students so that there can be a maximum of discussion and independent work. But although a seminar is an advanced course in our curriculum, it is often no more than the third occasion for our students to encounter literary texts of any kind at the college level. A few will have had the course on Romantic poetry or will have studied poetry of some kind in another literature course, but more are there simply because they once read a Blake poem and liked it. Although I assign little if any secondary reading, two or three weeks into the term I circulate a list of the Blake materials available in our library and suggest specific readings to students individually in conference. In class, however, we concentrate on Blake's plates. Normally I begin the first day with a brief lecture on Blake's career as poet and artist, touching on his view of the artist as prophet and on the mixed history of his public reception. Then I assign for the first night's work a single plate from the *Songs of Innocence*, whose visible characteristics (of picture and lettering alike) they are to describe in writing as completely as they can. At the next class meeting I put a slide of the plate on the screen, and we compare what people have seen. The effect is electrifying. These students are trained observers who pride themselves on scientific accuracy and meticulous attention to detail. But each has seen some minute particular that the others have not, and the resulting discussion is at once humbling to each and exhilarating to all. They are learning a new way to see, and from my point of view the less they know about Blake the better, for most of them are having their first adult experience of struggling to interpret in the absence of a preformulated system. Only now do we begin to pay attention to Blake's poetic text, which, as they are quick to recognize, only complicates the task of interpretation. The next night I assign the same exercise, but choose a companion poem from the *Songs of Experience*. And we're off.

And now to why MIT students find Blake a dizzying subject of study (and here I will often be quoting or paraphrasing their own words). Blake appeals to scientists because he is a system builder. Like most serious readers of his work, these students begin by being eager to break Blake's code. But perhaps more than most, they are troubled and yet filled with admiration as they begin to recognize that Blake's puzzles do not solve, though the questions they raise are of the most crucial kind. The mathematician Gödel proved that no logical system can be both complete and self-consistent. These students' understanding of Gödel and their complex sense of living among indeterminacies help them comprehend Blake's distinction between allegory (which appears complete and self-consistent in direct proportion to its triviality) and the constant "going forward, forward irresistible" of vision. Writes one student,

> There is some circuitry in the brain that short-circuits at a paradox. What distinguishes a really creative scientist is that this produces pleasure, while it produces pain or numbness in other people. I have come to think that perhaps scientists are addicted to this kind of mental sensation, and like visionaries are spurred by it to greater efforts of concentration.

The symmetries of Blake's art and ideas are also important, since, as the students observe, visual symmetry and logical symmetry are akin, and our assumptions about pattern influence the way we perceive and think. There's a lot of interest now in the role of pictorial analogy in scientific model making, in the way Kepler, for example, took the almost visual concept of the Trinity as a basis for his model of the solar system with its complexly balanced forces. Accordingly, Blake's emphasis on "vision," on the eye as the organ that "organizes," seems peculiarly modern and pertinent. Similarly important to these young people is Blake's emphasis on the distinction between the infinite and the indefinite. As one student, Hugh Blumenfeld, explains it,

> Infinite has never been the same for me since I learned to think of it in Blakean terms. It has somehow lost its terrifying and boring abstractness and has entered the realm of the human, of aesthetics and form. It seems to me that an understanding of this kind has been a key factor in every endeavor of modern scientific work, from calculus and number theory to biochemistry to astrophysics.

In conclusion, as Blumenfeld again notes,

> Blake is important for the scientist because he launches a vehement attack on Newton, and by extension on the atomistic analytical vision that informs most scientific work. Yet Newton was not a simple villain

for Blake, but a giant. He figures in the Apocalypse as well as the Fall. "Single vision and Newton's sleep" is a haunting image for the analytic mind, and I remember it taking a lot of work for us in class to redeem Newton. His power to give a definite form to error so that it can be cast out is part of his stature, but the possibility of his waking is, I think, even a greater part of it.

I always encourage students to apply Blake's vision to their own work, and they are quick to do so in fields as varied as biochemistry, neurophysiology, and artificial intelligence. But it is usually a two-step process. First they are pleased by his impulse toward integrative system building, because it is so congenial to their own. But then his critique of the materialistic and the instrumental invites them to resee the systems that organize their disciplines and the assumptions that underlie them, and to explore the ways in which "the whole business of man" is implicated in the view one takes of those systems and assumptions. The most adventurous of the students are then led to rethink what they want from their education. As Blake observed, "Study sciences till you are blind. . . . Yet science cannot teach intellect." It is of course intellect that shapes science, in shaping all human experience. And that, more than anything else, is what MIT students have to learn from Blake.

The Piper and the Physicist

Jenijoy La Belle

In 1969 I began teaching literature at the California Institute of Technology, a university whose primary purpose is to train scientists and engineers. When Blake wrote "sweet science reigns," he was not envisioning Caltech. There is nothing very sweet about the institution, although I did hope to bring some playful joy into scientific lives through the *Songs of Innocence* and thereby to extend the students' horizons. Since the late sixties and early seventies were, in most schools, a period of great experimentation, I initially tried to go along with the trend and create courses on Blake that would appeal to the students' interests. I went around campus putting up posters of Urizen reaching down with his dividers (Caltechers love instruments) and tried to lure pupils into the Blake circle through references to geometry.

I yearned to be able to speak in the seventies as T. R. Henn had in the forties when he gave his Cambridge "Lectures on Poetry designed (in the Main) for Science Students," published in his *The Apple and the Spectroscope.* Henn's basic approach was to convert the language of poetic metaphor into supposedly homologous structures in science. For instance, in his discussion of imagery, he cites Burns's simile "My love is like a red red rose," and then suggests: "If we look at the problem in terms of a valve, we have the girl and the rose represented by anode and cathode respectively. What in fact has happened is that certain particles of meaning, or electrons, have streamed across from the rose and attached themselves to the girl" (3). This analogy seemed remarkably silly to me, but I was still convinced that if I could talk in scientific terminology like an updated Henn and could somehow work the "invisible worm" and "howling storm" of Blake's "The Sick Rose" into an electrical system, I could have the students (anode) eating out of my hand (cathode).

When Donald Ault's *Visionary Physics* appeared in 1974, I was delighted. I decided I would steal his subtitle and call my course Blake's Response to Newton. Ault's book would be required reading. The students would see the volume in the bookstore and immediately be attracted by the dust jacket of Blake's face (in psychedelic blue) with his left eye removed from its socket and replaced by the tiny head of Sir Isaac (in psychedelic orange). Perhaps I would team-teach the course with someone from the department of physics. All the students would flock to my class, thousands of little boys and girls raising their innocent hands.

Of course, at this point, I hadn't even opened the book. But I purchased two copies, started to read one, and took the other to my colleague Richard P. Feynman, one of the world's greatest theoretical physicists and an admirer of Blake (his favorite poem being "Fair Elenor"). Soon after, "away the vapour flew." Feynman valiantly struggled with the book for several days; then, somewhat baffled, he returned it to me and said, "I don't know what this is, but it isn't physics." Several students, whom I had also engaged as samplers of Ault, had similar responses. A few more experiences of this kind, both in and out of the classroom, disabused me of any naive notion about getting scientists interested in Blake directly through science. Ault's book is as much literary criticism as history of science, and neither field is much closer to the interests of scientists than poetry itself. Indeed, I found that Techers were willing to approach poetry recreationally, as a pleasant diversion from the real business of life. What they found most peculiar was taking poetry seriously (particularly examples such as *Songs of Innocence*) and as central rather than peripheral to anyone's academic career.

With these hard-won lessons, I decided to build on a foundation of differences rather than (supposed) similarities. This approach was more strategic than honest, for I still clung to the notion of underlying similarities, but I would admit to them only after warning (and, I hope, intriguing) the class with the idea that what was to follow was strange, totally unlike what they would encounter in their other classes, and perhaps even a little dangerous.

At a fairly early stage in their university work, Caltech's apprentice scientists encounter the notion of alternative models for the explanation of physical phenomena. I have frequently seen my faculty colleagues in the sciences solve a problem in mathematics or present an explanation of a subatomic event and then say, "Another way of solving this problem is . . ." or something to that effect. Even civil engineers have more than one way to bridge a river. In some cases, particularly in the more theoretically oriented fields, the instructor could not come to a conclusion about the one right or best way of finding a solution. And this sense of undecidability increases as one approaches the frontiers of science.

Here, then, was the portal through which I could introduce students to Blake. Not only do Blake's *Songs* provide an alternative range of thoughts and sensibilities to those promoted by science courses, they also prompt us to seek alternative perspectives as an intrinsic part of their structure. My opening gambit ("and now for something completely different") thus led into a detailed consideration of the poems themselves, stressing point of view and context as organizing principles for class discussion. This approach is hardly revolutionary, and there is nothing particularly "scientific" about it, but one can introduce it to science students quickly and efficiently and engage their attention in traditional literary activities in such a way that they no longer see them as trivial. To put the matter in Hennish terms, the "two contrary states of the human soul" and the study of the poems arranged according to those contraries exercise the same need for double perspective as does the scientific study of light—sometimes a wave, sometimes a particle. For instance, one might compare and contrast "The Divine Image" in *Innocence* with "A Divine Image" in *Experience*. In the first poem, Blake presents the human body as an image of four virtues and an embodiment of God. In the second poem, the anatomy lesson takes a different point of view and offers us a body of cruel sins. One can also explore the contrast in tone as a way of complementing and underscoring the contrast in perspective. Blake has observed and made poetic use of the same object in two different ways, but neither poem is "truer" than the other in any scientific sense.

After pursuing conventional literary approaches to several poems in *Songs of Innocence* and their opposites in *Experience*, I often find it helpful to return to my initial leitmotiv—the differences between Blake and science, at least classical science. The latter has for several centuries stressed an absolute distinction between subject and object as a necessary prerequisite to the discovery of objective truth. This precept is tantamount to a kind of "purity" theory. The chemical sample or the organism must be untainted by other substances, much as the objective investigation must be untainted by the personality and prejudices of its investigator. The much heralded Heisenberg principle (it has almost become a cliché, even in certain kinds of literary studies) tends to break down the doctrine of noninterference, but in the vast majority of their studies my students are not encumbered by any philosophical doubts prompted by Heisenberg. Thus Blake provides a strong contrast to the theory of knowledge implicit in classical science. In *Songs of Innocence*, to know something is to be part of it, and this participatory mode breaks down the subject-object dichotomy. The continual impulse toward a unity of being in *Innocence* questions—and thereby reveals—the epistemology that my students bring to class but of which they are generally unaware. The next pleasant shock that Blake's *Songs* can offer the interested scientist is the way in which the fall into Experience is both cause and consequence of a perspective instituting the split between subject and object. Even a brief comparison of the child's relation with the lamb and its creator in *Innocence* and the speaker's relation with the beast and its creator in "The Tyger" can bring this point home. In "The Lamb," the child, the animal, and Jesus all tend toward a single mode of being. The child identifies with the lamb and, through it, with the Christ child, thus gaining spiritual knowledge through identification with the object of observation. Although one may say that the speaker in "The Tyger" projects his or her psychological condition onto the beast, the terror with which the speaker beholds the tiger creates a pattern of dissociation between the human world and the material cosmos and its origins. A discussion of the two poems in these terms can lead a class of budding scientists to a consideration of the way they see the forces of nature. Do the students see humanity as one with nature, a part of all that we behold?

Or does the objective world of science exist only through a suppression of the subjective or of the spiritual? After these heady questions, I have generally found it wise to return to the poems themselves, regrounding our speculations in the particulars of Blake's text.

The preceding represents the main features of my method of introducing the *Songs* to the young scientists at Caltech. Students frequently respond, however, to another property of Blake's poems. Many of them are engineering majors and thus have a primary interest in technology rather than in the outer reaches of theoretical science. They can respond to the notion of Blake as a craftsman—like many of them, a worker with metals and acids. A brief digression from purely literary concerns into the relief etching techniques Blake used to publish the *Songs* often attracts student interest. This topic also provides a method for introducing Blake's illustrations to the technologically oriented. All one needs in the way of materials are a blackboard and a piece of chalk for sketching a copper plate, seen face on and in cross section. It is then easy enough to show how Blake painted letters and designs onto his plates, just as one might paint watercolors on a piece of paper, and to contrast these processes with the conventional way of cutting lines through varnish on a plate. Most art-supply shops have etching tools and small zinc or copper plates, which can be used to flesh out an introduction to the technical aspects of the *Songs*, a subject covered in detail by Joseph Viscomi in his essay for this volume.

I have now been teaching at Caltech for almost twenty years: innocence has given way to experience. I have come to expect less of myself as a pseudoscientist but have found that I can expect more of my students as readers of Blake. I endeavor to introduce scientists to Blake's *Songs* in ways that preserve the intellectual seriousness that the students usually reserve for their chosen fields. By indicating a few points of contact of the sort I have discussed here between thought processes essential to science and those engaged in a reading of Blake's *Songs*, one can lead even students who think poetry trivial to take a different view. After that, science students at Caltech—and, I suspect, elsewhere—are capable of learning about and enjoying *Songs of Innocence and of Experience* without continued references to physics or chemistry.

Taking Risks in Teaching *Songs*

Stephen Cox

It's seldom hard to interest students in Blake's *Songs*, but it is often hard to help them see the *Songs* as a challenge to independent thinking and judgment. The poems come to them enshrined in deluxe editions, adorned with respectful notes and commentaries, and further embellished by admiring lectures about their theology, sociology, epistemology, and so forth. No wonder students tend to regard the *Songs* as unquestionably perfect expressions of perfectly respectable ideas—as museum pieces, in short. No wonder students begin writing their essays about "The Tyger" with the conviction that the poem is a flawless realization of profound concepts and then ransack their lecture notes to discover just what those concepts were said to be. No wonder many students discuss *Innocence* as if it were merely a set of innocuous poems about sweet little creatures, and *Experience* as if it were merely a set of prim editorials against reassuringly obvious moral evils. The genuine interest that students feel on first encountering the *Songs* too often fails to produce a permanent, fully conscious, and articulate enthusiasm.

If our students are to achieve the intellectual engagement and independent thought that Blake intended his works to foster, we may need to take some risks in teaching the *Songs*. We may need to direct attention principally to the apparent problems rather than to the apparent triumphs of the work—to the artistic devices that may not quite succeed, to the ideas that are not quite plain and obvious, to the interpretations that we favor but for which sufficient evidence may be hard to find. Often, the issues that most challenge students are not contained in such general questions as that of the essential relation between Innocence and Experience. Of course I discuss with my students the various answers available to this question, but I do not want them to be primarily engaged in choosing a general interpretation that they can use to "explain" most of what they see in the poems; I prefer that they spend their time exploring specific problems—some of them, perhaps, ultimately insoluble—regarding (1) the content of the *Songs*, (2) the evaluative judgments we make of them, and (3) the literary and artistic evidence we employ in constructing interpretations and evaluations. These three types of problems are closely related: when students do some hard thinking about what ideas a poem may express, they begin naturally to evaluate the poem's success in realizing those ideas, and they usually have to do some hard thinking about the evidence they can use in judging and interpreting.

Let me start, however, with problems of content. Because we as teachers are anxious to make the *Songs* readily accessible to our students, we often spend our class discussions insisting upon the collection's most basic and consistent ideas. What our audience remembers, however, may be only a group of thinly edifying "messages." The sense that Blake is dealing with difficult moral and intellectual questions somehow gets lost; the *Songs* begin to look like nothing but a lengthy exposition of the abstract but universally acceptable idea that love is better than hatred, and freedom is better than oppression. To do justice to the scope and complexity of Blake's thought, perhaps one should refer briefly to the importance of such concepts as love and freedom, and then go right to the specifics, particularly if those specifics indicate complications or seeming contradictions. How many types of "love" do we find in the *Songs?* Lyca's parents clearly love her and want to protect her—but what about Ona's father? Does he "love" his daughter, too? Is love, as the *Songs* represent it, a problem as well as a solution to problems? And what about the "love" expressed by the little boy lost in *Experience?* What, if anything, does this form of love have to do with the love of Ona or the little black boy or the chimney sweeper in *Innocence?*

But almost any line of Socratic questioning, this one included, can serve merely as a longer and duller version of a dogmatic lecture, with students being coerced into noticing certain things but never provoked into thought. The most spirited discussions in my courses sometimes result from lectures in which I argue for a thesis—not necessarily one that I accept, but one that can produce an argument about specifics. I may assert, for instance, that despite Blake's emphasis on freedom and his sympathy for rebellion, many of the *Songs* implicitly advocate a patient, even a passive, acceptance of injustice and suffering. I may claim that this sort of acceptance is implicitly advocated in several of the *Songs of Innocence* ("The Little Black Boy," "The Chimney Sweeper," and "Night") and in those *Songs of Experience* that describe the apparent failure of efforts to rebel against oppression or to improve life ("Introduction" and "Earth's Answer," "A Little Boy Lost," "A Little Girl Lost," and "Infant Sorrow"). Having presented this case, I can try to get my students to question it. I can remind them, for instance, of characters in the *Songs* who struggle for and achieve a spiritual triumph, even in the midst of material "failure." (Usually, however, students are agile enough at finding such evidence on their own). The final product of the discussion can be an improved perception of the *Songs'* complexity and a livelier sense of Blake's involvement with tough problems, of his refusal to advocate ideals without considering the difficulties that beset their realization.

To help students get an impression of Blake's mind at work on complex literary problems, it is sometimes as useful to consider what is not in the *Songs* as what is actually in them. One can illustrate his activity as conscious architect of the collection by discussing poems that appear in his notebook but never get into *Experience*—"I saw a chapel all of gold," for example.

What effect would this poem have if it were included in the *Songs*? Would it clarify and expand Blake's ideas about love, or would it reveal their ambiguities or contradictions? Are there psychological conflicts in the "Chapel" poem for which none of the *Songs* indicates a manner of resolution and that Blake accordingly excludes from the collection? (On using notebook materials, teachers may wish to consult Greenberg, "Shared Struggles.")

If we are willing to look closely at problems of inclusion and exclusion, we can make good use of the seemingly slighter songs—those that provide us with less attractive material for philosophical disquisitions than does "London" or "The Tyger," those that students often glance at and forget, supposing that they will not turn up on the final exam. Try asking: What, if anything, does "The Blossom," or "Laughing Song," add to *Innocence*? Students can usually find three or four ways in which such poems make a contribution. Now ask: Is this poem *necessary* to the sequence? That question is harder, less likely to elicit the sort of stock answers that could be used to justify the inclusion of virtually any poem. If the answer is no, broader questions can follow. One might say, for instance: "A time-honored literary theory holds that if something is not necessary to a work of art, its inclusion actually detracts from the work by lessening its intensity. Can this theory properly be used to criticize the poem that we're discussing?"

There's a turn toward evaluation in that last line of questioning, and I mean there to be. We teach Blake because we consider his work tremendously valuable. But we should encourage our students to make their own judgments of value and should aid them in doing so by dispelling the impression that the presence of a work of literature on a college syllabus is sufficient proof of that work's perfection. This is why it is useful to test the *Songs* against standards (such as the standard of necessity that I just mentioned) that might not reflect favorably on some of them, or against critical theses that can stimulate a variety of evaluative responses. We risk having to defend the author or (closer to my point) acknowledge flaws or missed opportunities in his work. Such risks are worth taking when teaching great literature. I sometimes ask my students to take a minute and read to themselves "The Divine Image" or "On Another's Sorrow." Then, after discussion of its ideas, I suggest that the poem appears to be little more than a static array of stanzas embodying a fairly simple theme. If I put this statement in sufficiently blunt terms, I can expect to provoke some opposition. The students and I argue back and forth: What does it mean to call a poem "static"? Must every poem include some dramatic change? Next, I ask someone to read the poem aloud: Does it gain anything from oral presentation? What, specifically, does it gain? Finally we look carefully at the illustration: Does seeing the work in its composite form answer the particular objections we've considered?

Many types of evaluative questions can emerge from discussion of the tensions—or strains—that exist between poems. The two "Holy Thursday" poems are, of course, "contraries" of each other—but precisely what kind of contrary ideas do they suggest, and how effective is the contrast developed? Is the second poem a cogent criticism of the first, or does it amount merely to a brusque dismissal of the "innocent" view? While comparing *Songs of Experience*, one might say,

> There are several songs—"Holy Thursday," "Earth's Answer," "The Garden of Love"—in which the speaker pictures external forces or institutions as responsible for the evils of life. In others—"Ah! Sunflower," "The Angel"—individuals seem to be held responsible for their own plight. In still others—the "Nurses Song," "The Sick Rose"—something as vague as "the nature of things" seems to be the culprit. Is there a conflict of principles here, or is Blake simply allowing some of his speakers to present flawed or partial explanations of the world as it appears from their perspectives? If the latter, can we distinguish clearly between "true" and "false" perspectives, "adequate" and "partial" views? Can we discern more than the dim outlines of an underlying explanation of Blake's own?

If we ask questions like these, however, we have obviously advanced from problems of evaluation to problems of literary evidence. Problems of evidence are perhaps the most difficult to address, but they are of exceptional importance. In teaching the *Songs* (or any other great literature), we should try to do much more than equip our students with some facts and some patented interpretive methods. We should give them practice in the critical use of literary evidence; we should help them develop an intellectual skill that they can transfer to the study of many other works. So rich and various are the *Songs* that it is hard to think of another literary work that can exercise thought in as many ways as they can—if we are prepared to risk opening up the question of evidence to begin with.

To do so, one can construct for the class a plausible interpretation of "The Clod and the Pebble," relying on other songs (or *The Book of Thel*) to maintain that we should regard sympathetically the attitude of the unselfish clod. One can then construct a plausible interpretation that relies on "A Little Boy Lost" (or some of *The Marriage of Heaven and Hell*) to support the pebble's notions. Now we have "external" evidence on both sides of the question, of the kind that may provide grounds for caution in the use of external evidence. Can we get any help from the "internal" evidence of the poem's illustration—the sheep, the duck, and the other fauna? Should the narrative element be given weight—the fact that the altruistic clod gets "trodden" underfoot? And consider the question of tone: can we tell whether the reference to "metres meet" is a compliment to the pebble or a sarcastic condemnation? A third plausible interpretation may arise: perhaps Blake's normative concept of love is neither the pebble's nor the clod's (my view). Can we adequately ground this interpretation in the poem, or must we seek, once more, for external evidence? But what, after all, constitutes "external" evidence? *Thel* and *The Marriage* may be external, but aren't all the poems published as the *Songs of Innocence and of Experience* designed to be read together and allowed to comment on one another? Under what circumstances are we justified in altering our interpretation of one song because of what we believe the other songs mean? What safeguards can we use to keep from forcing every problematic song to fit some general and "consistent" meaning of our own device?

Other disturbing questions can arise, if we let them, from comparatively simple problems of judgment. "Seated in companies they sit" ("Holy Thursday," *Innocence*): this tautology looks like an obvious literary error. But it might be a successful attempt at projecting a naively enthusiastic speaker. What kind of evidence can we find to indicate Blake's intentions here? Does he use similar verbal devices for apparently similar purposes elsewhere in the *Songs*? But to what degree should evidence about Blake's intentions influence our judgment of his performance? When is the usefulness of a device destroyed by the difficulty of determining whether it is a device? Additional questions can be brought up when we are comparing published *Songs* with manuscripts. By looking at the manuscripts of "London" or "The Lilly" or "The Sick Rose" (each presents its own problems of evidence), do we learn more about what the completed poem means, or more about what Blake decided it should not mean?

These lines of investigation can alter our conception of familiar poems; they can open students' minds to unorthodox conclusions; they can even produce some surprising changes in the work we plan to publish. It's risky to reconsider our interpretations and to look closely, once again, at our ways of handling evidence. But exciting things can happen when we deliberately introduce risks into our teaching.

APPROACHES EMPHASIZING LITERARY CONTEXT AND THE IDEA OF CONTEXT

Teaching the Variations in *Songs*

Robert N. Essick

In recent years it has become almost mandatory to take note of the designs, and their impact on our understanding of the poems, when teaching *Songs of Innocence and of Experience.* Slides are projected, or facsimiles passed from hand to hand, even in sophomore survey classes. Yet reproductions of a single copy are no better than a typographic text at indicating the manifold variations among all copies of the *Songs.* Should this undeniable fact about Blake's lyric collections be introduced into the classroom as more than a passing reference, and if so to what end?

A general concern with differences among copies introduces the problems and rewards of a historical perspective on Blake's composition, arrangement, and production of the *Songs* over a period of more than thirty-five years. We lose our sense of the individual copy as an unchanging and completely authoritative icon as it is recontextualized back into its material and temporal origins and seen as only one of many versions. But discussions that remain on this level of generality can leave a class out of touch with specific, observable differences. Students rightfully demand ocular demonstration in such matters. Further, we need to treat each type of variant in turn, for each is a product of a different stage of production and has a different impact on our reading of text and design. I think we can accomplish these goals without vast photographic resources and without producing profound bibliographical yawns.

The various arrangements of the plates in both *Songs of Innocence* and the combined *Songs* constitute the most obvious differences among copies. Blake's frequent reordering of his plates included even the shift of a few poems from the *Innocence* to the *Experience* section of the book (this and other bibliographic facts, plate numbers, and copy designations derive from Bentley, *Books* 364–432). He moved "The Little Girl Lost" and "The Little Girl Found" from the former to the latter section shortly after he created the composite *Songs* in 1794. "The School Boy" first moved to *Experience* in three copies (L–N) of ca. 1800–06, returned to *Innocence* in five copies (O–Q, R, S) ranging in dates up to 1808, and shifted back to *Experience* in 1815 or later. "The Voice of the Ancient Bard" did not move until this same late period. The last poem, along with "The School Boy," continued to appear in separately issued copies of *Songs of Innocence* until Blake ceased its publication no earlier than 1808.

It takes only a few minutes to introduce these simple facts to a class; discussion of their conceptual significance can—and should—take much longer. These changes not only alter the context for our reading of the poems in question but can also influence our understanding of the binary concepts Blake used to structure the entire work. Clearly, *Experience* evolved out of issues first raised in *Innocence*, not in absolute contrast to them. Students with an excessively rigid sense of Blake's contraries must reconsider their assumptions. The states of the human soul are not mutually exclusive: their boundaries overlap, like the Zoas in the diagram on plate 32 of *Milton*, and they unite into cycles, like those in the "Lost" and "Found" poems of the *Songs* and in "The Mental Traveller." If some poems can be placed in either section because they have features of both states, might not others in *Innocence* bear traces of the contrary state? The question can lead a class to consider the way Experience insinuates itself into Innocence and thus to the possibilities for ironic readings of poems such as "Holy Thursday" and "The Chimney Sweeper" in *Innocence*. As they come to learn that Blake's contraries are more a matter of point of view than of content, students can entertain multiple and transformative perspectives on the designs as well as the texts. The vine lovingly entwined about the tree on the title page to *Innocence* can become, when seen with the eyes of Experience, a threatening serpent in another garden.

The sequences of plates in extant copies of *Innocence* and the combined *Songs* present a bewildering variety. While some may have resulted from rebinding activities, many have the authority of Blake's autograph numbers.

A few plate clusters remain fairly stable in separate copies of *Innocence* issued before about 1800 (groupings recorded in Erdman, *Illuminated Blake* 69–70). Two copies of *Songs of Innocence and of Experience* (T, U) printed on paper watermarked 1815 have almost the same order of plates throughout both sections. The sequence of copy U reappears in the last five known copies of the combined *Songs* (W–AA), all on 1825 paper. Standing between these two groups is copy V on 1818 paper, the only copy for which Blake provided a manuscript "Order in which the Songs of Innocence & of Experience ought to be paged & placed." This arrangement is unique to copy V and varies considerably from that exemplified by other late copies.

Might we take, and present to our students, the arrangement of Blake's final five copies of the *Songs* as definitive? I think not. Their arrangement may well be a consequence of the chronology of production rather than of Blake's decision to establish a single authoritative order for conceptual reasons. All five copies may have been printed at about the same time in no more than two press runs, as the ink colors indicate, and assembled and numbered in contiguous operations. Instead of presenting students with a privileged sequence of plates, or spending valuable class time debating the issue of final intentions, I have found it far more fruitful to present structural variation as a constitutive feature of a Blakean book. Students can then (following a suggestion first made by Erdman in his 1965 *Poetry and Prose* 714) proceed to an oral or written exercise in which they extend Blake's activities by producing their own arrangements of the *Songs* with clusters of plates that emphasize various motifs or themes: birth and death, sexuality and repression, animals, social institutions, Christian faith, the family, education, and many others. Listing such clusters in two columns preserves essential interchanges between the contrary states. Taken together, the many possible arrangements demonstrate how all are implicit within the spatial form of Blake's book and are authorized by his multiple orderings. For more advanced classes, this assignment can also become the introduction for studying the alternative plate sequences in *The Book of Urizen* and chapter 2 of *Jerusalem*, as well as a practical demonstration of the unity of conception and execution so central to Blake's aesthetic theories.

Different orderings of the plates are only one variation Blake introduced into the format of his *Songs*. He printed independent copies of *Innocence* on both sides of each leaf until about 1802, when he began to print on one side only. Four early copies of the combined *Songs* (B–E) are printed recto and verso, but all later copies have the plates on rectos only. From about 1806, Blake began numbering each plate and painting transparent color washes over text areas. Between 1808 and 1819 he began drawing framing lines around the plates. Thus, as Viscomi notes (*Art* 17–18), the *Songs* gradually shifted from a standard book format, with each opening of the leaves revealing two (potentially linked) picture-poems, to a series of individual framed prints. This change would seem to have little impact on readings of individual poems and designs (although facing designs may be construable as mutually illuminating), but it is well worth introducing this fact to more advanced classes because it constitutes an important evolution in Blake's conception of the kind of artifact he was producing and the amount of interchange between contiguous plates he wished to promote.

Pictorial differences among impressions of the same plate result from several different types of variation; each should play a somewhat different role in the classroom. Blake's method of inking his plates with a dauber created many unavoidable variations even among uncolored impressions. Subsequent hand work with pen or brush is not subject to such accidents, but I think it wrong to assume that all (or even most) differences in outlining and coloring have symbolic import. Here again, the mode of production is crucial in generating, and determining the significance of, variation. Blake colored each copy of the *Songs* as a unit, and over the years his skills and sensibilities as a colorist changed, mostly in the direction of deeper, richer colors applied with the minute brushstrokes of the miniature portraitist. The choice of pigments for each copy and Blake's sense of its chromatic unity established the range of color effects, and thus it is unlikely that he was much concerned with detailed differences in coloring between one impression and another in a copy long since sold. How would Blake remember in 1825 every color on a print colored in 1795 and no longer in his hands, and to whom in his contemporary audience could he be signaling different meanings through color differences known to us only by comparing reproductions of two or more copies?

Instead of wrestling with these thorny issues in an undergraduate class, I prefer to introduce students to the fact of color changes and to exemplify it with one or two plates. I have found it helpful to show slides and/or facsimiles of the frontispiece to *Innocence*—a plate that introduces us to the coloring of all that follow—from an early copy of *Songs of Innocence* (B or I), a much later copy (L), and copies B or C (both ca. 1795), E (ca. 1800–06), and Z (1825) of the combined *Songs* (for information on obtaining these copies, see the essay in this volume by Grant and Johnson). The point, it is worth noting, can be made with only three copies—early, middle, and late—each available on slides. The important goal is to get students to respond to the visual qualities of each version, but a brief (and admittedly subjective) discussion can follow on the relationship between color tonality and verbal "tone" as the artist-author's attitude toward his subject.

The addition or elimination of a pictorial motif offers yet another category of variation. In at least one case—the pink, gray, or brown coloring of the child on the left in the second plate of "The Little Black Boy"—a simple change in tinting becomes a change in motif. This variation offers one of the best examples for class discussion, for all the students need is the text of the poem and the information that the boy is white in early copies and more or less black in most prints colored after about 1800. Evidently Blake first intended the design as an illustration of the moment when the black boy will be "free" from his "black . . . cloud." Yet the other child simultaneously becomes free of his "white cloud," indicating that "cloud" signifies the body, not simply skin coloring or race. Thus the text presents an obvious difficulty for the artist, who must show the boys in their bodies if he is to show them at all. To put the black boy in a white body belies the spiritual transformation in the text, and accordingly Blake returned his children to their natural colors in later copies. The change does not materially influence our reading of the poem, but it can lead to a discussion of the different capabilities and limitations of Blake's two media: verbal metaphor and pictorial image.

The most common motif variations in the *Songs* are the painting in of sunbursts in skies, haloes around heads, and water below the etched images on several plates in late copies. Such additions are invariably interesting, but I find in practice that they rarely have a significant impact on our readings of the poems or even on the central features of text-design relations. Blake consistently painted a hat on the child in "The Little Boy Lost," thereby creating a variant from the etched image on the plate, but do we need the headgear to know that he is one of Blake's spiritual travelers? And surely we already know that the streets of "London" are duplicitous and fallen before noticing the fork-tongued snake painted below the text in copy N of *Experience*. (Except for this addition in copy N, all motif variants mentioned here are noted in Bentley, *Books* 388–403, or Erdman, *Illuminated Blake* 42–68.) The crown on the woman pictured above "The Angel" is painted out in many early copies, but that does not make her any less a "maiden Queen" or more receptive to love. The halo added in seven copies to the head of the figure standing lower right in "The Divine Image" helps us identify him as Christ raising a fallen (Lazarus?) figure, but we do not assume that the absence of the halo indicates that he is someone else. Less notable changes, including the addition of more stars or tendrils to plates already bearing them in their etched images, seem even less productive of new readings. In his prospectus "To the Public" of 1793, Blake boasted that his illuminated books were "in a style more ornamental, uniform, and grand, than any before discovered." Many drawn and painted changes in his designs for *Songs of Innocence and of Experience* may have been made for the sake of these visual qualities rather than as directives on how we should convert everything we see into interpretations of Blake's thoughts.

I fear that the foregoing may project a negative thesis about my titular subject, one that offers reasons for *not* teaching copy variations in the *Songs*.

Rather, it should give us more confidence in what we can realistically expect to accomplish in undergraduate courses. It is helpful to introduce the fact and the concept of difference, even in survey courses. The various orderings of plates in the *Songs* can initiate discussions of such key matters as the structure of contrariety and the interweaving of multiple perspectives. Even a brief consideration of pictorial variations leads us closer to Blake's materials and processes of production. Classroom time can be spent more profitably on these concerns than on the cataloging of countless specific variants under the assumption that all are replete with iconographic significance.

Teaching the Biblical Contexts of *Songs*

Leslie Tannenbaum

In *Songs of Innocence and of Experience,* as in his prophetic books, Blake looked to the Bible as a main source of inspiration. A look at the picture of Adam and Eve on the title page tells us that biblical themes, images, and symbols contribute to the meaning and method of Blake's collection of lyrics. Since most undergraduates cannot be counted on to have much knowledge of biblical matters, however, teachers of Blake must decide how much biblical background is really necessary for an understanding and appreciation of Blake's *Songs.* The extent of the students' interest partially determines how far I stress this background in the interpretation of individual poems, yet I feel that certain biblical contexts are essential to give students the framework they need to apprehend Blake's meaning.

The first context that I discuss is the Christian interpretation of the Fall, as narrated in Genesis 3. I usually quiz the students on the Genesis story and then discuss with them its implications, especially the idea of eating from the Tree of Knowledge. Next, I invite them to consider the story of Adam and Eve as psychological myth, adopting the interpretations of Erich Fromm and Northrop Frye. I explain the correlation between Adam and Eve's separation from God and children's growing sense of alienation from their parents and from the world in general. Just as Adam and Eve in Eden were happy but essentially dependent on God, so the child's Eden is a state of being innocent yet dependent on parents. Young children feel secure and totally connected with the world, because they know no distinction between the self and the world. In other words, there is no separation between self and other, as everything is perceived as part of the self (as seen in a baby's attempts to absorb everything into its mouth). The development of consciousness—the awareness of the separation of self and other—results when children realize that the external world is no longer totally responsive to their desires or needs, and eating of the Tree of Knowledge can symbolize this awareness of separation.

To illustrate this psychological interpretation of the Fall, I have the students look at "The Lamb" and "The Tyger." They are quick to notice that in "The Lamb" the speaker, God, and nature (as represented by the lamb) form a totally coherent and integrated unity. Moreover, the speaker sees God as a protective and nurturing parent figure. The child is totally unconscious of the logical implications of his or her thinking and of the heresy of the poem's primitive theology (if God equals child equals lamb, then the child made the lamb). In Innocence, the entire universe is absorbed into—or is a projection of—the self. The speaker of "The Tyger," by contrast, is all too concerned with logic and theological issues, having fallen into consciousness and having experienced God and nature as other. It is clear that this speaker has eaten of the Tree of Knowledge and no longer experiences the sense of inner coherence and of connection with the external world that the speaker of "The Lamb" does. This contrast in point of view is underscored by Blake's illustration to "The Tyger," which shows an innocent-looking animal-cracker tiger; the fallen speaker's horrific image of the animal reflects the fallen vision of Other.

After going over these two poems, I ask students to point out others that exemplify the idea of Innocence and Experience as psychological states, thus reinforcing Blake's internalized interpretation of the Genesis story of the Fall from Eden. For instance, it is interesting to discuss the reasons behind the tortured logic of "The Fly." At this point I also expand the issue by introducing (if the students haven't already brought it up) a discussion of Blake's pastoral imagery. We discuss, or I lecture on, pagan and biblical ideas of pastoral, relating the myth of the golden age in pagan tradition to the idea of the promised land (with its accompanying pastoral imagery) as an analogue of Eden in the Bible, tying this material in with the typological pattern of biblical history—the promise and loss of Canaan as another Eden and the use of shepherd and lamb imagery to describe Christ, who will restore the lost Eden. Thus the students are able to see how the biblical images and themes in Blake's *Songs* develop religious, psychological, and historical meanings.

Having established some essential meanings of Innocence and Experience, I then attempt to make students aware of Blake's prophetic purpose in the *Songs*. Here I focus on the "Introduction" to *Songs of Experience*. Pointing out the allusion to Genesis 3.8 in line 5 of the "Introduction," I ask the students to relate the issue of the Fall to the bard's identity and rhetorical purpose in the poem. We end up relating these issues to biblical prophecy, and I provide whatever background information the students are unable to supply. I emphasize that the Old Testament prophets, St. John of Revelation, and ultimately Christ himself sought to heal the separation between humankind and God, to get the fallen world to "return." The aim of all this discussion is to see that since the Fall is defined as fragmentation—separation of human from God and of self from other—Blake's purpose in the *Songs* is to make his readers understand the prelapsarian state of Innocence and the fallen state of Experience, to see the nature and causes of the Fall, and to "return" to a new Eden, to become reintegrated.

This prophetic stance in the "Introduction" to *Experience* is markedly different from the stance of the piper in the "Introduction" to *Innocence*, but the bard in *Experience* claims to have the more inclusive view. This topic can provoke lively discussion, but it also leads to a more important issue that relates to Blake's prophetic function: Blake's reasons for providing multiple speakers and multiple perspectives in *Innocence* and *Experience*. One explanation lies in a corollary of Blake's perception of Innocence and Experience as psychological states: the mind itself creates reality, as is explicitly expressed in "the mind-forg'd manacles" of the inhabitants of "London." Another explanation, which relates to the previous one in terms of its emphasis on vision, is that Blake's use of multiple perspectives in *Songs* (and in his prophecies) is derived from biblical prophecy. The Old Testament prophets and St. John in Revelation employ perspectivism to widen their audience's comprehension of the issues concerning our fallen state and to stimulate the kind of mental activity necessary for fallen humanity's redemption.

As the discussion of this redemptive process proceeds, we inevitably have to deal with another important biblical issue in order to understand Blake's notion of a "return" to Eden: Blake's use of the Incarnation as a theme in the *Songs*. This theme is already implied in "The Lamb," in the "Introduction" to *Experience*, and in "Earth's Answer." Here students, especially those who are Christian, become fascinated with Blake's radical reinterpretation of traditional Christian doctrine. As I have already mentioned, the students come to see that the innocent speaker of "The Lamb" universalizes the idea that God became a little child, to the point where every child is God. The point is reiterated in "A Cradle Song," where the mother identifies her sleeping child with the infant Christ. This idea of the potential identity of God and human being also surfaces in the "Introduction" to *Experience*, where Blake's mention of the Holy Word alludes to the treatment of the Incarnation in John 1 and where the subject of the phrase "calling the lapsed soul" may be deliberately ambiguous, referring to the bard and the Holy Word (since the bard is the living embodiment of the Word in the present situation). Finally, Blake's idea of the Word made flesh is most explicitly expressed in "The Divine Image," which celebrates "the human form divine." All these poems show that Blake interprets the Incarnation to mean that "God becomes as we are, that we may be as he is" (*There Is No Natural Religion* [b]; E 3).

Blake further develops this idea of the Incarnation through his representation of the godhead in *Songs*. We see in *Experience* and in some of the illustrations to *Innocence* that Blake places greater value on God as the Son, because the Son represents God as human. This preference is most apparent in the "Introduction" to *Experience* and in "Earth's Answer." In the former poem, Blake reinterprets Genesis 3.8 by having the Son (the Holy Word) rather than the Father walk among the ancient trees of Eden. Conversely, in "Earth's Answer," he represents Earth's experience of God as other by having her perceive God as the Father, the jealous God of the Old Testament and of traditional Christian dogma ("the Father of the ancient men").

Thus Blake is expressing in numerous songs that God and humanity were once unified, that a state of Innocence includes divinity, that humanity's fallen condition includes loss of godhead, and that the Incarnation showed that reintegration or redemption can come about when God and humanity are, quite literally, one again. Once we establish Blake's idea that God must be humanized and that fallen humanity must recover its lost divinity, I lead students to explore Blake's ideas about what keeps humanity in its fallen state and what leads to potential regeneration. In this context we begin to discuss Blake's social and political criticism in such poems as "The Chimney Sweeper" of *Innocence*, "London," and "The Garden of Love." For poems that point toward regeneration, I emphasize "To Tirzah," "Holy Thursday" in *Innocence*, and "The Little Girl Found." Here again the issues of point of view and Blake's notion of vision become important. I usually introduce Blake's concept of apocalypse at this point, showing the students or reading to them Blake's famous statement in "A Vision of the Last Judgment": "Whenever an Individual Rejects Error & Embraces Truth, a Last Judgment passes upon that Individual" (E 562). An apocalypse is a matter of vision and can take place at any time; since the mind creates reality, humanity can reunite itself with God through an alteration of vision.

This notion of achieving an apocalypse through vision is perhaps most strongly developed in "To Tirzah," which explicitly points out the contrast between fallen vision and the possibility of achieving a redemptive vision. I have the students explore the implications of Blake's allusion, in the illustration to the poem, to Paul's idea of a "spiritual body" in 1 Corinthians 12. Here it is important to see that Blake's speaker is casting off the error of believing that natural vision is the only vision and is realizing the kind of last judgment that Blake wants his reader to experience.

In this context of apocalyptic vision, Blake's allusions to Revelation and the messianic visions of the Old Testament prophets in other poems in *Songs* become relevant. For instance, I point out the allusions to the peaceable kingdom described in Isaiah 11 (where the wild beasts become tame) in "The Little Girl Found," "Night," and the illustration to "The Tyger." In these poems the taming of the wild beasts implies the fulfillment of prophetic promise through a change of vision. Similarly, the echoes of Revelation in "Holy Thursday" and "The Chimney Sweeper" in *Innocence* are important as intimations of an apocalyptic reversal of oppressive situations. Tom Dacre's dream of a resurrection and bathing in the waters of life represents a vision of a new heaven and earth realizable in the present if this vision were not clouded over by traditional theology. The "harmonious thunderings" of the children in "Holy Thursday," which echo the "thunderings and lightnings and voices" of the four-and-twenty elders around the throne of God in Revelation (4.5), indicate not only that the present situation is an ironic reversal and judgment upon the elders in Blake's poem but also that innocence has the potential power to overthrow the established order.

By the time we reach these visions of possible redemption, the students have come to grasp some essential themes and symbols in *Songs of Innocence and of Experience*. They have moved from an understanding of Blake's notion of the Fall to a sense of his prophetic purpose and ultimately to a fuller idea of his theology concerning the Incarnation, the causes of human suffering, and the means of redeeming humankind's fallen state. They have also come to a better understanding of the workings of Blake's imagination, of the ways in which his work is creatively engaged with the Bible, the one book that Blake regarded as "the Great Code of Art."

Songs and the Bible

Philip J. Gallagher

I teach selections from Blake's *Songs of Innocence and of Experience* in a variety of classes, ranging from a freshman composition course called Research and Critical Writing, through a sophomore survey of English literature, to a noncredit continuing-education offering called The Bible and English Literature. These different contexts require a variety of approaches to the lyrics, but throughout I have found it possible—and indeed profitable—to focus on the allusive and thematic relations between the *Songs* and Holy Scripture, especially the Book of Genesis. (To do so is manageable even within the framework of my composition class, whose deliberately irritating subtitle is Christianity and Other Myths.) To be sure, biblical motifs do not inform all the *Songs*, but the sacred text frequently illuminates—or is illuminated by—a Blake poem, and in the juxtaposing of the two, even the "simplest" lyrics sometimes acquire a complexity often denied them by student readers and professional critics alike.

To begin with the title of these collected poems, one might reasonably expect a volume preoccupied with the contraries Innocence and Experience to be parasitic upon (and also critical of) Genesis 2.25–3.24 (where the innocent naked unashamedness of Adam and Eve changes into self-awareness and humiliation) and Romans 5.12–21 (where the hereditary curses of Genesis become explicitly moralized in the doctrine later called "original sin"). For Blake, the Pauline dichotomies of guiltlessness and sin, which have eschatological and legalistic rather than psychological implications, become the largely perceptual categories of childlike naïveté and adult sophistication (*Shewing the Two Contrary States of the Human Soul*), and Blake's lyrics are less Pauline instruments of exegetical casuistry than dramatic vehicles of social criticism. I do not, however, begin my teaching of the *Songs* and the Bible by suggesting such a global interconnectedness as I have just sketched. Instead, I elucidate a number of easy—and easily identifiable—Blakean allusions to well-known biblical verses, thereby setting the stage for more ambitious forays into the *Songs'* biblical parasitism.

Songs of Innocence

The first two *Songs of Innocence* (in Erdman's ordering)—"Introduction" and "The Shepherd"—transcend the secular tropes of conventional pastoral poetry that they clearly embody and point toward the Bible. The shepherd persona of *Innocence* is enjoined in the first poem to "Pipe a song about a Lamb" ("Introduction"), usage reminiscent of John 1.29 ("Look, there is the lamb of God that takes away the sins of the world"). The verse thus suggests an identification between Blake's pastoral animal and Jesus. The same speaker, who naturally (if naively) believes that "sweet is the Shepherds sweet lot" ("The Shepherd"), may echo Jesus's trenchant metonymy "I am the good shepherd" (John 10.11, 14) and its eschatological adaptation in 1 Peter 5.4: "When the chief shepherd [i.e., Christ] appears, you will be given the crown of unfading glory." I do not press the argument for biblical allusiveness very far in poems like these, in part because, for many of my students, Scripture enjoys a privileged status, and in part because the universality of the images involved ("lamb," "shepherd") makes precise identification of supposed literary sources impossible. But this very universality also makes the scriptural connection *plausible*, and my students— indeed, all beginning students of literature—need to learn to approach the Bible as "mere" literature, as a system of conventions available for "deconstruction" by later generations of poets. Thus "Introduction" and "The Shepherd" provide innocuous entries into more thorough and compelling exegesis of Blake's biblical parasitism in the *Songs*.

I typically turn from these poems to such other *Songs of Innocence* as "The Divine Image," whose title clearly echoes Genesis 1.26–27 ("Let us make man in our own image . . ."), and whose final line ("There God is dwelling too") recalls the New Testament doctrine of the deity's indwelling in the upright heart and pure (see, for example, 2 Cor. 3.3). Precisely because this poem is filled with pious Christian platitudes, my students readily accept its biblical echoes at face value and wrongly infer that Blake was a typical and orthodox Christian. The first version of "The Chimney Sweeper" does nothing to change this view, even though the childish eschatological dream of "little Tom Dacre" institutionalizes and certifies the oppression of the poor (21–23), whom "You have . . . with you always" (John 12.8), by endorsing an Augustinian otherworldliness and an otherworldly eschatology epitomized in the poem's ominous final line: "So if all do their duty they need not fear harm."

I find it virtually impossible at first to make students see that, in poems like "The Chimney Sweeper," Blake is deploying Christian commonplaces and biblical tropes to expose the exploitativeness of antichrists who dilute the power of Scripture for their own selfish ends. How, then, can one show that the *Songs of Innocence*, however frequently they may echo the Bible, are revisionist critiques of biblical tradition rather than mere iterations of it? The solution is to look at other Blake lyrics that rely on Scripture both more systematically and less straightforwardly. The first "Holy Thursday" poem is a good place to begin. My students again do not find this poem a threat to their own (partly hermeneutic) innocence; they are comforted by its emphasis on liturgical ritual, and they endorse its climactic aphorism ("Then cherish pity, lest you drive an angel from your door") as a fit moral to a poem so obviously orthodox.

At this juncture I inform them that this "blameless" moral probably alludes to the destruction of Sodom at Genesis 19 and to its more hideous analogue at Judges 19, where a hospitable Gibeahite door offers a concubine to "certain sons of Belial" to avoid homosexual rape. The impact of these sources is significant: students at once recognize the darker side of Scripture and the possibility that, in Blake, apparent biblical platitudes imply less a symbiotic than a parasitic relation between the Bible and the poet. The possibility is reinforced (if not confirmed) when I point out that the final pietistic line of "Holy Thursday" is virtually identical in tone to the sententious conclusion of "The Chimney Sweeper."

Having thus persuaded my students both that the Bible impinges on Blake's lyrics and that the poems in turn might impinge on the Bible (would that the work of persuasion were as systematic or as successful as my writing implies), I take up perhaps the most complex instance of this interanimation in the *Songs of Innocence*: "The Little Black Boy." Harold Bloom has explicated the ironies of this poem, so I will confine myself to its biblical resonances. My students—black and white alike—fail to discern the inadequacies of the lyric's literal argument: instead, they accept the word of a little boy as if it were the *verbum Dei* and endorse his mother's account of the origin of blackness as if it were a mixture of hard science and sophisticated biblical orthodoxy. The mother's myth (9–20) and her son's misconstrual of it (23–28), however, are closer to pious catechistics (Q: "Why did God make you?" A: "God made me to know him, to love him, and to serve him in this world and to be happy with him in the next.") than to rigorous hermeneutics. Moreover, the form of her naive etiology of black skin rehearses, in its simplicity, such transparent and repressive etiologies of Genesis 3 as those of labor, death, pain in childbearing, and the subjugation of women.

The mother's arguments thus confirm this poem's affinity with the Judeo-Christian tradition, but they do not make it orthodox. For instance, the woman promises her son that when they die, God will invite them to "come out from the grove [i.e., the body] . . . , / And round my golden tent like lambs rejoice." She probably has in mind Revelation 7.15, where Christians who have been persecuted on earth (the mother and her son?) will be dressed in white robes in heaven and will serve God, who "will spread his tent over them." This biblical passage seems to confirm the mother's otherworldliness, but only at first sight: her tent image embraces other biblical passages as well, including Exodus 25.8–9, where the Israelites are enjoined to make a tent so that God can dwell among men, and John 1.1, "The Word was made flesh, he pitched his tent among us." Both passages, especially the latter, confirm a Judeo-Christian truth often obscured in such unrealized eschatologies as the mother's: instead of supplying the liberation from materiality that she desiderates, the tent-pitching incarnate Word implies, by the very fact of its incarnation, God's inextricable involvement in human history. Freedom must be sought in the world and time, not in the otherworld and eternity. This is (in part) the Bible's message, and it is Blake's too, once we have learned to grasp certain insights implicit in his poem (if not in his characters' reductionist thinking). My students are amazed to find such complexity in "The Little Black Boy," and many of them take satisfaction in learning to differentiate "authentic" Blakean Christianity from the sorts of institutionalized perversions of it that this "simple" lyric dramatizes. Such awareness requires juxtaposing the *Songs of Innocence* with the biblical passages they feed on, an approach equally effective in the *Songs of Experience*.

Songs of Experience

The relevance of the Bible to the *Songs of Experience* is easy to demonstrate to students: to begin with, this collection of lyrics is overseen by a visionary "Bard / Who Present, Past, and Future sees," and "Whose ears have heard, / The Holy Word, / That walked among the ancient trees" ("Introduction"). The bard thus claims intimacy with the events behind Genesis (if not the whole Bible), wherein "Yahweh God walk[ed] in the cool of the day" (Genesis 3.8) and "Call[ed to] the lapsed Soul" ("Introduction"; Genesis 3.9a), "Where are you?" (3.9b). As we might expect of a speaker so familiar with "The Holy Word" of God, the bard informs the lyrics with significant references to Scripture. Even so unlikely a candidate as "The Sick Rose" echoes and recontextualizes a biblical passage—the prophet's strident denunciation of decadent Judah: "And you, what are you going to do? You may dress yourself in scarlet, put on ornaments of gold, enlarge your eyes with paint but you make yourself pretty in vain. Your lovers disdain you, your life is what they are seeking" (Jer. 4.30). As a scriptural source may be doubted for a poem so obviously parasitic on the carpe diem tradition, however, I prefer to rest my case for the biblicism of the *Songs of Experience* on two more explicit instances: "The Tyger" and "A Poison Tree."

It is misleading to teach "The Tyger" apart from its companion poem "The Lamb," so I teach the two lyrics as paradigms of the comparativist approach to the *Songs of Innocence and of Experience*. Both lyrics have their origin in the creation accounts of Genesis 1 and 2, as filtered (in the "The Lamb" especially) through a tradition of catechistical questions and answers. The danger of a comparative reading, however, is naively to conclude that the lamb and the tiger symbolize and confirm the moral dichotomies **"good"** and **"evil."**

One can neutralize this misinterpretation (epidemic in persons encountering Blake for the first time) by calling students' attention to the poems' redeployment of the messianic prophecy of paradise regained: "The wolf lives with the lamb, the panther lies down with the kid, calf and lion cub feed together with a little boy to lead them. The cow and the bear make friends, their young lie down together. The lion eats straw like the ox" (Isa. 11.6–7; cf. *Paradise Lost* 4.340–45). This passage, with its audacious and almost simplistic denial of the contrariety between human beings and domestic animals on the one hand and wild animals on the other (cf. Gen. 9.1–4), encourages Blake (so I urge on my students) to explore, through two radically different poetic personae, the ontogeny of beings as different as his lamb and his tiger. The poet in effect undoes the reconciliatory gesture of Isaiah by replacing the prophet's fantastic projection of social unanimity among the animals with his bard's uncertain questions about the supposed unity of their creator: "Did he who made the Lamb make thee?" ("The Tyger"). This problem, of course, returns us to the creative mysteries of Genesis, for Blake recapitulates in his poetic act the eternal act of creation.

My final example of the biblicism of the *Songs of Experience* is "A Poison Tree" (a poem I have studied in detail in "The Word Made Flesh"). In all my classes I reserve a full hour for discussion of this powerful indictment of the biblical account of the Fall. Its original title, "Christian Forbearance," encourages an allegorical or parabolic interpretation of the fable, in which the trope of a poison tree conveniently illustrates the radical moral principle that the supposed virtue of turning the other cheek is really the vice of psychological repression. Students familiar with Freud prefer to rest in such a figurative reading, especially since they find it impossible to take seriously this lyric's literal argument. Nevertheless, armed with the decisive evidence of Genesis 1–3, I insist on just such an approach to "A Poison Tree": having traced the grammatical and psychological processes by which the narrator's unspoken word becomes the poisonous flesh of a tree, I turn to the implications of the poem's controlling symbol, interpreting the lyric as a countermyth that exposes the biblical narrative of the Fall as a fraud by revealing the "true" etiology of the Tree of the Knowledge of Good and Evil. The exegetical effort is lost on some students, but it liberates others by illuminating Blake's bold and subtle assault on the supposed inerrancy of the first book of the Bible. They come to see that for the poet Holy Scripture, a foundation of the Western tradition, is less a solution to be embraced than a problem to be explored. Blake repeatedly urges students to such insights, which is why I teach his *Songs* as parasitic in varying degrees on the Bible. The method works, and, what is more, it promotes a liberal education. I recommend it highly.

The Grounding of the *Songs*

Wallace Jackson

Though it is now customary to regard Blake as a Romantic poet (it was not always so), there are excellent reasons to approach the *Songs of Innocence and of Experience* through the poetry of the mid–eighteenth century. The *Songs* take their inception in the earlier poetry and are summoned into existence by Blake's desire to locate for himself a place to stand. Thus the *Songs*, whatever else they may do, engage the tradition of which he is a part. It is not unusual for Blake's poetry to assume this corrective or dialogic function (think, for example, of his *Milton* and the encounter on which that poem is based). In the few pages available to me here I want to suggest some ways a teacher may explore this subject and by doing so locate the *Songs* within an immediate historical and thematic context.

During the middle years of the eighteenth century, a body of poetry appeared that is loosely classified as meditative-descriptive. It includes work by James Thomson, Thomas Gray, the Wartons, Goldsmith, and other lesser figures. To some extent this poetry incorporates elements of pastoralism and primitivism, and it provides some essential reality principles that Blake's *Songs* challenge, satirize, and repudiate—a rejection in effect of certain articles of faith dear to the mid-century poets. In surveying the traditional pastoral of innocence, the poetry of Arcadian idyll, Renato Poggioli proposes that the form "tends to express itself in collective, or plural, terms" and may therefore "look at the human condition from the standpoint of the family" (58). Clearly aware of this tradition in his careful reading of eighteenth-century poets, Blake writes such *Songs of Innocence* as "The Shepherd," "The Little Black Boy," and "A Cradle Song," in which a loving guardianship is evident. Yet even as he accepts the principles governing the pastoral of innocence, in the *Songs of Experience* he turns the tradition upside-down to write deliberately antipastoral—and hence anti-Thomsonian or anti-Wartonian—poems. He does not burlesque the tradition, as Gay does in *The Shepherd's Week* or as Swift does in "Baucis and Philemon," nor does he submit the pastoral of innocence to the mere corrective of a realistic appraisal of village life, as Crabbe provides in *The Village*. Poggioli observes that "the task of the pastoral imagination is . . . to reconcile innocence and happiness, to exalt the pleasure principle at the expense of the reality principle" (14). In Gray's "Ode on a Distant Prospect of Eton College," the speaker remarks of the children at play:

> Alas, regardless of their doom,
> The little victims play!
> No sense have they of ills to come,
> Nor care beyond today. (51–54)

The speaker, who knows the reality of the human condition, looks on such wisdom as of dubious value: "where ignorance is bliss, / 'Tis folly to be wise." Moreover, earlier ages of primitive innocence are preferable to later times of sophisticated wit and sociality. Thus, when Thomas Warton, in "The Pleasures of Melancholy," conceives the difference between Spenser's Una and Pope's Belinda, he tends to imagine the former as consistent with a romantic primitivism, whereas the latter is all superficial glitter:

> Yet does my mind with sweeter transport glow,
> As at the root of mossy trunk reclin'd,
> In magic Spenser's wildly-warbled song
> I see deserted Una wander wide
> Thro' wasteful solitudes, and lurid heaths,
> Weary, forlorn; than when the fated fair
> Upon the bosom bright of silver Thames
> Launches in all the lustre of brocade,
> Amid the splendours of the laughing sun.   (152–60)

The numerous examples of this sentiment in mid-eighteenth-century poetry commonly evoke a set of related preferences—the fond wish for the "sweeter transport" of natural idyllicism rather than the waking reality of a "true" or sophisticatedly "false" reality. The strong desire for innocence, however, is "no longer possible for the modern—either because the bowers have been destroyed or because they have been hidden," as Thomas Weiskel reminds us in *The Romantic Sublime*. He is speaking of the close of William Collins's "Ode on the Poetical Character" and of the "unhappy progress of consciousness away from the ampler power of Innocence" (131). Innocence thereby becomes either the domain of the child, to which the adult, like Gray, mournfully condescends, or becomes the haunt of pseudo–woodland nymphs like Una, whose sexuality is beguiling because innocent (unlike Belinda's). The deliberate transformations of such attitudes in Blake's *Songs* indicate his concerted critique of an entire tradition.

Take for another example Goldsmith's aging beauty in "The Deserted Village":

> As some fair female unadorned and plain,
> Secure to please while youth confirms her reign,
> Slights every borrowed charm that dress supplies,
> Nor shares with art the triumph of her eyes;
> But when those charms are passed, for charms are frail,
> When time advances and when lovers fail,

> She then shines forth, solicitous to bless,
> In all the glaring impotence of dress.   (287–94)

Insofar as the poet prefers artless charm to tasteless artifice, the situation resembles the relation between Una and Belinda; both passages have to do with the deception and duplicity consequent on loss and alteration or, more simply, on mere temporal progress. We recognize such formulas in the notion that youth is better than age, the past better than the present, ignorance better than knowledge, simplicity superior to complexity—that, in sum, there are golden ages in history and in the individual life, and that when we lose those we have lost much that is valuable in the human condition. This point is also relevant to the familiar retirement poem in the eighteenth century, wherein purling brooks and shady nooks are desired above cities, the toils of humanity, and ambition. Thus there is a body of well-known poetry in the period, much of which Blake clearly knew, that depends heavily on antitheses of the sort I have indicated and that builds its major emotional effects on the validity of the oppositions or contraries I have identified. Within such a poetry, time is inevitably the enemy, history is the record of loss, and the reality principle is predicated on the notion that we become less than we were. Inevitably, a longing for the mother haunts the nostalgic reversalism that fuels much of this vision.

It is equally true, as Blake recognized, that to become less is to know more, to understand better the reality principles on which our lives are based; but the evidence of maturity and wisdom is the recognition that what is lost is superior to what has been gained—an understanding to which those within the pastoral of innocence do not and cannot come. A poetry aware in this way is bound to have strong elegiac impulses, and this fact alone helps us understand something of Wordsworth's exploration of pastoral elegy in the Lucy poems. Blake's *Songs of Innocence*, however, tend not to memorialize the state of innocence, because this state is not yet embalmed in his imagination. He writes as from within it, nowhere more convincingly perhaps than in "Laughing Song" or "A Cradle Song." In other words, he does not yet deny the adequacy or permanence of innocence, though the presence of the *Songs of Experience* changes things considerably. Northrop Frye long ago pointed out that "The *Songs of Experience* are satires, but one of the things that they satirize is the state of innocence. . . . Conversely, the *Songs of Innocence* satirize the state of experience, as the contrast which they present to it makes its hypocrisies more obviously shameful" (*Fearful Symmetry* 237).

If Frye is right, as I think he is in general, the poems enforce the limitations of possibility and vision that characterize each state (one can lead students to this perception by examining each state from the perspective of the other). Blake's pastoral of Innocence and his antipastoral of Experience propose different conceptions of reality, which is one reason why a speaker contemplating Innocence from the standpoint of Experience has such trouble understanding it. This insight explains the bewilderment of the speaker of "The Tyger." How could a god who made a lamb make a tiger? And why would a god want to do so? But the lamb is not a sentimental pastoral notion, nor is the tiger a terrible fact to be shunned. The meaning of Blake's tiger, then, emerges only as students come to see that the state of Experience has its inevitable terrors and challenges, the recognition of which signifies not decline and loss but the opportunity for growth and gain. A normative eighteenth-century proposition, such as the one traced above, posits not only loss but closure: Innocence dies, but Experience succeeds and determines the way we live within the world, determines even our idea of reality. In teaching Blake against that background, I try to point out that for him, when we take either state to be better or more real than the other we directly transform it into a trap or prison, the state in which no further growth in imagination or vision is possible. To see Innocence as totally desirable and experience as wholly negative is to create the reality that we have envisioned. Students readily understand that no one can stay within Innocence, for it is finally inconsistent with our humanity, but it is more difficult for them to appreciate that the desire to do so dehumanizes Experience and renders it frightful and sterile.

My point is that Gray and Collins, Warton and Goldsmith present "truths" of inevitable decline; this is the function of their wisdom, and it should not be surprising that their appraisal of reality so stultified their imaginations that they became, in large measure, victims of the reality they perceived. They suffered the closure they proclaimed. When we look to Blake, however, we see that the nature of the real as offered by the speakers of the *Songs of Experience* arises from the notion that division is the essential fact of the human condition. From this recognition derives the justification for antipastoral; division is what antipastoralism exists to rationalize (as, for example, for the speaker of "The Human Abstract"). Separation, exclusion, and difference all define the real, and the sensible evidence of one's grasp of reality is the ability to articulate this perception as absolute. Some speakers within Experience do not like this fact, but most of them base their lives on it. The speaker of the "Nurses Song" of *Experience* is both envious of Innocence and contemptuous of it, and her contempt is a part of her disappointment that Innocence is lost to her forever (though of course it need not be). Blake's point, then, inheres in her *perception* that she must lose it. Blake therefore brings under scrutiny several key assumptions informing the reality principle that descends from the poetry of the mid– to late eighteenth century.

Before concluding, I would like to offer teachers of Blake's *Songs* a corollary to this position. Within the individual life a rough justice disposes things so that what may seem a loss offers something of a gain and, conversely, what may seem initially to be all gain involves some loss. While this principle seems only paradoxically related to what I said at the outset about eighteenth-century poetry, I take it to be an occasion for those poets' optimism, covertly offering another justification for resigning oneself to the order of reality. Such a "submission" is authorized in Pope's magisterial "Whatever is, is Right," and is based on the presumed fact of compensation or alternation. The familiar Enlightenment version of the idea is independent of specific religious or theological contexts and serves to justify the chiaroscuro of pleasure and pain, good and bad.

Eighteenth-century writers offer this proposition in many forms. Meditating on the disproportionate gifts bestowed on different countries, Goldsmith observes in "The Traveller":

> And yet perhaps if countries we compare,
> And estimate the blessings which they share,
> Though patriots flatter, still shall wisdom find
> An equal portion dealt to all mankind,
> As different good, by Art or Nature given,
> To different nations makes their blessings even.   (75–80)

In the "Elegy Written in a Country Churchyard," Gray remarks the limits consequent on the obscurity of rural life:

> Their lot forbade: nor circumscribed alone
> Their growing virtues, but their crimes confined;
> Forbade to wade through slaughter to a throne,
> And shut the gates of mercy on mankind.   (65–68)

The principle of compensation dictates an equality of sorts that arises from an inherent system of checks and balances. If every virtue has its defect, every defect has its virtue. To recognize this principle is the function of wisdom (Goldsmith so identifies it in the passage above), and wisdom discovers that a ruling justice oversees loss and gain within the lives of nations and humble folk. Blake builds "The Human Abstract" on this notion; manipulated by his speaker, such ideas become a bizarre apologia for deprivation and ultimately for the "mystery" religions that are based on such schemes.

The greatest of the poets arising in the late eighteenth century, Blake and Wordsworth, begin their careers by reimagining the pastoral. Wordsworth reinvents pastoral as a way of exploring fidelity to the deeply-impressed truths of the human imagination. Blake begins somewhat differently. By deliberately juxtaposing pastoral and antipastoral, unfallen and fallen worlds, he shows that the pastoral helps invent its antithesis; the decline of freedom and Innocence promotes the disillusion and cynicism of Experience, from which some minds never recover. This reaction to the closure of Innocence is just as likely as those responses that, by way of protecting against the attractions of Innocence, either parody it or expose it to realistic appraisal. For Blake neither state of the soul is permanent or total. The fallen world is merely the wilderness through which the journeying soul progresses. Blake's grasp of the imaginative reality of human life has therefore nothing to do with the bitterness that closure may sponsor or with the idea that a providentially disposed law of distributive justice makes of human life a thing of checks and balances, of vicissitude, as Gray (who wrote an ode to this eighteenth-century "deity") would have it. Inevitably, in any number of passages Gray's ode reads like a song of Experience:

> Still, where rosy Pleasure leads,
> See a kindred grief pursue;
> Behind the steps that Misery treads,
> Approaching Comfort view.   (33–36)

Against the backdrop of eighteenth-century poetry, the Songs reveal the necessities that summoned them and become a formidable document for charting Blake's awareness of, and distance from, his predecessors.

APPROACHES EMPHASIZING INDIVIDUAL SONGS

The Point-of-View Approach to *Songs*: Classroom Implications

Brian Wilkie

Despite my unflagging interest in Blake and ever-increasing delight in teaching his *Songs of Innocence and of Experience* in upper-division under-graduate, honors, and graduate courses, I have long been reluctant to in-clude the *Songs* on lower levels, such as the introduction-to-poetry courses I sometimes teach, unless my students and I have time to spend a week or so in sustained study of at least several of them. This tactic may sound fastidi-ously elitist, but I would like to think it is the reverse. It springs from dis-comfort with what philosophers call the "doctrine of the two truths"—that is, the doctrine, or at least working assumption, that the plebs are capable of absorbing only falsely simplified versions of a more complex truth accessible to sophisticated initiates only. Even the most thoroughgoing analysis of "London" or "The Garden of Love" in isolation must, almost inevitably, ei-ther treat these poems as straightforward social protest or introduce, from a source invisible to introductory-level students, nuances of the speaker's per-sonality that are all too likely to elicit some form of that most depressing of queries: "Aren't you reading all that into the poem?"

Such nuances—which epitomize what makes Blake's *Songs* one of the two or three greatest integrated volumes of lyric poetry in English—arise mainly from an awareness of the speakers' mind-sets and of how they illustrate what the volume's subtitle calls "the two contrary states of the human soul." One can persuasively teach "London" and "The Garden of Love" as protest poems and no more. But Blake did have more in mind, in these poems as in the other *Songs*, namely, a form of personal and social psychiatry in terms of which the innocent and experienced viewpoints are perennial *formae mentis*, intimately related to the objective conditions of the speakers' worlds but also to some extent self-sustaining and independent of external social facts.

Thus the world of "London" and of "The Garden of Love" is indeed corrupted by commercial greed, monarchy, militarism, loveless marriage, priestcraft, and other manacles, but the persons whose minds have forged the manacles include not only the framers of exploitative institutions but also the protesters themselves. For some profoundly mysterious reason, these protesters have come to define their personalities in terms of social evils without which they would virtually forfeit their identities. The repeated "every" in "London" can be heard as unflinching honest anger, but it can also be heard as a kind of shrill stubbornness, a willful determination that social evils *shall* exist, without qualification or mitigation. The statement in "The Garden of Love" that the priests are binding the speaker's desires must be read (unless we regard it as evidence of sloppy control of his language by Blake) as a telltale double entendre. If we have in mind the nausea accompanying the graphic sexual symbolism of the closely related manuscript poem "I saw a chapel all of gold," we can understand that the shut gates of the chapel (why, if this newly raised edifice is evil, should the speaker want the gates to be open?) are also the sexual portals of women from whom the speaker is alienated not only by the priestly worshippers of death but by his own complicated, and partially self-imposed, inhibitions.

Almost all, and perhaps literally all, the poems in both *Innocence* and *Experience* can be read in this bifocal way, as descriptions of the world or as revelations, usually less than fully conscious, of the states of the speakers' souls. "The Chimney Sweeper" of *Innocence* is a description of the lives of exploited sweeps but also the self-revelation of a sweep older enough than Tom Dacre to be on the verge of experienced bitterness. The poem's counterpart in *Experience* is both an attack on the monarchy and the church and a piece of ventriloquism in which the experienced adult persona uses the "little black thing" as a dummy through which radical adult rhetoric can vent itself. "The Sick Rose" attacks the evil of secret, shame-ridden love, but it also projects the voice of an alarmist who is himself sick with desire. "The Lamb" and "The Tyger" are descriptions of, respectively, a paradisal and a demonic world, but they are also the voices of trustful confidence and self-induced terror. "The Clod and the Pebble" acknowledges that love takes both unselfish and selfish forms, but it also reveals a speaker who cynically and irresponsibly shrugs off the whole question of what love should truly be—or is content with the illusory simplicity of either-or propositions. The "Holy Thursday" poems create a composite picture of official public philanthropy, but they also delineate the contrasting psychologies of sentimental complacency and compulsive rage. "My Pretty Rose Tree" describes an unappreciative wife but also reveals a speaker whose mind is twisted by a combination of guilt, self-righteousness, insensitivity, and cowardice. (For more detailed reading of most of these poems, see Wilkie.)

These alternatives, stated rather baldly here and all capable of endless refinements of emphasis and of detailed explication, will seem to many students the merest fancifulness unless the class starts from a broad base, from having read at least a dozen of the lyrics. (One need not discuss more than a few of them, of course, and one will seldom have time for more than that even in specialized Romantics courses.) Ideally, one should assign all the *Songs*, since any single poem in the volume is a ganglion from which nerves extend to several other poems. The notion that the *Experience* "Chimney Sweeper" is an exercise in ventriloquism will seem more tenable when students are aware that in two related poems, the *Innocence* version of the "Sweeper" and "The Little Black Boy" (who parallels those white "little black boys," the sweeps), the dubiously reliable transmission of a heard message also takes place. One cannot feel the full force of "The Lamb" and "The Tyger" unless one has gotten used to the Experience speakers' habit of asking rhetorical or (as they believe) unanswerable questions and the antithetical Innocence habit of solving all problems and resolving all disputes with effortless ease, as in "Nurse's Song."

The most important practical implication of this approach for classroom procedure is in the manner of group explication. Most great lyric poetry can be made to yield its meaning, with progressive refinement toward a single composite interpretation, through the Socratic method, suggestions coming from all quarters of the classroom as one goes along. Blake's *Songs*, of course, has the richness that calls for such refinement and honing of meaning, but the poems are unusual in that they do not merely reveal progressively richer overtones and complexities of meaning as one examines them more closely; rather, they can turn themselves completely inside out in the way I have been trying to illustrate. No group explication of any one of the richer songs, therefore, can get far before reaching bifurcations that lead in utterly different directions. One cannot get past the third line of "Ah! Sunflower" ("Seeking after that sweet golden clime") without deciding whether the speaker is in sentimental sympathy with the flower or is being sarcastic, and to proceed toward further explication of the subsequent lines is not to mediate between refinements of meaning suggested by different students but to umpire a toe-to-toe fight between radically different orientations to the poem and its speaker. An analogous branching occurs with the first words of "Infant Sorrow": "My mother groand! my father wept" forces us to choose between hearing the rather demonic voice of a child suffering the trauma of birth and hearing the voice of an embittered adult, whose imagination is soured like Lear's, reflecting that we have good reason to wawl and cry the first time that we smell the air.

Bifurcations such as these are only the beginning; typically, each of the alternative paths forks again, sometimes several times, so that discussion can approach chaos. The usual method of line-by-line cooperative explication is clearly not a practical way to handle poems that repeatedly force us to choose between moving straight ahead, making right-angle turns, and doing about-faces. The best solution I have found to the difficulty is to have one person, the teacher or a single student, give an uninterrupted straight-through reading. One can then throw open the discussion, considering objections to the reading on its own terms or refinements that support it. After that, one can give the floor to another student for a fundamentally different reading of the poem, then invite objections and refinements to this new reading. It may be best, in approaching the first song or two on the agenda, for the teacher to provide the straight-through reading, so as to get the students thinking in the terms called for by Blake's characteristic diction (his penchant for puns, for example) and by the recurrent images of the *Songs* in general.

Individual students cannot be expected to come up with such holistic readings on the spur of the moment. At the very least, one must alert them at a previous class meeting that they will be called upon to give a reading of the whole poem—say, a five-minute talk on it. Better still, one can make this project a short (say, two-page) paper assignment. After reading these papers, the instructor can select the authors of representative competing interpretations to read or summarize their papers as starting points for the kind of discussion I have been suggesting.

Described schematically, this method may sound like an encouragement of mass solipsism, each person listening only to the sound of his or her voice, prejudices, or intuitions. In practice, that need not and probably will not be the result. Usually no more than three or four fundamentally different readings will emerge, each with its own partisans who, even while agreeing with one another, want to steer the poem in slightly different ways. Of course, arguments can become heated between students who disagree fundamentally in their interpretations, and it is positively desirable to elicit the prejudices and intuitions of individual students. One can argue that Blake crafted the *Songs* deliberately in such a way as to make his readers commit themselves to and then become conscious of their stock responses to the aspects of life considered in the poems.

The point-of-view approach to the *Songs* has its dangers, of which two seem to me worth special mention. One is the danger that a concentration on the speakers' flawed states of mind, especially in *Songs of Experience*, will drain the social protest of all its power—a result that, one feels sure, Blake did not intend. The resolution of this difficulty raises fundamental questions of interpreting Blake that go far beyond the scope of this essay— particularly the question, which I have had to beg here for lack of space, of the extent to which Blake is in fact practicing individual as distinct from so- cial psychiatry. The dilemma can be resolved to some teachers' satisfaction if one regards society itself as largely to blame for the distortion of the speak- ers' perspectives; the belief that damage done to imagination is as evil as damage done to the outward conditions of one's life is a thoroughly Blakean position. The second danger is that Blake may emerge as a relativist, which all Blakeans would agree he is not. One can obviate this danger by getting students to see that, although Blake expects his poems to be performed dif- ferently in different people's minds, these responses are not all equally well founded on genuinely human and humane values.

The various reader-response theories of literature that have gotten atten- tion in recent years are clearly pertinent to the point-of-view approach to the *Songs*. In a way this timeliness is unfortunate, however, since the texts of the *Songs* suggest that Blake systematically composed them in such a way as to invite alternative readings. Therefore, even teachers unsympathetic to re- cent trends in criticism can concentrate on persona and point of view with some confidence that, if authorial intention ought indeed to govern, they are approaching the *Songs* in the way Blake the author intended.

Teaching Blake's Psychology of Redemption in *Songs*

Harold Pagliaro

In teaching *Songs of Innocence and of Experience* I use a variety of points of view, but I subordinate them to this consideration: What do the songs, taken as a whole, imply about how the mind works psychologically? To answer, I consider the characters, including the speakers. Who are they? What is their predicament? What are their responses to natural, social, and psychological forces? I also pay attention to the social justice Blake calls for; to his uses of pastoral tradition; to the irony implicit in many songs, especially *Songs of Innocence*; to recurring religious metaphors; to relations between text and illustration; to the consistency of ideas from *Songs* through major prophecies. My chief aim, however, is to get "inside" individual characters in the songs, to expose their psychologies, and to see how those psychologies help us learn about the two contrary states of the human soul and the relation of those states to redemption—what in Blake's view humans must do to be saved.

Most characters in *Songs* seem utterly exposed to experience, vulnerable to the people and things around them, but few seem aware of what they endure. Blake helps us see that the unembroiled regard of this exposure to pain is possible, even necessary, first by encouraging us to so regard it, and then by showing us some characters who share this view—chiefly speakers like those of "The Clod and the Pebble" and "The Human Abstract" in *Songs of Experience*.

Death is the subject on which Blake draws to identify the basis of human vulnerability. In his world, it is death that limits us to mortal vision, makes us accommodate to the natural world or perish, defines the natural world and the natural human being in all of us. In *Songs* death appears in many forms: the garden of love is filled with graves; chimney sweepers are locked in coffins of black; the Raven of death nests in the human-made tree of holy Mystery; the cycle of life in London begins in the Marriage hearse: man and fly are married in death; the little black boy thinks he will be free of prejudice only after he leaves his unalterable black body; some nameless power has dared to grasp the Tyger's deadly terrors.

Factors outside *Songs* reinforce this first powerful impression. At Thel's grave plot, the vision of life as hostile and deadly, like much of Blake's poetry, seems to combine human vulnerability and the steady regard of threatening forces. Though the two functions are often divided (the young harlot of "London" is vulnerable, but the poem's speaker, also vulnerable in a way, looks steadily at her vulnerability), Thel experiences both. True, she is able to flee the world of death, but until she does, she sees death everywhere defining life. Neither blaming her for running nor congratulating her for avoiding a bad scene seems reasonable; there is no simple solution for the problem she faces. Death is all around Thel, and to see it as starkly as she does is to run away, Blake seems to say. On the other hand, the combination of vulnerability and the capacity to see clearly is necessary for Self-examination and Self-annihilation.

The view that much in the poetry turns on death is not new to Blake studies, but it is more important than the time spent on it in the criticism implies. In his preface to the Blake *Concordance* Erdman remarks on the unexpectedness of the poet's frequent use of *death*: "Each new concordance brings its . . . surprises, those most immediately accessible being some of the words that come out at the top of the frequency count. . . . We may have expected to find MAN, LOVE, ETERNAL, and EARTH among Blake's most used words, but not DEATH so near the top . . . " (1: vii). In fact, the only words of substance more frequent than *death* in the poetry are *all, Los, Albion,* and *man.* But how Blake uses the word (and related words) is most important—they almost never refer to physical death. Without morbidity, Blake associates *death, dead,* and their proxies with the fallen world we move through as we live our lives, stumbling ". . . all night over bones of the dead" ("The Voice of the Ancient Bard"). He uses the word to characterize our natural and our social context or to suggest a sense of ourselves or a point of view we have unconsciously adopted as a result of being imposed upon— ("They clothed me in the clothes of death" as the chimney sweeper in Experience says). Aware that we are intimidated by death, Blake treats it dynamically, as a conditioning force we incorporate into our beings as we unconsciously accommodate to its threat. And he makes clear we do so in order to survive.

It is with this background in view that I approach *Songs.* Usually I begin with one of the few poems in *Songs of Innocence* that present characters unaffected by physical or emotional danger—the "Introduction" or "The Lamb"—and I try to show that the children in these poems are in a state such that people and forces outside them seem "continuous" with, not inimical to, themselves, as Gleckner (*Piper* 45), Holloway (62), Erdman (*Illuminated Blake* 48), and others have shown. The child speaker of "The Lamb" is made "identical" with the Lamb and with Christ: "I a child & thou a lamb / We are called by [Christ's] name. . . ."

Having established the psychology of this child as an obvious model of Innocence, I turn to songs that do not conform to the model—the great majority of *Songs of Innocence.* In what sense is the chimney sweeper—who, far from being "continuous" with his environment, has been "cut off" from his

dead mother and "cut off" by the father who sold him—in a state of Innocence? And what about the little black boy, who is "cut off" from the white?
Do not their songs, and many others of Innocence, register a world of sorrow
and disillusion? The answer depends on whose point of view one takes. The
reader may see in such poems a world of sorrow. Obviously both children
are driven hard by a cruel society. Or Blake the man may be understood to
be using irony to express his anger at their treatment. The last line of each
poem certainly undercuts the palliating vision earlier presented by each
child. "So if all do their duty, they need not fear harm" may be read as
Blake's ironic way of rendering the comfort of Tom Dacre's dream illusory.
"And be like him and he will then love me" may similarly render the comfort
of the black mother's lesson futile; if the black boy wants more to be loved by
the white than to accept as valuable his mother's view of him (and all blacks)
as especially benefited by experience, what good is her lesson after all?

Despite the logic of Bloom's view that *Songs* includes many ironies
(*Blake's Apocalypse*, e.g., 50–51), it is also reasonable to consider these
poems from the point of view of the children who experience their action. It
is the children, finally, who dwell in Innocence or leave it. It is their point of
view, in and out of Innocence, that helps us to understand their psychology.
Let us assume that both chimney sweeper and black boy speak for themselves consistently (as well as for the poet's irony). Then we would have to
conclude that the sweep's "So if all do their duty, they need not fear harm"
was literally intended, and it would follow that he had been taken in by Tom
Dacre's dream. That is, we would understand that the speaker accepts the
rationalization the dream represents, masking and transforming his deadly
social present with a promise of a transcendent heaven.

Read with the same expectations for consistency, the black boy's "And be
like him and he will then love me" underscores a similar presentation of social evil and the speaker's evasion of it. The black boy's last line permits the
reader to see the child's mind working at two levels, quite self-deceivingly.
At one level he recalls the occasion of his mother's lesson with unself-
conscious pleasure—"She took me on her lap and kissed me"—and then he
repeats the lesson verbatim, surely an act of faith in its truth and efficacy.
But at another level, he makes of the lesson something very different from
what the mother claims it to be: the promise of a future state in which his
spiritual superiority—which, she tries to make him realize, he enjoys in the
present life—will enable him to help the English boy. Instead, he finds in it
a reason for believing he can become enough like the white boy for the white
boy to love him. In effect, the black boy believes he has accepted his
mother's lesson, but in fact he unconsciously repudiates it, using it to cope
with a problem it was intended to transcend. The problem still controls him,
and he is unaware of the fact.

In contrast with these children of Innocence, characters in *Songs of Experience* are typically self-conscious of the dangers they face, or they are somehow urged or otherwise moved to become conscious of it; they confront their troubles or they feel pain without the relief of illusion. Psychologically the "obverse" of his counterpart in Innocence, the chimney sweeper of Experience knows he has been imposed upon, and he resents the fact: ". . . because I am happy, & dance & sing, / They think they have done me no injury." Not only does he have an unvarnished view of his own predicament, he has also begun to appraise the mental operations of his mother and father, who, as he sees it, believe they have done him no injury, when of course they have "clothed [him] in the clothes of death." He shows a further psychological sophistication by associating his parents with other creators of a false heaven—"God & his Priest & King / Who make up a heaven of our misery."

It may be important to ask whether the voices of speakers, which I have understood to represent "characters," are not after all disembodied, in which case I have invented an implausible critical fiction: I think the answer is that no completely characterized mind is to be found in any single voice in *Songs*, or in a simple compositing of all the voices to build the "one mind" of *Songs*. The voices vary enormously in emotional strength, intelligence, sensitivity, and temperament; but they all collect to suggest a continuing mental process which, if not complete, is certainly full. It seems reasonable, finally, to think of the voices as speaking for characters, because so understood they give us a full sense of Blake's vision of the human predicament. And the representation of this vision, dynamic as it is, invites us as much to participate in the process it identifies as to consider it analytically.

In fact, as I argue in *Selfhood and Redemption in Blake's "Songs,"* *Songs* represents a continuous psychological process, an inevitable movement from the state of Innocence, in which (from the child's point of view) one enjoys an unself-conscious unity with one's surroundings, to an encounter with strong evidence that one's life is endangered; such evidence is for a time displaced by rationalization (chimney sweeper, little black boy) but later intrudes into consciousness. At this point the mind may be thought of as in Experience because of its inability to rationalize evidence of danger (the nurse of *Experience*) or, a very different matter, because of its willingness to accept this evidence (the chimney sweeper of *Experience*). Where the mind cannot rationalize the evidence and yet cannot cope with the problem it represents, it registers as fear, pain, guilt, or a sense of defeat (the sick rose). Where the mind receives the evidence with knowledge enough to give it "meaning," it becomes a problem understood to need a solution (the speaker of "The Tyger") or a problem for which a solution is sometimes sought and found (the speaker of "To Tirzah"). In sum, danger in the world of nominal

Innocence results in the mind's formation of a self-protective mechanism or conditioned self that not only protects life (reducing it to what is safe) but leaves the protected unaware that a larger life is available. *Songs* indicates that this self, which Blake later names "Selfhood," must first be formed (Thel in Har had no chance to do so) and then confronted and done away with. But the task is very difficult, not only because in the confrontation we give up our defenses, so that death comes at us, but also because we believe (irrationally) that Selfhood is the "true self," and when it is threatened, we are afraid we will cease to be.

It is not usual to think of characters in *Songs of Experience* as caught in the process of transformation (Self-examination), so it is hard to illustrate the process briefly. Here are necessarily curtailed readings of "The Fly," "A Poison Tree," and "The Tyger." The first is a poem about someone liberated from his conditioned self (the self that dies) who takes the experience seriously, though he finally treats it comically. An unself-conscious gesture usually viewed as inconsequential, the brushing away and death of a fly, has moved the man responsible to consider his own life and death. First, his dominant sense is that he and the fly are one; next, that he and the fly are mortal. The two views are not mutually exclusive. The fly's death informs the speaker so immediately of his own vulnerability and death that the usual ways of distinguishing himself from the fly dissolve. In more Blakean terms, he becomes continuous with the fly, having moved through the boundaries of Selfhood.

The second stanza identifies the climax of this liberation. Its sentences, questions, register not doubt but reverent recognition of the heretofore unknown: "Am not I / A fly . . . ? / . . . art not thou / A man . . . ?" He knows, of course, that he is still a man—"thou [art] / A man like me"—but he feels for the moment at least a redefinition of his usual self. The speaker marks his sense of identity with the fly as if there were no difference not only between a fly's being and a man's but also between a dead being and a live one: "art not thou [dead] / A man like me [alive]?" The two issues, being and mortality, are for him parts of the same whole. If thought is life, and its want death, he argues, then he is a happy fly if he lives—that is, he has known a sense of oneness with the happy (unself-conscious) fly as a function of his new-won consciousness. And he is a happy fly if he dies in that the same consciousness of identity with the unself-conscious fly makes it comically reasonable for him to claim that his death will be like the fly's, unself-conscious. The illustration provides the clearest sign of this change from man to fly. The speaker is not there, it seems, only a boy, controlled by a woman who almost surrounds him, and a girl playing battledore. All are located inside arching barren limbs of adjacent trees, whose tops just miss touching. About to pass between the not-quite-met branches of confinement is a butterfly—the missing speaker, I believe.

"A Poison Tree" may appear at first to be a poem about the destructive consequences of repressed feelings. But the watering of suppressed wrath and the sunning of it with deceitful wiles imply the speaker's consciousness of the predicament. The result of momentary repression and clandestine nourishment is an interior garden world, imagined as attractive to the speaker's foe. In a way, the clear and growing shape of energy, neither expressed externally nor repressed, makes the speaker a minor Satan, comic but by no means trivial. What such a character might have rationalized in Innocence eventually flourishes in Experience. The speaker's tone suggests pleasure in recounting an experience that began badly and ended well. Informing us that he or she had been frightened into silence by a foe, who now is dead, the speaker displays a confidence in facing up to external events. It is "in the morning," the start of a new day, that the speaker concludes the action of this initially interior adventure, which has led to the threshold of outward things, to a sense of continuity between inside and outside the mind. One might say the speaker has endured the death of that part which feared the foe too much to permit the expression of anger.

Blake's illustration reinforces this reading. Erdman identifies "a hand [just above the fourth stanza] that seems to grasp the trunk above it as by the leg of an elongated human torso" (*Illuminated Blake* 91). A hand there seems unlikely, and I suggest to my students that it is the head of a happy-looking serpent, from whose mouth issues a giant forked tongue, part of which underlines and brackets the poem's title and part of which extends the entire length of the poem to become continuous with the "y" of "my" in the last line. The garden is the serpent-speaker's, as are the Tree of the Knowledge of Good and Evil, the deceitful (spiritually productive) behavior, the dead foe, and the promise of a new day. But the speaker is, finally, neither proprietary nor murderous, only psychologically enlarged by the destruction of an inhibition, like someone who has taken the advice of the devils in *The Marriage of Heaven and Hell*.

The first four stanzas of "The Tyger" register the depth of the speaker's recognition of the Tyger's deadly terrors, chiefly by showing him or her to be incredulous to the point of disorientation. The speaker has come to know but can hardly believe that these terrors have been incorporated into a living form of the creation. Making no effort to repudiate the Tyger's deadliness, or to explain it in the handy terms of proverbial or domestic truth, like the first chimney sweep or the black boy's mother, the speaker accepts the idea of the beast as terrible. This painful accommodation seems not to be entirely conscious, but it is nonetheless systematic and effective. Such dislocations result from the recognition of things in unplumbed depths of the mind and their movement into consciousness. In perceiving the Tyger thus, the speaker is compelled to define Tyger, Creator, Lamb, and human being anew and somehow to integrate them into a new shape of understanding. Given the question "Did he who made the Lamb make thee?" one must conclude that the speaker once believed unconsciously that its answer was no and is on the verge of changing that answer to yes and of acknowledging that Tyger, Lamb, and observer are parts of a single system, however discrete they seemed. The change implies a passage to a new self-knowledge.

Obviously, the Tyger first recognized by the speaker is very different from the Tyger of the illustration. The Tyger there is not fierce, but neither is it a cat essentially; it is a cat with human features. He who made the Lamb made the Tyger, and he made humanity as well, who is Tyger, Lamb, and more. In this perception of creation, it is appropriate that the Tyger should be humanized. Paradoxically increased and diminished by this exhausting experience, the speaker is for the moment in the condition of rest and hope as the poem ends. But we have read the sign of potential redemption in his or her changing definition of self and world.

Songs of Innocence and of Experience has yielded full and satisfying responses from my students—not exclusive, confined, or otherwise reductive—when they consider its poems from the point of view of the psychological model I have suggested. A closely related result has proved to be the students' understanding of the dynamic processes represented in *Songs*, primarily as a function of their becoming involved in those processes as they try to grasp the living predicament of each character they encounter.

Hearing the Songs

Thomas A. Vogler

> We have heard with our ears . . .
> (Psalms 44.1)

Even more than their conventional-sounding title suggests, Blake's *Songs* call for attention to the practice of "hearing," both as thematized in the poems and as applicable on various levels to our mode of engagement with them in a responsive reading. If we look first at the "Introduction" to the *Songs of Innocence*, we notice that it calls attention to its graphic form, as a "writing" that is the trace of a prior phonetic-linguistic phenomenon, itself the trace of a prior prelinguistic moment evoked by the onomatopoeic word *piping*. The move from a prelinguistic utterance to its representation and amplification in written language is accompanied by hints that the process may contaminate its source ("I stain'd the water clear") or lose it altogether (if the ink-filled pen replacing the breath-filled "hollow reed" of the "pipe" produces only a "hollow read"). The announced aim of writing (that "Every child may joy to hear") pits itself against the contrary force and possible effects of writing, calling attention to the programmatic aspect of the volume's title as *Songs*.

The emphatic first word, *piping*, takes the grammatical form of a modifying participle, with the combined force of an adjective and a verb, so that the action of the verb (*to pipe*) is generalized and ongoing. Our visual recognition of the word, producing an image of the primitive musical instrument, needs to be supplemented by its etymology in the Latin *pipare*, meaning "to peep, cheep, or chirp." As an instance of onomatopoeia, the word represents bird noise, and through associations developed in the *Songs of Innocence* it comes to stand for the "infant noise" of Innocence as evoked in "Spring": "Cock does crow / So do you." The latent force of the verb in this poem's title evokes kinetic utterance appropriate to both "infant noise" and "bird noise." When the little peeper breaks through its shell to enter the world, the force of its pecking becomes the force of its piping, something innate and expressive, undetermined and uninfluenced by the world outside, which it has not yet experienced.

A contrary view is forcefully presented in "Infant Sorrow" from *Songs of Experience*. There what we might call the "parent noise" ("My mother groaned; my father wept.") precedes and influences the birth of the infant, so that the same word, *piping*, offers itself to a contrary hearing. A metrical struggle in the poem between iambs and trochees reflects and reinforces this difference, embodying rhythmically the contrast between the high seriousness of eighteenth-century iambic-pentameter verse and the jump-rope chant of a child, expressed in the trochaic rhythm that Thrall and Hibbard claim is "perversely popular with children and undeveloped minds" (496). The "parent noise" of the beginning of "Infant Sorrow" is clearly expressed in iambic tetrameter. The second line is suggestively ambiguous, the weak first stress of the expected iamb overcome by the eruptive force of two dactyls. Lines 3–7 seem to break free into a clear and insistent pattern of trochees until, as if exhausted, the poem returns to its beginnings in an iambic rhythm.

Most approaches to Blake's *Songs* begin with the *Songs of Innocence*, assuming that they represent a primal state that somehow leads to or falls into Experience. I prefer to start with the *Songs of Experience*, because I think that if we are to be "introduced" to (i.e., "led into") Innocence, we must be led *from* somewhere. Since there are only two contrary states, that somewhere must be the state of Experience. Like Innocence, Experience is presented as a scene of hearing. The last word of the "Introduction" to the *Songs of Innocence* becomes the imperative first word of the "Introduction" to the *Songs of Experience*: "Hear." Two lines of emphasis open here: first, we should listen differently to the two categories of songs—second, our modes of hearing may themselves actively constitute the songs as "of" Innocence or "of" Experience.

The "Introduction" to *Experience* asks us to "hear" the voice of a bard who himself has heard a prior "Word." The much-debated question of whether the bard's "Word" is the judgment of the Old Testament or the redemption of the New Testament is less important here than the situational model, which presents a bard whose hearing is at all points mediated and influenced by a prior text. All the speakers or singers in Experience exemplify this situation, so that the bard becomes a higher or more elaborate version of the speaker of "Infant Sorrow," whose prior "Word" was the parental groaning and weeping. Once we have heard the sounds of Experience *as* "Experience," our ability to hear differently may be permanently impaired. We may ask rhetorically, like the speaker in "Holy Thursday" (*Experience*), "Is that trembling cry a song? / Can it be a song of joy?" expecting only a negative response. Hearing is markedly different in the realm of Innocence, where the shepherd's happiness is related to his ability to hear "the lambs innocent call," which makes his tongue "filled with praise."

A clear and informative example of "contrary" hearing is that of the two nurses' songs, which demand a side-by-side reading. We can "hear" them as if sung by two nurses standing in the same green but responding differently because of differences of hearing, or we can imagine a single nurse at different times, exhibiting contrary states. One nurse hears "laughing" on the hill, the other "whisperings" in the dale. One tells the children to come home because it's bedtime; the children say no, because they have been alert to signs that she has missed—the birds are still flying and the sheep are still covering the hills. This nurse hears the children (echoing their responsiveness to nature, the birds and sheep), and her response allows the "echoing" on the green to continue at least for a while. The nurse in Experience hears differently; unlike the first nurse and the children, she has heard some "holy word," perhaps Genesis 3, where the verdict is announced that "labor," in the form of work for males and childbearing for females, is the human destiny. Thus days without work are "wasted" and nights without sex (to produce children) "disguised."

In addition to the many differences of hearing in the *Songs*, I like to call attention to the many different hearings *of* the *Songs* in the critical literature. One example will have to suffice here. The bard's ears have heard the "Holy Word, / That walk'd among the ancient trees." Some readers of this poem "hear" that "Word" as the word in Genesis 3, where "the voice of the Lord God walking in the garden in the cool of the day" challenges Adam for his sin and pronounces the verdict on him and his mate. Others hear this "Word" as the chronologically later but ontologically prior "Word" revealed in the Gospel of John: the Word of God's love for humankind made incarnate for human redemption in Jesus, the Word that *was* "In the beginning" (John 1.1). In either case, the critic's "hearing" of a prior word informs and constitutes the bard's song.

If we try to approach the *Songs of Innocence* from the state of Experience, "London" is perhaps our best test case for the difficulty of hearing "infant noise" as innocent. This song is not a representation of London per se so much as a "hearing" of London, where the all-seeing, all-hearing speaker of the poem may be trapped in and trapped by limited powers of perception. As readers and potential hearers, we are in danger of being overcome by the tropes of weakness, tropes of woe, and by the mind-forged rhetoric we hear in the poem. The poem itself may be like the "blackning" churches in the poem, either growing black from the marks of coal smoke as a consequence of the industrial revolution, or itself a source of blackness, putting its black Pauline mark on the infant "Word" of Christianity and on the physical world (every blackning Church a Paul's). The speaker "marks" marks of weakness, marks of woe—but does this mean the speaker remarks them (i.e., observes them) or puts them there by seeing them, through a semiology that is not necessarily in the nature of things but rather a "forgery" of the mind?

It is perhaps easier to point to the visual than to the acoustic manifestations of the speaker's immobilizing intelligibility, but the latter are crucial to the poem. Many readers have noted the pervasive paronomasia of "London." Words like *charter, mark, forg'd, ban, manacles,* and *appalls* echo and reecho with multiplied meanings and resonances the longer we "hear" the poem. In the process, our own hearing ability expands toward the amazing auditory power of the speaker, who can *hear* the "mind-forg'd man-acles" in "every cry of every Man, / In every infant's cry of fear, / In every voice: in every ban." But in this expansion we run a paradoxical risk that our hearing may become manacled, trapped in the pervasive sound pattern so that the poem becomes a "word" that shapes our potential hearing, drowning out any possibility of hearing that "infant noise" which cannot speak to us in words (*infans* 'not capable of speech'). In this field of sound the chimney sweeper's cry can only be a "weep weep" as the rhyme words become a miniature poem within a poem.

Both the acoustic and the visual effects of the poem's emphasis on the ear (*near, where, fear, hear, hear, tear, hearse*) recall the imperative beginning of the *Songs of Experience* and call our attention to the auditory dimension of our responses to the poem. In particular, the framing of the poem's third stanza by the verb *hear* and the anagrammatic inscription of the verb in the initial letters of that stanza confirm the power of a hearing that can detect in London the sound of a sigh running in blood down palace walls in France:

> . . . I *hear*
>
> *H*ow the Chimney-sweepers cry
> *E*very blackning Church appals,
> *A*nd the hapless Soldiers sigh
> *R*uns in blood down Palace walls
>
> . . . I *hear* (emphasis added)

We are in danger of taking this power of hearing as the inevitable truth and of succumbing to the speaker's perception of the whole world as chartered in and by the streets of London. His words may "impose" on us (in the sense of that word used in *The Marriage of Heaven and Hell*) and determine the potential for our own experience, limiting us to ironic readings of the *Songs of Innocence*. Does anything in the poem alert us to this danger? There are two clues. By careful attention to the rhythm of the poem we can hear a tension that might potentially subvert the immobilizing intelligence of the speaker—an ongoing rhythmical tension between strong and weak initial stress in the metrical feet that provide the pace for the feet wandering through the streets.

Another clue appears in the illustration, especially when one compares the "London" plate with its counterpart from *Jerusalem* (plate 84), where the lamenting daughters say: "I see London blind & age-bent begging thro the Streets / Of Babylon, Led by a child." In both cases we are left to imagine what might be behind a mysterious door. Is it the door of death, toward which the child is already pointing as a child, his infant's tear blasted by the "Harlot's curse"? Or is the child pointing to a door that opens into the contrary state of Innocence, still there if we can hear it: "He that hath ears to hear, let him hear" (Mark 4.9, Luke 14.35, 8.8).

If we hear the *Songs of Innocence* only through the ears of Experience, we will never hear "infant noise" *as* innocent. While I do not make the psychological or philosophical or religious claim that infant noise is innocent, I suggest that Blake's *Songs* emphasize the danger that our ability to hear may be dominated by the mediated state of Experience, by our having heard a prior "Word" that determines how we hear all subsequent words. If our hearing were not impaired, we might be able to "hear" Innocence even in the chartered midnight streets of a London that is not the ancient and presumptively primal Babylon, echoing the fallen babble of chartered language, but the *Baby*lon of a "baby" London, in which there can still be an infant cry that is a "song" of Innocence. Our ability to hear "infant noise" may even enable us to detect traces of Innocence in "The Tyger," in spite of almost two centuries of "contrary" readings. To bring out this possibility, I suggest we try an emphatic reading of the poem's trochees. Those feet, described as "perversely popular with children and undeveloped minds," may still be there walking "upon England's mountains green" (*Milton*) for those who have ears to hear:

> Tyger, Tyger, burning bright,
> Twinkle, twinkle, little star,
> Barber, barber, shave a pig,
>
> In the forests of the night;
> How I wonder what you are.
> How many hairs to make a wig?
>
> What immortal hand or eye,
> Way up in the sky so high
> Four and twenty, that's enough
>
> Could frame thy fearful symmetry?
> Like a diamond in the sky.
> Give the barber a pinch of snuff!

Unreading "London"

Donald Ault

Pedagogical difficulties (as well as opportunities) inevitably occur when we use even the best of typeset editions of Blake's poetry, David Erdman's *Complete Poetry and Prose*. In its attempts to approximate through conventional printing methods the subversive materiality and visual dimension of variant copies, this text acknowledges not only the radical openness of Blake's poems to conflicting readings but also, in a profound sense, the resistance of these poems to being "read" at all, in the conventional sense of that verb. Thus, twenty years after the first appearance of Erdman's edition of Blake's poetry, "corrected" or "normalized" versions of Blake's poems persist in most anthologies. This urge to homogenize Blake's heterogeneous texts is a residual manifestation of the powerful inertial (ontological and perceptual) principle Blake called "Single vision & Newtons sleep" (E 722): by drawing attention away from the apparently anomalous qualities of Blake's poems, it undermines the processes through which the act of reading is able to rehabilitate "Single vision" by "cleansing" the "doors of perception" (E 39).

A crucial dimension of Blake's poetic program implicitly insists that readers enact the process of cleansing their perceptions, an act that resists any reductive foundationalist account of the vision onto which the doors of perception may open once they are "cleansed." Because a primary goal of Blake's defiance of "Single vision & Newtons sleep" is the perceptual and ontological reorganization of the reader, a "reader-response" or "affective-stylistics" method of approaching the *Songs* is necessary to expose the anti–single vision, anti-Newtonian strategies of the work. To be true to Blake's texts, however, such a reader-response pedagogy must emphasize reading as a sequence of events and the writtenness of textual marks (or the absence of them) while devaluing the poem's role as utterance or speech act (a role that many reader-response accounts have invoked to preserve the primacy of the temporal dimension of reading). Blake's poetic strategies, especially as they emerge from a study of his revisions, push to their limits the presuppositions of those reader-response methods essential to disclosing the reading processes Blake's poetry opposes.

"London" is one of the best poems for introducing students to such radical "reading," for it exemplifies several of Blake's visual-textual strategies that open up otherwise closed texts and dethrone their authoritative gestures in relation to the individual reader. Most directly, "London" provokes its readers to create, through the act of reading, the "mind-forg'd manacles" its manifest content opposes. The poem's anti-Newtonian (i.e., antiatomistic) texture systematically defies the male-dominated institutions of church, state, and marriage, which the poem, considered as an utterance by either a neurotic persona or Blake as prophet, criticizes.

Some different textbook versions of "London" (each readily available to students) reveal the consequences of Blake's strategies and the dangers inherent in normalizing Blake's poems to make their message less obstructed to the student. I use for my examples: (1) Erdman's typeset reconstructed text of Blake's variant copies in *Complete Poetry and Prose* (which I take to be primary, although it varies from the 1970 to 1982 editions), (2) a normalized text (as it appears, for example, in *The Norton Anthology of Poetry*), (3) Erdman's typeset version of Blake's notebook revisions in *Complete Poetry and Prose*, and (4) the copy in Erdman's *Illuminated Blake*.

In Erdman's reconstructed version, the period after "flow" (2) marks the end of a sentence, initially forcing "And mark" (3) to be imperative: "And [you] mark[!]"—as in "Mark well my words!" (*Milton* 7.16)—a reading that we must then revise as the syntax unfolds, for it is "in every face *I* meet" (emphasis added) that the absent subject must do the marking. In the Keynes facsimile version of the *Songs*, however, the absence of punctuation at the end of line 2 hurls the reader forward, creating the initial impression that "the Thames does flow / And mark"—a certain boundary of London, for example. But this reading, too, is thwarted by the words that immediately follow in the text. Because both of these options create disturbances for the reader, the standardized version places a comma at the end of line 2. This editorial elimination of the previous options invites the reader to search backward and choose the obvious subject of "mark," the "I" of line 1, repressing the optative action of the reader by shifting attention to the fictional "I" of the text. Blake's wording clearly permits us to reconstruct a normalized version (by the substitution of punctuation), but that "version" neutralizes or forestalls the reader's awareness of being engaged in an act of revisionary reading—a reading of a poem that, unless revised, is unreadable, an awareness that requires at least a two-fold vision.

Blake's notebook reveals that "London" underwent severe revision in the traditional sense, a compositional struggle that in itself serves to undermine the possibility of a "Single vision" reading and hence of a unified theme extractable from the textual web in which it is embedded. Most obviously, Blake twice changed the predictable adjective "dirty" to the unlikely "charter'd" (1–2), a revision that should draw the student's attention to "street" and "Thames" as details of a written text rather than as referential names for places in a city external to the poem. Again, Blake changed "see" in line 3 to "mark," another word that asserts the writtenness of the text, the marks on the page.

Probably the aspects of Blake's final punctuation of "London" that are most frustrating and yet most rewarding to a reader-response analysis involve his placement of apostrophes where they are not necessary (i.e., where he does not always use them) and his refusal to place them where they seem most essential (i.e., in possessives, where he often but not always omits them). Though the apostrophes in "thro' " (twice), "charter'd" (twice), and "mind-forg'd" may indicate pronunciation, they also call attention to their role as visible marks of omitted letters. In "every Infants cry" (6), however, the reader is obliged to revise the text by inserting a missing apostrophe, since "Infants," being preceded by "every," must be singular possessive. In "the Chimney-sweepers cry" (9), "the hapless Soldiers sigh" (11), and "the youthful Harlots curse" (14), the absence of apostrophes leads the reader initially to assume that "Chimney-sweepers," "Soldiers," and "Harlots" are plural nouns followed naturally by verbs ("cry," "sigh," "curse"). The syntactic constraints of the lines make this choice seem inevitable until, in each case, the next line of the poem undermines this natural assumption and causes the reader to revise the poem retroactively by inserting mental apostrophes. This mental insertion converts each collective social group into a (grammatical) state of possession and transforms the nouns into adjectives and the verbs into nouns. Yet a "Single vision" reading of the poem urges us to perform this act of revision to make the syntax settle down into a recognizable and stable order. That is, unless we add the apostrophes (thus preempting this revisionary reading process), the lines stand as unreadable, syntactically unclosed. It is precisely this unreadableness (or the coexistence of incommensurable readings) that creates problems even for those forms of reader-response criticism that see readers as constituting or creating the text through the interpretive conventions they bring to bear on the marks on the page. It is as if Blake's text calls attention to the readers' need to anchor their perspectives at all costs in some set of reading conventions, as if such anchoring were an inevitable condition of being in a language. It is also significant that this process occurs primarily in the act of visually processing the lines: there is no auditory difference between the two versions of these lines when read aloud.

The absence of periods at the end of stanzas other than the first reinforces the text's resistance to closure, as it defies the stability of grammatical categories of English. The absence, especially, in Blake's final text of a period after "I hear" (8) allows this subject and verb to act as the main clause for both the second and third stanzas, a sort of fulcrum point in the poem, which is sufficiently obstructive to "Single vision" reading to have tempted all editors of normalized texts to supply a period (or a dash) there to close off that possibility. In Erdman's *Illuminated Blake* a period follows "manacles," which could cause the reader to search backward (past the only stable period in the poem, at the end of line 4,) to locate the subject and verb in the problematic "[I] mark" of line 3.

In Blake's notebook, "But most" originally followed "I hear." That arrangement replaces the need for punctuation at the end of line 8 by sharply shifting the direction of the syntax; the revision to "How every" in line 9 encourages the reader to continue the syntax between lines 8 and 9 ("I hear / How every . . ."). Also the original juxtaposing of "cry / Blackens" allows the reader to correct "cry" to a noun immediately, while the revised version places the verb at the end of line 9, farthest from "cry," postponing retroactive revision. (The comma situated at the end of line 11 in Erdman's 1970 reconstructed text, but absent in the most recent edition, serves to cut off the connection between "Sigh" and "Runs" prematurely, where the verb's position immediately corrects the initial reading of "sigh" as a verb.) Absence of a period at the end of line 12 invites students to interpret the syntax as continuous: "Runs in blood down palace walls / But most through midnight streets[.]" In this case, the location of "But most" encourages continuous reading, whereas at the beginning of the third stanza it would have closed off that possibility.

Students can easily be shown that, in "London," the visual images illuminating the verbal text cannot be at all predicted from the words, just as the words could not be predicted from the illustrations. The graphic elements supplement the verbal text by including dimensions that the words exclude, even dimensions that contradict the words. Although the polyvalent energy of the verbal text subverts the linguistic (patriarchal) authority that originates the misery of the poem's manifest plot, the words themselves are dominantly and obsessively negative. The visual illumination, however, suggests an alternative vision of "London." Students can be taught to see, then, that Blake creates a gap between image and text by means of the spatial positioning of the graphic design in relation to the visible layout of the words, producing thereby a movement of the imagination beyond "Single vision."

Attempting to resolve the gap between visual and verbal texts by resorting to the fiction of the poem as a "speaker's" utterance only creates more problems for reading and interpretation. If we take a clue from *Jerusalem* 84.11 ("I see London, blind & age-bent begging thro the Streets / Of Babylon, Led by a child"), where an inverted image of the upper portion of the "London" plate occurs (Erdman, *Illuminated Blake* 363), then we can equate the "speaker" with "London," presented as a fictional character. In this case, however, the visual image contradicts the verbal text, for the speaker is "wander[ing]," not being led. Furthermore there is on the face of the (androgynous) child in the illumination no evidence of the pain and terror that the speaker so vividly "marks" and "hears." (The revision from "sees" to "marks," as well as the pervasive emphasis on hearing, could confirm that the speaker is blind and thus is more graphically "marking," literally scarring, the faces he or she meets than the verbal text suggests.) Conversely, if the "child" is speaking, "wander[ing]" seems inappropriate since the child seems to be leading the aged man to some definite destination. To avoid the pitfalls of such a reduction of the poem to a speech act, the students need to return to the way the events "depicted" in the visual text relate to the process of reading the poem.

The figures in the upper portion of the page stand atop the word "London," which thereby visually constitutes a "charter'd [written] street" composed of graphic stones seeming to congeal from the two-dimensional image of smoke (rising from an equally two-dimensional fire) that conforms to, yet opposes, the fluid right margin of the verbal text. This arrangement invites the reader to construct, among other things, a possible allegory that centers on the act of reading the text of "London" itself: the perceptually aged (habituated) "Single vision" (patriarchally indoctrinated) reader, leaning on a single crutch that pivots on the space between (the all-capitalized) "Lon" and "don" (calling attention to the near symmetry of the two halves of the word), is being guided in the direction of the flow of reading by an open (androgynous, childlike) text across the "charter'd" (written) streets (lines) of "London" (the poem). This allegorical interpretation, however, itself risks becoming the kind of "Single vision" reduction the poem strives to defy and so must not be taken as a definitive closure of the poem's conflicts. Indeed, it calls attention to new anomalies in a kind of infinite regress of retroactive revision of an unreadable poem.

Like the defiant punctuation that undermines the stability of grammatical categories and the revisions and variations that conspire with the punctuation to make the poem unreadable as it stands, the visual illumination to "London" draws attention to the act of reading and to the text's power to perform subversive perceptual functions precisely because it is a written, printed, visible text. By opening up multiple options of reading "London"— especially by repeatedly offering the option that the poem is literally unreadable—Blake hopes to rouse his readers from "Single vision & Newtons sleep," and teachers of "London" can at least aspire to rouse their students against the interpretive risks of such a reading.

PARTICIPANTS IN SURVEY OF BLAKE INSTRUCTORS

The following scholars and teachers of Blake generously agreed to participate in the survey of approaches to teaching *Songs of Innocence and of Experience* that preceded and then informed preparation of this volume. Without their assistance, this volume would not have been possible.

Michael Ackland, Monash Univ.; Donald Ault, Vanderbilt Univ.; Rodney M. Baine, Univ. of Georgia; Stephen C. Behrendt, Univ. of Nebraska; James R. Bennett, Univ. of Arkansas; G. E. Bentley, Jr., Univ. of Toronto; James Bieri, Univ. of Texas, Austin; James Bogan, Univ. of Missouri, Rolla; Betsy Bowden, Camden Coll., Rutgers Univ.; Stephen L. Carr, Univ. of Pittsburgh; Paul Cohen, Southwest Texas State Univ.; Thomas E. Connolly, State Univ. of New York, Buffalo; Stephen D. Cox, Univ. of California, San Diego; Pamela Dembo–Van Schaik, Univ. of South Africa; Stefania D'Ottavi, Univ. of Rome; Landon Downey, Washington, DC; Morris Eaves, Univ. of Rochester; Helen B. Ellis, Univ. of Waterloo; Robert N. Essick, Univ. of California, Riverside; Julie Fawcus, Trianon Press, Paris; Paula R. Feldman, Univ. of South Carolina; Anthony J. Franzese, Oklahoma City Univ.; Thomas R. Frosch, Queens Coll., City Univ. of New York; Steven H. Gale, Missouri Southern State Coll.; Philip J. Gallagher, Univ. of Texas, El Paso; Jerry Caris Godard, Guilford Coll.; Sidney Gottlieb, Sacred Heart Univ.; John E. Grant, Univ. of Iowa; Mary Lynn Johnson Grant, Univ. of Iowa; Michael Grenfell, Langley Univ., London; Ronald L. Grimes, Wilfrid Laurier Univ.; David Gross, Univ. of Oklahoma; George Mills Harper, Florida State Univ.; Nelson Hilton, Univ. of Georgia; Joseph Holland, Los Angeles, CA; Wallace Jackson, Duke Univ.; David James, Occidental Coll.; Jenijoy La Belle, California Inst. of Technology; D. W. Lindsay, University Coll. of North Wales; Jane McClellan, South Georgia Coll.; James McCord, Union Coll.; Anne K. Mellor, Univ. of California, Los Angeles; Paul Miner, Wichita, KS; O. S. Mitchell, Trent Univ.; W. J. T. Mitchell, Univ. of Chicago; James K. P. Mortensen, Univ. of Texas, El Paso; Karen Mulhallen, Ryerson Inst. of Technology; Hans Ostrom, Univ. of Puget Sound; Judith W. Page, Millsaps Coll.; Harold E. Pagliaro, Swarthmore Coll.; Morton D. Paley, Univ. of California, Berkeley; Stuart Peterfreund, Northeastern Univ.; Valli Rao, Flinders Univ. of South Australia; James Reaney, Univ. of Western Ontario; Mark Reynolds, Jefferson Davis Junior Coll.; David

Simpson, Univ. of Colorado; Warren Stevenson, Univ. of British Columbia; Leslie Tannenbaum, Ohio State Univ.; Irene Tayler, Massachusetts Inst. of Technology; Judith Taylor, Northern Kentucky Univ.; Michael John Tolley, Univ. of Adelaide; William Van Pelt, Univ. of Wisconsin, Milwaukee; Frank A. Vaughan, Campbell Univ.; Joseph Viscomi, Univ. of North Carolina; Thomas A. Vogler, Univ. of California, Santa Cruz; David Wagenknecht, Boston Univ.; Winston Weathers, Univ. of Tulsa; Dennis M. Welch, Virginia Polytechnic Inst. and State Univ.; Brian F. Wilkie, Univ. of Arkansas; John Wright, Univ. of Michigan; Toby Silverman Zinman, Philadelphia Coll. of Art.

WORKS CITED

Unless otherwise noted, all references to Blake's writings derive from Erdman, *Complete Poetry*, abbreviated throughout as "E." The abbreviation "K" refers to Keynes, *Complete Writings*.

Abrams, M. H., gen. ed. *The Norton Anthology of English Literature*. 5th ed. 2 vols. New York: Norton, 1986.

Ackland, Michael. "Blake's Problematic Touchstones to Experience: 'Introduction,' 'Earth's Answer,' and the Lyca Poems." *Studies in Romanticism* 19 (1980): 3–17.

———. "The Embattled Sexes: Blake's Debt to Wollstonecraft in *The Four Zoas*." *Blake: An Illustrated Quarterly* 16 (1982–83): 172–83.

Adams, Hazard. "Reading Blake's Lyrics: 'The Tyger.' " *Texas Studies in Literature and Language* 2 (1960): 18–37.

———. "Revisiting Reynolds's *Discourses* and Blake's Annotations." Essick and Pearce 128–44.

———. *William Blake: A Reading of the Shorter Poems*. Seattle: U of Washington P, 1963.

———, ed. *William Blake:* Jerusalem, *Selected Poems and Prose*. New York: Holt, 1970.

Adlard, John. "Blake's 'The Little Girl Lost and Found.' " *Archiv* 210 (1973): 330–34.

———. *The Sports of Cruelty*. London: Woolf, 1972.

Adler, Jacob H. "Symbol and Meaning in 'The Little Black Boy.' " *Modern Language Notes* 72 (1957): 412–15.

Aers, David. "Blake: Sex, Society, and Ideology." Aers, Cook, and Punter 27–43.

———. "William Blake and the Dialectics of Sex." *ELH* 44 (1977): 500–14.

Aers, David, Jonathan Cook, and David Punter, eds. *Romanticism and Ideology*. London: Routledge, 1981.

Ault, Donald D. "Incommensurability and Interconnection in Blake's Anti-Newtonian Text." *Studies in Romanticism* 16 (1977): 277–303.

———. *Narrative Unbound*. New York: Station Hill, 1986.

———. *Visionary Physics: Blake's Response to Newton*. Chicago: U of Chicago P, 1974.

Baine, Rodney M. "Blake's 'Tyger': The Nature of the Beast." *Philological Quarterly* 46 (1967): 488–98.

Baine, Rodney M., and Mary R. Baine. "Blake's 'Blossom.' " *Colby Library Quarterly* 14 (1978): 22–27.

———. "Blake's Other Tygers, and 'The Tyger.' " *Studies in English Literature* 15 (1975): 563–78.

Barker, Francis, ed. *Reading, Writing, Revolution: Proceedings of the Essex Conference on the Sociology of Literature.* Essex: U of Essex P, 1982.

Basler, Roy P. *Sex, Symbolism, and Psychology in Literature.* New Brunswick: Rutgers UP, 1948.

Bass, Eban. "*Songs of Innocence and of Experience*: The Thrust of Design." Erdman and Grant 196–213.

Bateson, F. W. "Myth—A Dispensable Critical Term." *The Binding of Proteus: Perspectives on Myth and the Literary Process.* Ed. Marjorie W. McClune, Tucker Orbison, and Philip M. Withim. Lewisburg: Bucknell UP, 1980. 141–52.

——, ed. *Selected Poems of William Blake.* London: Heinemann, 1957.

Beeching, H. C. "Blake's Religious Lyrics." *Essays and Studies* 3 (1912): 136–52.

Beer, John. *Blake's Humanism.* Manchester: Manchester UP, 1968.

——. *Blake's Visionary Universe.* Manchester: Manchester UP, 1969.

——. "Brief Riposte." *Blake Newsletter* 6 (1972): 22–23.

——. "A Reply to Irene Chayes." *Blake Newsletter* 4 (1971): 144–47.

Bellin, Harvey F., and Darrell Ruhl, eds. *Blake and Swedenborg.* New York: Swedenborg Foundation, 1985.

Bender, John, and Anne K. Mellor. "Liberating the Sister Arts: The Revolution of Blake's 'Infant Sorrow.'" *ELH* 50 (1983): 297–319.

Benjamin, Walter. "The Work of Art in an Age of Mechanical Reproduction." *Illuminations.* Ed. Hannah Arendt. Trans. Harry Zohn. New York: Schocken, 1969. 217–51.

Bentley, G. E., Jr. *Blake Books: Annotated Catalogues of William Blake's Writings . . . , Reproductions of His Designs, Books with His Engravings, Catalogues, Books He Owned, and Scholarly and Critical Works about Him.* Oxford: Clarendon, 1977.

——. *Blake Records.* Oxford: Clarendon, 1969.

——, ed. *William Blake: The Critical Heritage.* London: Routledge, 1975.

——, ed. *William Blake's Writings.* 2 vols. Oxford: Clarendon, 1978.

Bentley, G. E., Jr., and Martin K. Nurmi. *A Blake Bibliography.* Minneapolis: U of Minnesota P, 1964.

Berninghausen, Thomas F. "The Marriage of Contraries in 'To Tirzah.'" *Colby Library Quarterly* 20 (1984): 191–98.

Berwick, F. J. "'The Sick Rose': A Second Opinion." *Theoria* 47 (1976): 77–81.

Bier, Jesse. "A Study of Blake's 'The Tyger.'" *Bucknell University Studies* 1 (1949): 35–46.

Bindman, David. *Blake as an Artist.* Oxford: Phaidon; New York: Dutton, 1977.

——. "Blake's Theory and Practice of Imitation." Essick and Pearce 91–98.

——. *The Complete Graphic Works of William Blake.* London: Thames; New York: Putnam's, 1978.

Binyon, Laurence, ed. *Poems of Blake*. London: Macmillan, 1931.

Birenbaum, Harvey. *Tragedy and Innocence*. Lanham: UP of America, 1983.

Blackstone, Bernard. *English Blake*. Cambridge: Cambridge UP, 1949.

Blake, William. *Songs of Experience*. Facsimiled by Joseph Patrick Trumble, Sophia Elizabeth Muir, and William Muir. Blake Centenary. London: Muir, 1927.

———. *Songs of Experience*. London: Benn, 1927.

———. *Songs of Experience*. Ed. Joseph Wicksteed. New York: n.p., [1947?].

———. *Songs of Experience*. New York: Dover, 1984.

———. *Songs of Innocence*. [*Reproduced by Photography from a Perfect Black and White Copy of the Original Issue of 1789, Containing All the Poems Afterwards Called* Songs of Innocence, *and Three More Which Were Afterwards Issued among the* Songs of Experience]. Boston: n.p., 1883.

———. *Songs of Innocence*. London: Hollyer, 1923.

———. *Songs of Innocence*. London: Benn, 1926.

———. *Songs of Innocence*. Facsimiled by Joseph Patrick Trumble and William Muir. London: Muir, 1927.

———. *Songs of Innocence*. Introd. Ruthven Todd. New York: n.p., [1947?].

———. *Songs of Innocence*. New York: Dover, 1971.

———. *Songs of Innocence and of Experience*. Norwood: Norwood Eds., n.d.

———. *Songs of Innocence and of Experience*. London: Falcon; New York: United Book Guild, 1947. Rpt. Folcroft: Folcroft Library Eds., 1973.

———. *Songs of Innocence and of Experience*. Bibliographical statement by Geoffrey Keynes. London: Trianon Press for the Blake Trust, 1955.

———. *Songs of Innocence and of Experience*. New York: Orion, 1967. Rpt. Oxford: Oxford UP, 1970.

———. *Songs of Innocence and of Experience*. Huntington Library Facsimiles. San Marino: Huntington Library, 1976.

Bland, David. *A History of Book Illustration*. Cleveland: World, 1958.

Blondel, Jacques. "William Blake: 'The Chimney Sweeper': De l'innocence à la violence." *Langues modernes* 40 (1966): 162–67.

Bloom, Harold. *Blake's Apocalypse: A Study in Poetic Argument*. Garden City: Doubleday, 1963.

———, ed. *Modern Critical Views: William Blake*. New York: Chelsea, 1985.

———. *Poetry and Repression: Revisionism from Blake to Stevens*. New Haven: Yale UP, 1976.

———. *The Visionary Company: A Reading of English Romantic Poetry*. New York: Anchor-Doubleday, 1962.

Blunt, Anthony. *The Art of William Blake*. New York: Columbia UP, 1959.

Bodden, Horst, and Herbert Kausser. "William Blake's 'London.' " *Modellanalysen englischer Lyrik: Shakespeare, Marvell, Milton, Blake, Keats, Shelley, Hopkins, Yeats, Hughes*. Stuttgart: Klett, 1974. 66–79.

Bodkin, Maud. *Archetypal Patterns in Poetry*. London: Oxford UP, 1934.

Bolt, S. F. "William Blake: The *Songs of Innocence*." *Politics and Letters* 1 (1947): 15–23.

Borck, Jim S. "Blake's 'The Lamb': The Punctuation of Innocence." *Tennessee Studies in Literature* 19 (1974): 163–75.

Bottrall, Margaret, ed. *William Blake: Songs of Innocence and Experience: A Casebook*. London: Macmillan, 1970.

Bowra, C. Maurice. *The Romantic Imagination*. Cambridge: Harvard UP, 1949.

Brenkman, John. "The Concrete Utopia of Poetry: Blake's 'A Poison Tree.' " *Lyric Poetry: Beyond New Criticism*. Ed. Chaviva Hosek and Patricia Parker. Ithaca: Cornell UP, 1985. 182–93.

Brisman, Leslie. "Re: Generation in Blake." *Romantic Origins*. Ithaca: Cornell UP, 1978. 224–75.

Bronowski, Jacob, ed. *William Blake: A Selection of Poems and Letters*. Harmondsworth: Penguin, 1958.

———. *William Blake, 1757–1827: A Man without a Mask*. London: Secker, 1944.

Brooks, Cleanth, et al., eds. *An Approach to Literature*. New York: Crofts, 1940.

Brower, Reuben. *The Fields of Light: An Experiment in Critical Reading*. New York: Oxford UP, 1951.

Butler, Marilyn. *Romantics, Rebels, and Reactionaries*. Oxford: Oxford UP, 1982.

Butlin, Martin. *The Paintings and Drawings of William Blake*. 2 vols. New Haven: Yale UP, 1981.

Butter, Peter H. *Selected Poems: William Blake*. London: Dent, 1982.

Carr, Stephen Leo. "William Blake's Print-Making Process in *Jerusalem*." *ELH* 47 (1980): 520–41.

Chamberlain, Walter. *Etching and Engraving*. New York: Viking, 1972.

Chayes, Irene. "Blake and Tradition: 'The Little Girl Lost' and 'The Little Girl Found.' " *Blake Newsletter* 4 (1970): 25–28.

———. "Brief Riposte." *Blake Newsletter* 6 (1972): 23–24.

———. "Little Girls Lost: Problems of a Romantic Archetype." *Bulletin of the New York Public Library* 67 (1963): 579–92.

———. "A Rejoinder to John Beer." *Blake Newsletter* 5 (1971): 211–13.

Christensen, Bryce J. "The Apple in the Vortex: Newton, Blake, and Descartes." *Philosophy and Literature* 6 (1982): 147–61.

Coleridge, Samuel Taylor. "Letter to C. A. Tulk" [12 Feb. 1818]. *The Collected Letters of Samuel Taylor Coleridge*. Ed. Earl Leslie Griggs. 6 vols. Oxford: Clarendon, 1959. 4: 833–38.

Connolly, Thomas E. "Point of View in Interpreting 'The Fly.' " *English Language Notes* 22 (1984): 32–37.

———. "The Real 'Holy Thursday' of William Blake." *Blake Studies* 6 (1975): 179–87.

Connolly, Thomas E., and George R. Levine. "Pictorial and Poetic Design in Two Songs of Innocence." *PMLA* 82 (1967): 257–64.

———. "Recognizing Mother." *Blake Newsletter* 1 (1967): 17–18.

———. "Two Songs of Innocence II." *PMLA* 84 (1969): 138–39.

Coombes, Henry. *Literature and Criticism.* London: Chatto, 1953.

Corti, Claudia. "Acque natali e acque lustrali nei *Songs of Innocence* di Blake." *Rivista di letterature moderne e comparate* 30 (1977): 5–19.

Cox, Stephen D. "Adventures of 'A Little Boy Lost': Blake and the Process of Interpretation." *Criticism* 23 (1981): 301–16.

Crehan, Stewart. *Blake in Context.* London: Gill and Macmillan; Atlantic Highlands: Humanities, 1984.

———. "Blake's 'Tyger' and the 'Tygerish Multitude.'" *Literature and History* 6 (1980): 150–60.

Culler, Jonathan. "Prolegomenon to a Theory of Reading." *The Reader in the Text: Essays in Audience Interpretation.* Ed. Susan R. Suleiman and Inge Crosman. Princeton: Princeton UP, 1980. 46–86

———. *The Pursuit of Signs.* Ithaca: Cornell UP, 1981.

Curtis, F. B. "Blake and the 'Moment of Time': An Eighteenth–Century Controversy in Mathematics." *Philological Quarterly* 51 (1972): 460–70.

———. "William Blake and Eighteenth-Century Medicine." *Blake Studies* 8 (1979): 187–99.

Damon, S. Foster. *A Blake Dictionary: The Ideas and Symbols of William Blake.* Providence: Brown UP, 1965.

———. *William Blake: His Philosophy and Symbols.* 1924. Gloucester: Smith, 1958.

Damrosch, Leopold. *Symbol and Truth in Blake's Myth.* Princeton: Princeton UP, 1980.

Davidson, Clifford. "Blake's *Songs of Experience* and 'Rebel Nature.'" *Research Studies* 44 (1976): 35–41.

Davies, J. G. *The Theology of William Blake.* 1948. Hamden: Archon, 1965.

Davis, Michael. *William Blake: A New Kind of Man.* Berkeley: U of California P, 1977.

de Selincourt, Basil, ed. *Selected Poems by William Blake.* Oxford: Oxford UP, 1927.

Dickstein, Morris. "The Price of Experience: Blake's Reading of Freud." *The Literary Freud: Mechanisms of Defense and the Poetic Will.* Ed. Joseph H. Smith. New Haven: Yale UP, 1980. 67–111.

Dike, Donald A. "The Difficult Innocence: Blake's *Songs* and Pastoral." *ELH* 28 (1961): 353–75.

Dilworth, Thomas. "Blake's Argument with Newberry in 'Laughing Song.'" *Blake: An Illustrated Quarterly* 14 (1980): 36–37.

DiSalvo, Jackie. *War of Titans: Blake's Critique of Milton and the Politics of Religion.* Pittsburgh: U of Pittsburgh P, 1984.

Dorfman, Deborah. *Blake in the Nineteenth Century: His Reputation as a Poet from Gilchrist to Yeats.* New Haven: Yale UP, 1969.

Downer, A. S., ed. *English Institute Essays 1950.* New York: Columbia UP, 1951.

Doyno, Victor. "Blake's Revision of 'London.' " *Essays in Criticism* 22 (1972): 58–63.

Durrant, G. H. "Blake's 'My Pretty Rose Tree.' " *Theoria* 30 (1968): 1–5.

Dyson. A. E. " 'The Little Black Boy': Blake's Song of Innocence." *Critical Quarterly* 1 (1959): 44–47.

Eaves, Morris. "Blake and the Artistic Machine: An Essay in Decorum and Technology." *PMLA* 92 (1977): 903–27.

——. "Blake and Ginsberg on ABC-TV's 'Directions.' " *Blake Newsletter* 5 (1971): 164.

——. Rev. of Allen Ginsberg, " 'Songs of Innocence and Experience' by William Blake, Tuned by Allen Ginsberg." *Blake Newsletter* 4 (1971): 90–97.

——. *William Blake's Theory of Art.* Princeton: Princeton UP, 1982.

Edwards, Gavin. "Mind Forg'd Manacles: A Contribution to the Discussion of Blake's 'London.' " *Literature and History* 5 (1979): 87–105.

Edwards, Thomas R. *Imagination and Power: A Study of Poetry on Public Themes.* New York: Oxford UP, 1971.

Eliot, T. S. "Blake." *The Sacred Wood.* London: Methuen, 1920. 151–58.

Ellis, Edwin John, and William Butler Yeats, eds. *The Works of William Blake: Poetic, Symbolic, and Critical.* 3 vols. London, 1893.

England, Martha W. "Wesley's *Hymns for Children* and Blake's *Songs of Innocence and of Experience.*" *Bulletin of the New York Public Library* 70 (1966): 7–26.

Epstein, E. L. "Blake's 'Infant Sorrow'—An Essay in Discourse Analysis." *Current Trends in Stylistics.* Ed. Braj B. Kachru and Hubert F. W. Statilke. Edmonton: Linguistic Research, 1972. 231–41.

——. "The Self-Reflexive Artefact: The Function of Mimesis in an Approach to a Theory of Value for Literature." *Style and Structure in Literature: Essays in the New Stylistics.* Ed. Roger Fowler. Ithaca: Cornell UP, 1975. 40–78.

Erdman, David V. *Blake: Prophet against Empire.* Princeton: Princeton UP, 1954. Rev. ed., 1969. 3rd ed., 1977.

——, ed. *The Complete Poetry and Prose of William Blake.* Newly rev. ed. Commentary by Harold Bloom. Berkeley: U of California P, 1982.

——, annotator. *The Illuminated Blake.* Garden City: Anchor-Doubleday, 1974.

——, ed. *The Poetry and Prose of William Blake.* Garden City: Doubleday, 1965.

——, ed. *William Blake: Selected Poetry.* Signet Classics. New York: NAL, 1976.

Erdman, David V., et al. *A Concordance to the Writings of William Blake.* 2 vols. Ithaca: Cornell UP, 1967.

Erdman, David V., and John E. Grant, eds. *Blake's Visionary Forms Dramatic.* Princeton: Princeton UP, 1970.

Erdman, David V., and Donald K. Moore, eds. *The Notebook of William Blake: A Photographic and Typographic Facsimile*. Oxford: Clarendon, 1973. Rev. ed. New York: Readex, 1977.

Essick, Robert N. "Blake and the Traditions of Reproductive Engraving." *Blake Studies* 5 (1972): 59–103.

————. "Review of the Manchester Etching Workshop Blake Facsimiles." *Blake: An Illustrated Quarterly* 18 (1985): 39–51.

————. *The Separate Plates of William Blake: A Catalogue*. Princeton: Princeton UP, 1983.

————, ed. *The Visionary Hand: Essays for the Study of William Blake's Art and Aesthetics*. Los Angeles: Hennessey, 1973.

————. *William Blake, Printmaker*. Princeton: Princeton UP, 1980.

————. "William Blake, William Hamilton, and the Materials of Graphic Meaning." *ELH* 52 (1985): 833–72.

————. *The Works of William Blake in the Huntington Collection*. San Marino: Huntington Library, 1985.

Essick, Robert N., and Donald Pearce, eds. *Blake in His Time*. Bloomington: Indiana UP, 1978.

Fairchild, B.H. *Such Holy Song: Music as Idea, Form, and Image in the Poetry of William Blake*. Kent: Kent State UP, 1980.

Ferber, Michael. "Blake's Idea of Brotherhood." *PMLA* 93 (1978): 438–47.

————. "'London' and Its Politics." *ELH* 48 (1981): 310–38.

————. *The Social Vision of William Blake*. Princeton: Princeton UP, 1985.

Fish, Stanley. *Is There a Text in This Class? The Authority of Interpretive Communities*. Cambridge: Harvard UP, 1980.

Fisher, Peter F. *The Valley of Vision: Blake as Prophet and Revolutionary*. Ed. Northrop Frye. Toronto: U of Toronto P, 1961.

Fox, Susan. "The Female as Metaphor in William Blake's Poetry." *Critical Inquiry* 3 (1977): 507–19.

Fraistat, Neil. *The Poem and the Book: Interpreting Collections of Romantic Poetry*. Chapel Hill: U of North Carolina P, 1985.

Freeman, Rosemary. *English Emblem Books*. London: Chatto, 1948.

Frosch, Thomas R. *The Awakening of Albion: The Revolution of the Body in the Poetry of William Blake*. Ithaca: Cornell UP, 1974.

Frye, Northrop, ed. *Blake: A Collection of Critical Essays*. Englewood Cliffs: Prentice, 1966.

————. "Blake after Two Centuries." *University of Toronto Quarterly* 27 (1957): 10–21.

————. "Blake's Introduction to Experience." *Huntington Library Quarterly* 21 (1957): 57–67.

——. "Blake's Treatment of the Archetype." Downer 170–96.

——. *Fearful Symmetry: A Study of William Blake*. Princeton: Princeton UP, 1947.

——. "Poetry and Design in William Blake." *Journal of Aesthetics and Art Criticism* 10 (1951): 35–42.

——, ed. *Selected Poetry and Prose of Blake*. Modern Library College Ed. New York: Random, 1953.

Gallagher, Philip J. "The Word Made Flesh: Blake's 'A Poison Tree' and the Book of Genesis." *Studies in Romanticism* 16 (1977): 237–49.

Gallant, Christine. *Blake and the Assimilation of Chaos*. Princeton: Princeton UP, 1979.

Gardner, Stanley. *Blake's* Innocence *and* Experience *Retraced*. London: Athlone; New York: St. Martin's, 1986.

——. *Infinity on the Anvil: A Critical Study of Blake's Poetry*. Oxford: Blackwell, 1954.

——, ed. *Selected Poems of Blake*. London: U of London P, 1962.

George, Diana Hume. *Blake and Freud*. Ithaca: Cornell UP, 1980.

——. "Is She Also the Divine Image? Feminine Form in the Art of William Blake." *Centennial Review* 23 (1979): 129–40.

Gibaldi, Joseph. *Approaches to Teaching Chaucer's* Canterbury Tales. New York: MLA, 1980.

Gilchrist, Alexander. *The Life of William Blake, Pictor Ignotus*. 2 vols. London: Macmillan, 1863. New and enl. ed. London: Macmillan, 1880.

——. *The Life of William Blake, Pictor Ignotus*. Ed. Ruthven Todd. London: Dent, 1974.

Gill, Frederick C. *The Romantic Movement and Methodism*. London: Epworth, 1937.

Gillham, D. G. *Blake's Contrary States: The* Songs of Innocence and of Experience *as Dramatic Poems*. Cambridge: Cambridge UP, 1966.

——. *William Blake*. Cambridge: Cambridge UP, 1973.

Ginsberg, Allen. "To Young or Old Listeners: Setting Blake's *Songs* to Music, and a Commentary on the *Songs*." *Blake Newsletter* 4 (1971): 98–103.

Glazer, Myra. "Blake's Little Black Boys: On the Dynamics of Blake's Composite Art." *Colby Library Quarterly* 16 (1980): 220–36.

Glazer-Schotz, Myra, and Gerda Norvig. "Blake's Book of Changes: On Viewing Three Copies of the *Songs of Innocence and of Experience*." *Blake Studies* 9 (1980): 100–21.

Gleckner, Robert F. "Blake and the Four Daughters of God." *English Language Notes* 15 (1977): 110–15.

——. "Blake and the Senses." *Studies in Romanticism* 5 (1965): 1–15.

——. *Blake and Spenser*. Baltimore: Johns Hopkins UP, 1985.

————. "Blake, Gray, and the Illustrations." *Criticism* 19 (1977): 118–40.

————. "Blake's 'Little Black Boy' and the Bible." *Colby Library Quarterly* 18 (1982): 205–13.

————. "Blake's 'My Pretty Rose Tree.' " *Explicator* 13 (1955): item 43.

————. *Blake's Prelude: Poetical Sketches*. Baltimore: Johns Hopkins UP, 1982.

————. "Blake's 'The Tyger' and Edward Young's Book of Job." *Blake: An Illustrated Quarterly* 21 (1987–88): 99–101.

————. "Blake's *Tiriel* and the State of Experience." *Philological Quarterly* 36 (1957): 195–210.

————. "Irony in Blake's 'Holy Thursday.' " *Modern Language Notes* 71 (1956): 412–15.

————. *The Piper and the Bard: A Study of William Blake*. Detroit: Wayne State UP, 1957.

————. "Point of View and Context in Blake's *Songs*." *Bulletin of the New York Public Library* 61 (1957): 531–36.

————, ed. *Selected Writings of William Blake*. New York: Crofts, 1967.

————. "The Strange Odyssey of Blake's 'The Voice of the Ancient Bard.' " *Romanticism Past and Present* 6 (1982): 1–25.

————. "William Blake and the Human Abstract." *PMLA* 76 (1961): 373–79.

Glen, Heather. "Blake's Criticism of Moral Thinking in *Songs of Innocence and of Experience*." Phillips, *Interpreting* 32–69.

————. *Vision and Disenchantment: Blake's* Songs *and Wordsworth's* Lyrical Ballads. Cambridge: Cambridge UP, 1983.

Goller, Karl H. "William Blake: '*Songs of Innocence*, Introduction.' " *Die englische Lyrik*. Ed. Goller. Düsseldorf: Bogel, 1968. 301–08.

Gouma-Peterson, Thalia, and Patricia Mathews. "The Feminist Critique of Art History." *Art Bulletin* 69 (1987): 326–57.

Grant, John E. "The Art and Argument of 'The Tyger.' " *Texas Studies in Literature and Language* 2 (1960): 38–60.

————, ed. *Discussions of William Blake*. Boston: Heath, 1961.

————. "The Fate of Blake's Sunflower: A Forecast and Some Conclusions." *Blake Studies* 5 (1974): 7–64.

————. "Interpreting Blake's 'The Fly.' " *Bulletin of the New York Public Library* 67 (1963): 593–615.

————. "Misreadings of 'The Fly.' " *Essays in Criticism* 11 (1961): 481–87.

————. "Recognizing Fathers." *Blake Newsletter* 1 (1967): 7–9.

————. "Two Flowers in the Garden of Experience." Rosenfeld 333–67.

Grant, John E., and Fred C. Robinson. "Tense and the Sense of Blake's 'The Tyger.' " *PMLA* 81 (1966): 596–603.

Graves, Robert. *"The Crane Bag" and Other Disputed Subjects*. London: Cassell, 1969.

Greco, Norma A. "Blake's 'The Little Girl Lost': An Initiation into Womanhood." *Colby Library Quarterly* 19 (1983): 144–54.

──────. "Mother Figures in Blake's *Songs of Innocence* and the Female Will." *Romanticism Past and Present* 10 (1986): 1–15.

Greenberg, Mark L. "Blake's 'Science.' " *Studies in Eighteenth-Century Culture* 12 (1983): 115–30.

──────. "Blake's 'Vortex.' " *Colby Library Quarterly* 14 (1978): 198–212.

──────. "Shared Struggles, Shared Triumphs: Watching Writers Write." *CEA Critic* 42 (1980): 3–9.

Greene, Gayle, and Coppélia Kahn, eds. *Making a Difference: Feminist Literary Criticism.* London: Methuen, 1985.

Hagstrum, Jean. " 'The Fly.' " Rosenfeld 368–82.

──────. "Rebuttal" [to Michael J. Tolley]. *Blake Studies* 2 (1969): 84–86.

──────. *The Romantic Body: Love and Sexuality in Keats, Wordsworth, and Blake.* Knoxville: U of Tennessee P, 1985.

──────. *William Blake, Poet and Painter: An Introduction to the Illuminated Verse.* Chicago: U of Chicago P, 1964.

──────. "William Blake Rejects the Enlightenment." *Studies on Voltaire and the Eighteenth Century* 25 (1963): 811–28.

──────. "William Blake's 'The Clod and the Pebble.' " *Restoration and Eighteenth-Century Literature.* Ed. Charles Carroll Camden. Chicago: U of Chicago P, 1963. 381–88.

──────. " 'The Wrath of the Lamb': A Study of William Blake's Conversions." Hilles and Bloom 311–30.

Harper, George Mills. *The Neoplatonism of William Blake.* Chapel Hill: U of North Carolina P, 1961.

──────. "The Source of Blake's 'Ah! Sunflower.' " *Modern Language Review* 48 (1953): 139–42.

Hazen, James. "Blake's Tyger and Milton's Beasts." *Blake Studies* 3 (1971): 163–70.

Heath, William, ed. *Major British Poets of the Romantic Period.* New York: Macmillan, 1973.

Heinzelman, Kurt. "William Blake and the Economics of the Imagination." *Modern Language Quarterly* 39 (1978): 99–120.

Henn, T. R. *The Apple and the Spectroscope.* London: Methuen, 1951.

Hill, Archibald. "Imagery and Meaning: A Passage from Milton, and from Blake." *Texas Studies in Literature and Language* 11 (1969): 1093–105.

Hilles, Frederick W., and Harold Bloom, eds. *From Sensibility to Romanticism: Essays in Honor of Frederick A. Pottle.* New York: Oxford UP, 1965.

Hilton, Nelson, ed. *Essential Articles for the Study of William Blake, 1970–1984.* Hamden: Archon, 1986.

──────. *Literal Imagination: Blake's Vision of Words.* Berkeley: U of California P, 1983.

————. "Some Sexual Connotations." *Blake: An Illustrated Quarterly* 16 (1982–83): 166–71.

————. "Spears, Spheres, and Spiritual Tears: Blake's Poetry as 'The Tyger.' " *Philological Quarterly* 59 (1980): 515–29.

Hinkel, Howard H. "From Pivotal Idea to Poetic Ideal: Blake's Theory of Contraries and 'The Little Black Boy.' " *Papers on Language and Literature* 11 (1975): 39–45.

Hirsch, E. D., Jr. *Innocence and Experience: An Introduction to Blake.* New Haven: Yale UP, 1964.

Hobsbaum, Philip. "A Rhetorical Question Answered: Blake's 'Tyger' and Its Critics." *Neophilologus* 48 (1964): 151–55.

————. *Theory of Criticism.* Bloomington: Indiana UP, 1972.

Hoeveler, Diane Long. "Blake's Erotic Apocalypse: The Androgynous Ideal in *Jerusalem.*" *Essays in Literature* 6 (1979): 29–41.

Hofmann, Werner, ed. *William Blake: Lieder der Unschuld und Erfahrung.* Frankfurt am Main: Prestel, 1975.

Hollander, John. "Blake and the Metrical Contract." Hilles and Bloom 293–310.

Holloway, John. *Blake: The Lyric Poetry.* London: Arnold, 1968.

Howard, John D. "Swedenborg's *Heaven and Hell* and Blake's *Songs of Innocence.*" *Papers on Language and Literature* 4 (1968): 390–99.

Iovine, Marcella Quadri. "La presia del desiderio: 'Ah! Sunflower' di W. Blake." *Annali Istituto Universitario Orientale: Anglistica.* Rome, 1979.

Ivins, William. *Prints and Visual Communication.* London: Routledge, 1953.

Jackson, Wallace. *The Probable and the Marvelous: Blake, Wordsworth, and the Eighteenth-Century Critical Tradition.* Athens: U of Georgia P, 1978.

Jakobson, Roman. "On the Verbal Art of William Blake and Other Poet-Painters." *Linguistic Inquiry* 1 (1970): 3–23.

Jakubec, Doris. " 'La rose malade' de William Blake." *Etudes de lettres* 3.5 (1972): 51–59.

Jameson, Fredric. *The Political Unconscious: Narrative as a Socially Symbolic Act.* Ithaca: Cornell UP, 1981.

Johnson, Mary Lynn. "Choosing Textbooks for Blake Courses: A Survey and Checklist." *Blake Newsletter* 10 (1976): 9–26.

————. "Emblem and Symbol in Blake." *Huntington Library Quarterly* 37 (1974): 151–70.

————. "William Blake." *The English Romantic Poets: A Review of Research and Criticism.* Ed. Frank Jordan. 4th ed. New York: MLA, 1985. 113–254.

Johnson, Mary Lynn, and John E. Grant, eds. *Blake's Poetry and Designs.* Norton Critical Ed. New York: Norton, 1979.

Johnston, Kenneth. "Blake's Cities: Romantic Forms of Urban Renewal." Erdman and Grant 413–42.

Juhl, Peter D. *Interpretation: An Essay in the Philosophy of Literary Criticism.* Princeton: Princeton UP, 1980.

Kaplan, Fred. *Miracles of Rare Device.* Detroit: Wayne State UP, 1972.

———. " 'The Tyger' and Its Maker: Blake's Vision of the Artist." *Studies in English Literature* 7 (1967): 617–27.

Kauver, Elaine M. "Landscape of the Mind: Blake's Garden Symbolism." *Blake Studies* 9 (1980): 57–73.

Kazin, Alfred, ed. *The Portable Blake.* New York: Viking, 1946.

Keith, William J. "The Complexities of Blake's 'Sunflower': An Archetypal Speculation." Frye, *Blake: A Collection* 56–64.

Kennedy, R. B., ed. Songs of Innocence and of Experience, *and Other Works.* London: Collins, 1970.

Keogh, J. G. "Two Songs of Innocence." *PMLA* 84 (1969): 137–38.

Kermode, Frank, and John Hollander, gen. eds. *The Oxford Anthology of English Literature.* 2 vols. New York: Oxford UP, 1973. ·

Keynes, Geoffrey. *A Bibliography of William Blake.* New York: Grolier Club, 1921.

———, ed. *Blake: Complete Writings, with Variant Readings.* London: Oxford UP, 1966.

———. *Blake Studies: Essays on His Life and Work.* 1949. Rev ed. Oxford: Clarendon, 1971.

———. " 'Blake's Own' Copy of *Songs of Innocence and of Experience.*" *Book Collector* 29 (1980): 202–07.

———, ed. *The Letters of William Blake.* Cambridge: Harvard UP, 1980.

———, ed. *Songs of Innocence and of Experience.* 1967. Oxford: Oxford UP, 1970.

Keynes, Geoffrey, and Edwin Wolf II. *Blake's Illuminated Books: A Census.* New York: Grolier Club, 1953. Rpt. New York: Kraus, 1969.

Kiralis, Karl. " 'London' in the Light of *Jerusalem.*" *Blake Studies* 1 (1968): 5–15.

Kirschbaum, Leo. "Blake's 'The Fly.' " *Essays in Criticism* 11 (1961): 154–62.

Lambert, Susan. *Reading Drawings.* New York: Pantheon, 1984.

Landry, Hilton. "The Symbolism of Blake's Sunflower." *Bulletin of the New York Public Library* 66 (1962): 613–16.

Langland, Elizabeth. "Blake's Feminist Revision of Literary Tradition in 'The Sick Rose.' " *Critical Paths: Blake and the Argument of Method.* Ed. Dan Miller, Mark Bracher, and Donald Ault. Durham: Duke UP, 1987. 225–43.

Larrabee, Stephen A. "An Interpretation of Blake's 'A Divine Image.' " *Modern Language Notes* 47 (1932): 305–08.

Larrissy, Edward. "A Description of Blake: Ideology, Form, Influence." Barker 101–09.

———. *William Blake.* London: Blackwell, 1985.

Law, Phillip. "Innocence Renewed: The Divine Images of *Songs of Innocence and of Experience.*" *Theology* 89 (1986): 275–82.

Leader, Zachary. *Reading Blake's* Songs. Boston: Routledge, 1981.

Leavis, F. R. "A Reply." *The Importance of Scrutiny*. Ed. Eric Bentley. New York: Stewart, 1948. 30–40.

———. *Revaluation: Tradition and Development in English Poetry*. New York: Stewart, 1936.

Lefcowitz, Barbara F. "Omnipotence of Thought and the Poetic Imagination: Blake, Coleridge, Rilke." *Psychoanalytic Review* 59 (1972): 417–32.

Lindop, Grevel. "Blake: 'The Little Girl Lost' and 'The Little Girl Found.'" *Critical Survey* 6 (1973): 36–40.

Lindsay, Jack. *William Blake: His Life and Work*. New York: Braziller, 1979.

Linkin, Harriet K. "The Language of Speakers in *Songs of Innocence and of Experience*." *Romanticism Past and Present* 10 (1986): 5–24.

Lipking, Lawrence. *The Ordering of the Arts in Eighteenth-Century England*. Princeton: Princeton UP, 1970.

Long, Kay Parkhurst. "William Blake and the Smiling Tyger." Weathers, *William Blake* 115–21.

Lowery, Margaret Ruth. *Windows of the Morning: A Critical Study of William Blake's* Poetical Sketches. New Haven: Yale UP, 1940.

Maheux, Ann. "An Analysis of the Watercolor Technique and Materials of William Blake." *Blake: An Illustrated Quarterly* 17 (1984): 124–29.

Mahoney, John L., ed. *The English Romantics*. Lexington: Heath, 1978.

Majdiak, Daniel, and Brian Wilkie. "Blake and Freud: Poetry and Depth Psychology." *Journal of Aesthetic Education* 6 (1972): 87–98.

Mankowitz, Wolf. "William Blake: The *Songs of Experience*." *Politics and Letters* 1 (1947): 15–23.

Manlove, C. N. "Engineered Innocence: Blake's 'The Little Black Boy' and 'The Fly.'" *Essays in Criticism* 27 (1977): 112–21.

Mann, Paul. "Apocalypse and Recuperation: Blake and the Maw of Commerce." *ELH* 52 (1985): 1–32.

Margoliouth, H. M. *William Blake*. New York: Oxford UP, 1951.

Marks, Elaine, and Isabelle de Courtivron, eds. *New French Feminisms*. Amherst: U of Massachusetts P, 1979.

McCarthy, Shaun. "Riddle Patterns and William Blake's 'The Tyger.'" *Journal of English* 8 (1980): 1–11.

McConnell, Frank D. "Romanticism, Language, Waste: A Reflection on Poetics and Disaster." *Bucknell Review* 20 (1972): 121–40.

McGann, Jerome J. *The Romantic Ideology*. Chicago: U of Chicago P, 1983.

Mellor, Anne K. "Blake's Portrayal of Women." *Blake: An Illustrated Quarterly* 16 (1982–83): 148–55.

Meynell, Alice, ed. *Poems by William Blake*. London: Red Letter Library, 1911.

Middleton, Peter. "The Revolutionary Poetics of William Blake." Pt. 1: Barker 110–18. Pt 2: *Oxford Literary Review* 6 (1983): 35–51.

Mikkelsen, Robert. "William Blake's Revisions of the *Songs of Innocence and of Experience.*" *Concerning Poetry* 2 (1969): 60–71.

Miles, Josephine A. "The Language of William Blake." Downer 141–69.

Miller, Dan, Mark Bracher, and Donald Ault, eds. *Critical Paths: Blake and the Argument of Method.* Durham: Duke UP, 1987.

Miner, Paul. " 'The Tyger': Genesis and Evolution in the Poetry of William Blake." *Criticism* 4 (1962): 59–73.

Mitchell, W. J. T. *Blake's Composite Art: A Study of the Illuminated Poetry.* Princeton: Princeton UP, 1978.

———. *Iconology: Image, Text, Ideology.* Chicago: U of Chicago P, 1986.

———. "Style as Epistemology: Blake and the Movement toward Abstraction in Art." *Studies in Romanticism* 16 (1977): 145–64.

———. "Visible Language: Blake's Wond'rous Art of Writing." *Romanticism and Contemporary Criticism.* Ed. Morris Eaves and Michael Fischer. Ithaca: Cornell UP, 1986. 46–95.

Moi, Toril. *Sexual/Textual Politics: Feminist Literary Theory.* London: Methuen, 1985.

Montgomery, James, ed. *Chimney Sweeper's Friend and Climbing Boy's Album.* London, 1824.

Moore, Donald K. "Blake's Notebook Versions of 'Infant Sorrow.' " *Bulletin of the New York Public Library* 76 (1972): 209–19.

Munson, Rita. "Blake's 'Night.' " *UNISA English Studies* 22 (1984): 7–13.

Murray, E. B. "Thel, *Thelophthera* and the Visions." *Studies in Romanticism* 20 (1981): 275–97.

Nanavutty, Piloo. "Blake and Emblem Literature." *Journal of the Warburg and Courtauld Institutes* 15 (1952): 258–61.

Nathan, Norman. "Blake's 'Infant Sorrow.' " *Notes and Queries* ns 7 (1960): 99–100.

Neisser, Ulric. *Cognition and Reality.* San Francisco: Freeman, 1976.

Neubauer, John. "The Sick Rose as an Aesthetic Idea." *Irrationalism in the Eighteenth Century.* Ed. Harold E. Pagliaro. Cleveland: Case Western Reserve UP, 1972. 167–79.

Nurmi, Martin K. "Blake's Revision of 'The Tyger.' " *PMLA* 71 (1956): 669–85.

———. "Fact and Symbol in 'The Chimney Sweeper' of Blake's *Songs of Innocence.*" *Bulletin of the New York Public Library* 68 (1964): 249–56.

———. "Negative Sources in Blake." Rosenfeld 303–18.

Olivier, T. "The Voice of the Bard in Blake's *Songs of Experience.*" *Theoria* 33 (1969): 71–76.

O'Neill, Judith, ed. *Critics on Blake: Readings in Literary Criticism.* London: Allen; Coral Gables: U of Miami P, 1970.

Ortner, Sherry. "Is Female to Male as Nature to Culture?" *Women, Culture and Society.* Ed. Michelle Zimbalist Rosaldo and Louise Lamphere. Palo Alto: Stanford UP, 1974. 67–88.

Ostriker, Alicia. "Desire Gratified: William Blake and Sexuality." *Blake: An Illustrated Quarterly* 16 (1982–83): 156–65.

———. *Vision and Verse in William Blake*. Madison: U of Wisconsin P, 1965.

———, ed. *William Blake: The Complete Poems*. Harmondsworth: Penguin, 1976.

Pagliaro, Harold E. "Blake's 'Self-Annihilation': Aspects of Its Function in the *Songs*, with a Glance at Its History." *English* 30 (1981): 117–46.

———. *Selfhood and Redemption in Blake's "Songs."* University Park: Pennsylvania State UP, 1987.

Paley, Morton D. *Energy and the Imagination: A Study of the Development of Blake's Thought*. Oxford: Clarendon, 1970.

———, ed. *Twentieth Century Interpretations of* Songs of Innocence and of Experience. Englewood Cliffs: Prentice, 1969.

———. *William Blake*. Oxford: Phaidon, 1978.

Paley, Morton D., and Michael Phillips, eds. *William Blake: Essays in Honour of Sir Geoffrey Keynes*. Oxford: Clarendon, 1973.

Parsons, Coleman O. "Blake's 'Tyger' and Eighteenth-Century Animal Pictures." *Art Quarterly* 31 (1968): 296–312.

———. "Tygers before Blake." *Studies in English Literature* 8 (1968): 573–92.

Paterson, E. H. "Simple Thoughts on William Blake." *Theoria* 28 (1967): 63–65.

Pauchard, Jean. " 'The Blossom': Une visualisation." *Visages de l'harmonie dans la littérature anglo-americaine*. Reims: Centre de Recherche sur l'Imaginaire dans les Littératures de Langue Anglaise, Université de Reims, 1982. 61–70.

Paulson, Ronald. *Representations of Revolution, (1789–1820)*. New Haven: Yale UP, 1983.

Pechey, G. K. "Blake's Tyger." *Theoria* 26 (1966): 81–92.

Percival, Milton O. *William Blake's Circle of Destiny*. New York: Columbia UP, 1938.

Perkins, David, ed. *English Romantic Writers*. New York: Harcourt, 1967.

Peterfreund, Stuart. "Blake and Newton: Argument as Art, Argument as Science. *Studies in Eighteenth-Century Culture* 10 (1981): 205–26.

Pfefferkorn, Eli. "The Question of the Leviathan and the Tiger." *Blake Studies* 3 (1970): 53–60.

Phillips, Michael, ed. *Interpreting Blake*. Cambridge: Cambridge UP, 1978.

———. "William Blake's *Songs of Innocence* and *Songs of Experience*: From Manuscript Draft to Illuminated Plate." *Book Collector* 28 (1979): 17–59.

Pinto, Vivian de Sola, ed. *The Divine Vision: Studies in the Poetry and Art of William Blake*. London: Blake Bicentenary Comm., 1957.

Plowman, Max, ed. *Blake's Poems and Prophecies*. Everyman's Library. London: Dent, 1927.

Poggioli, Renato. *The Oaten Flute*. Cambridge: Harvard UP, 1975.

Price, Martin. *To the Palace of Wisdom*. Carbondale: Southern Illinois UP, 1965.

Punter, David. "Blake: Creative and Uncreative Labor." *Studies in Romanticism* 16 (1977): 535–61.

———. *Blake, Hegel, and Dialectic*. Atlantic Highlands: Humanities, 1982.

———. "Blake/Hegel/Derrida." *Blake: An Illustrated Quarterly* 18 (1984): 58–63.

———. "Blake, Marxism, and Dialectic." *Literature and History* 6 (1977): 219–42.

———. "Blake, Trauma, and the Female." *New Literary History* 15 (1984): 475–90.

———. "Blake and the Shapes of London." *Criticism* 23 (1981): 1–23.

Quilligan, Maureen. *The Language of Allegory*. Ithaca: Cornell UP, 1979.

Raine, Kathleen. *Blake and Tradition*. 2 vols. Princeton: Princeton UP, 1968.

———, ed. *A Choice of Blake's Verse*. London: Faber, 1970.

———. "The Little Girl Lost and Found and the Lapsed Soul." Pinto 17–63.

Rawlinson, David H. *The Practice of Criticism*. London: Cambridge UP, 1968.

Richardson, Alan. "Romanticism and the Colonization of the Feminine." *Romanticism and Feminism*. Ed. Anne K. Mellor. Bloomington: Indiana UP, 1988. 13–25.

Riese, Teut Andreas. "William Blake: 'The Little Girl Lost' und 'The Little Girl Found.'" *Verdichtung der englische Romantik*. Ed. Riese and Dieter Riesner. Berlin: Schmidt, 1968. 80–107.

Riffaterre, Michael. "The Self-Sufficient Text." *Diacritics* 3 (1973): 39–45.

Roberts, Peter. "On Tame High Finishers of Paltry Harmonies: A Blake Music Review and Checklist." *Blake Newsletter* 7 (1974): 91–99.

Robinson, Fred C. "Verb Tense in Blake's 'The Tyger.'" *PMLA* 79 (1964): 666–69.

Robinson, Henry Crabb. *On Books and Their Writers*. Ed. Edith J. Morley. 3 vols. London: Dent, 1938.

Rose, Edward J. "Blake's Human Insect: Symbol, Theory, and Design." *Texas Studies in Literature and Language* 10 (1968): 215–32.

———. "Blake's Metaphorical States." *Blake Studies* 4 (1971): 9–31.

Rosenblum, Robert. *Transformations in Late Eighteenth-Century Art*. Princeton: Princeton UP, 1967.

Rosenfeld, Alvin H., ed. *William Blake: Essays for S. Foster Damon*. Providence: Brown UP, 1969.

Rossetti, William Michael, ed. *The Poetical Works of William Blake, Lyrical and Miscellaneous*. London, 1874.

Roti, Grant C., and Donald L. Kent. "The Last Stanza of Blake's 'London.'" *Blake Newsletter* 11 (1977): 19–21.

Rumsby, R. L. "Trinities in 'The Tyger.'" *Cambridge Quarterly* 11 (1982): 316–28.

Salemi, Joseph S. "Emblematic Tradition in Blake's *The Gates of Paradise*." *Blake: An Illustrated Quarterly* 15 (1982): 108–24.

Sampson, John, ed. *The Lyrical Poems of William Blake*. Introd. Walter Raleigh. Oxford: Oxford UP, 1905.

———, ed. *The Poetical Works of William Blake*. Oxford: Clarendon, 1905.

Sánchez Pérez, Aquilino. *Blake's Graphic Work and the Emblem Tradition*. Murcia: U of Murcia, 1982.

Sanzo, Eileen. "Blake and the Great Mother Archetype." *Nassau Review* 3 (1978): 105–16.

Saurat, Denis. *Blake and Modern Thought*. New York: Dial, 1929.

Schorer, Mark. *William Blake: The Politics of Vision*. New York: Holt, 1946.

Schulz, Max. "Point of View in Blake's 'The Clod and the Pebble.' " *Papers in Language and Literature* 2 (1966): 217–24.

Shaviro, Steven. " 'Striving with Systems': Blake and the Politics of Difference." *Boundary 2* 10 (1982): 282–99.

Shepherd, R. H., ed. *Songs of Innocence and Experience*. London, 1866.

Showalter, Elaine. "Introduction: The Feminist Critical Revolution." *The New Feminist Criticism: Essays on Women, Literature, Theory*. Ed. Showalter. New York: Pantheon, 1985. 3–17.

———. "Women's Time, Women's Space: Writing the History of Feminist Criticism." *Tulsa Studies in Women's Literature* 3 (1984–85): 29–43.

Shrimpton, Nick. "Hell's Hymnbook: Blake's *Songs of Innocence and of Experience* and Their Models." *Literature of the Romantic Period, 1750–1850*. Ed. R. T. Davies and B. G. Beatty. English Texts and Studies. New York: Barnes, 1976. 19–35.

Siemens, Reynold. "Borders in Blake's 'The Little Girl Lost-Found.' " *Humanities Association Bulletin* 22 (1971): 35–43.

Simons, Joan O. "Teaching Symbolism in Poetry." *College English* 23 (1962): 301–02.

Simpson, David. "Blake's Pastoral: A Genesis for 'The Ecchoing Green.' " *Blake: An Illustrated Quarterly* 13 (1979–80): 116–38.

———. *Irony and Authority in Romantic Poetry*. Totowa: Rowman, 1979.

Singer, June K. *The Unholy Bible: A Psychological Interpretation of William Blake*. New York: Putnam's, 1970.

Sosnowski, T. Ford. "Meter and Form in Blake's 'The Lamb' and 'The Tyger.' " *Kwartalnik Neofilologiczny* 31 (1984): 407–16.

Stepto, Michael L. "Mothers and Fathers in Blake's *Songs of Innocence*." *Yale Review* 67 (1978): 357–70.

Stevenson, W. H., ed. *The Poems of William Blake*. Text ed. David V. Erdman. London: Longman, 1971. New York: Norton, 1972.

Stevenson, Warren. "Artful Irony in Blake's 'The Fly.' " *Texas Studies in Literature and Language* 10 (1968): 77–82.

———. " 'The Tyger' as Artefact." *Blake Studies* 2 (1970): 5–19.

Stone, Lawrence. *The Family, Sex, and Marriage in England: 1500–1800*. New York: Harper, 1977.

Storch, Margaret. "Blake and Women: Nature's Cruel Holiness." *American Imago* 38 (1981): 221–34.

Summerfield, Geoffrey. *Fantasy and Reason: Children's Literature in the Eighteenth Century*. Athens: U of Georgia P, 1984.

Sutherland, John. "Blake: A Crisis of Love and Jealousy." *PMLA* 87 (1972): 424–31.

Swinburne, A. C. *William Blake: A Critical Essay*. London, 1866.

Swingle, L. J. "Answers to Blake's 'Tyger': A Matter of Reason or of Choice?" *Concerning Poetry* 2 (1969): 61–71.

Tayler, Irene. "The Woman Scaly." *Midwestern Modern Language Association Bulletin* 6 (1973): 12–17.

Thompson, E. P. " 'London.' " Phillips, *Interpreting* 5–31.

——. *The Making of the English Working Class*. New York: Pantheon, 1964.

Thompson, J. B. "Blake's 'My Pretty Rose Tree'—An Interpretation." *Theoria* 24 (1965): 33–37.

Thrall, W. F., and Addison Hibbard. *A Handbook to Literature*. Rev. and enl. by C. H. Holman. New York: Odyssey, 1960.

Tillyard, E. M. W. *Poetry Direct and Oblique*. London: Chatto, 1934.

Todd, Ruthven, ed. *Blake: Selected Poetry*. New York: Dell, 1960.

——, ed. *Poems of William Blake*. London: Crown, 1949.

Tolley, Michael J. "Blake's Blind Man" and "Reply" [to Jean Hagstrum]. *Blake Studies* 2 (1969): 77–84, 86–88.

——. "Blake's Songs of Spring." Paley and Phillips 96–128.

——. "Remarks on 'The Tyger.' " *Blake Newsletter* 1 (1967): 10–13.

Trout, Henry. "A Reading of Blake's 'The Little Girl Lost' and 'The Little Girl Found.' " *West Virginia University Bulletin: Philological Papers* 23 (1977): 37–46.

Trumbach, Randolph. *The Rise of the Egalitarian Family: Aristocratic Kinship and Domestic Relations in Eighteenth-Century England*. New York: Academic, 1978.

Van Doren, Mark. *Introduction to Poetry*. New York: Columbia UP, 1951.

Viscomi, Joseph. *The Art of William Blake's Illuminated Prints*. Manchester: Manchester Etching Workshop, 1983.

——. "Recreating Blake's Illuminated Prints: The Facsimiles of the Manchester Etching Workshop." *Blake: An Illustrated Quarterly* 19 (1985): 4–23.

——. "The Workshop." *Studies in Romanticism* 21 (1982): 404–09.

Vogler, Thomas A., ed. *Blake and Criticism: A Conference at the University of California, Santa Cruz—20–22 May 1982*. Santa Cruz: Kresge Coll., U of California, 1982.

Vogler, Thomas A., and Nelson Hilton, eds. *Unnam'd Forms: Blake and Textuality*. Berkeley: U of California P, 1986.

Wagenknecht, David. *Blake's Night: William Blake and the Idea of Pastoral*. Cambridge: Harvard UP, 1973.

Walcutt, Charles Child, and J. E. Whitesell, eds. *The* Explicator *Cyclopedia*. Chicago: Quadrangle, 1968.

Ward, Aileen, ed. *Blake's Poems*. London: Limited Editions Club, 1973.

Wardle, Judith. " 'For Hatching Ripe': Blake and the Educational Uses of Emblem and Illustrated Literature." *Bulletin of Research in the Humanities* 81 (1978): 324–48.

———. "William Blake's Iconography of Joy: Angels, Birds, Butterflies and Related Motifs from *Poetical Sketches* to the Pickering Manuscript." *Blake Studies* 9 (1980): 5–44.

Warner, Janet. *Blake and the Language of Art.* Kingston: McGill-Queen's UP; Gloucester: Sutton, 1984.

Wasser, Henry H. "Notes on the *Visions of the Daughters of Albion* by William Blake." *Modern Language Quarterly* 9 (1948): 292–97.

Watson, J. R. *English Poetry of the Romantic Period, 1789–1830.* London: Longman, 1985.

Weathers, Winston. "The Construction of William Blake's 'The Tyger.' " *Style and Text.* Ed. Håkan Ringbom. Stockholm: Skriptor, 1975.

———, ed. *William Blake: "The Tyger."* Columbus: Merrill, 1969.

Webster, Brenda S. *Blake's Prophetic Psychology.* Athens: U of Georgia P, 1983.

Weiskel, Thomas. *The Romantic Sublime.* Baltimore: Johns Hopkins UP, 1976.

Welch, Dennis. "Blake's Response to Wollstonecraft's *Original Stories.*" *Blake: An Illustrated Quarterly* 13 (1979): 4–15.

Wellek, René. "A Letter [to F. R. Leavis]." *The Importance of Scrutiny.* Ed. Eric Bentley. New York: Stewart, 1948. 23–30.

Welsh, Andrew. *Roots of Lyric: Primitive Poetry and Modern Poetics.* Princeton: Princeton UP, 1978.

Wheeler, Charles B. *The Design of Poetry.* New York: Norton, 1966.

White, Helen C. *The Mysticism of William Blake.* Madison: U of Wisconsin P, 1927.

Whitehead, Fred. "William Blake and the Radical Tradition." *Weapons of Criticism: Marxism in America and the Literary Tradition.* Ed. Norman Rudich. Palo Alto: Ramparts, 1976. 217–36.

Wicksteed, Joseph H. *Blake's Innocence and Experience: A Study of the Songs and Manuscripts "Shewing the Two Contrary States of the Human Soul."* London: Dent; New York: Dutton, 1928. Rpt. Folcroft: Folcroft Library, 1973.

Wilkie, Brian. "Blake's *Innocence and Experience*: An Approach." *Blake Studies* 6 (1975): 119–37.

Wilkie, Brian, and James Hurt, eds. *Literature of the Western World.* 2 vols. New York: Macmillan, 1984.

Wilkinson, D. R. M. "Blake's *Songs*: Taking Stock, 1984." *English Studies* 66 (1985): 227–40.

Williams, Harry. "The Tyger and the Lamb." *Concerning Poetry* 5 (1972): 49–56.

Williams, Porter. " 'Duty' in Blake's 'The Chimney Sweeper' of *Songs of Innocence.*" *English Language Notes* 12 (1974): 92–96.

———. "The Influence of Mrs. Barbauld's *Hymns in Prose for Children* upon Blake's *Songs of Innocence and of Experience.*" *A Fair Day in the Affections: Literary*

    Essays in Honor of Robert B. White. Ed. Jack D. Durant and M. Thomas Hester. Raleigh: Winston, 1980. 131–46.

Williams, Raymond. *The Country and the City.* London: Chatto, 1976.

——. *Culture and Society 1780–1950.* New York: Oxford UP, 1958.

Wilner, Eleanor. *Gathering the Winds: Visionary Imagination and Radical Transformation of Self and Society.* Baltimore: Johns Hopkins UP, 1975.

Wilson, Mona. *The Life of William Blake.* 1927. Rev. ed. London: Hart-Davis, 1948. Rev. Geoffrey Keynes. Oxford: Oxford UP, 1971.

——. "The Twilight of the Augustans." *Empire Review* 45 (1927): 509–17.

Wimsatt, William K. "Genesis: An Argument Resumed." *The Disciplines of Criticism.* Ed. Peter Demetz et al. New Haven: Yale UP, 1968. 193–225.

——. *Hateful Contraries: Studies in Literature and Criticism.* Lexington: U of Kentucky P, 1965.

Witcutt, W. P. *Blake: A Psychological Study.* Port Washington: Kennikat, 1946.

Wittreich, Joseph Anthony, ed. *Nineteenth-Century Accounts of William Blake.* Gainesville: Scholars' Facsimiles and Reprints, 1970.

Wollstonecraft, Mary. *A Vindication of the Rights of Woman.* London, 1792.

Wright, John. "Blake's Relief-Etching Method." *Blake Newsletter* 9 (1976): 94–114.

——. "Toward Recovering Blake's Relief-Etching Process." *Blake Newsletter* 7 (1973): 32–39.

Yeats, William Butler, ed. *The Poems of William Blake.* London, 1893.

INDEX

Modern Language Association of America
Approaches to Teaching World Literature
Joseph Gibaldi, series editor

Achebe's Things Fall Apart. Ed. Bernth Lindfors. 1991.
Arthurian Tradition. Ed. Maureen Fries and Jeanie Watson. 1992.
Atwood's The Handmaid's Tale *and Other Works*. Ed. Sharon R. Wilson, Thomas B. Friedman, and Shannon Hengen. 1996.
Austen's Pride and Prejudice. Ed. Marcia McClintock Folsom. 1993.
Balzac's Old Goriot. Ed. Michal Peled Ginsburg. 2000.
Baudelaire's Flowers of Evil. Ed. Laurence M. Porter. 2000.
Beckett's Waiting for Godot. Ed. June Schlueter and Enoch Brater. 1991.
Beowulf. Ed. Jess B. Bessinger, Jr., and Robert F. Yeager. 1984.
Blake's Songs of Innocence and of Experience. Ed. Robert F. Gleckner and Mark L. Greenberg. 1989.
Boccaccio's Decameron. Ed. James H. McGregor. 2000.
British Women Poets of the Romantic Period. Ed. Stephen C. Behrendt and Harriet Kramer Linkin. 1997.
Brontë's Jane Eyre. Ed. Diane Long Hoeveler and Beth Lau. 1993.
Byron's Poetry. Ed. Frederick W. Shilstone. 1991.
Camus's The Plague. Ed. Steven G. Kellman. 1985.
Cather's My Ántonia. Ed. Susan J. Rosowski. 1989.
Cervantes' Don Quixote. Ed. Richard Bjornson. 1984.
Chaucer's Canterbury Tales. Ed. Joseph Gibaldi. 1980.
Chopin's The Awakening. Ed. Bernard Koloski. 1988.
Coleridge's Poetry and Prose. Ed. Richard E. Matlak. 1991.
Dante's Divine Comedy. Ed. Carole Slade. 1982.
Dickens' David Copperfield. Ed. Richard J. Dunn. 1984.
Dickinson's Poetry. Ed. Robin Riley Fast and Christine Mack Gordon. 1989.
Narrative of the Life of Frederick Douglass. Ed. James C. Hall. 1999.
Eliot's Middlemarch. Ed. Kathleen Blake. 1990.
Eliot's Poetry and Plays. Ed. Jewel Spears Brooker. 1988.
Ellison's Invisible Man. Ed. Susan Resneck Parr and Pancho Savery. 1989.
Faulkner's The Sound and the Fury. Ed. Stephen Hahn and Arthur F. Kinney. 1996.
Flaubert's Madame Bovary. Ed. Laurence M. Porter and Eugene F. Gray. 1995.
García Márquez's One Hundred Years of Solitude. Ed. María Elena de Valdés and Mario J. Valdés. 1990.
Goethe's Faust. Ed. Douglas J. McMillan. 1987.
Hebrew Bible as Literature in Translation. Ed. Barry N. Olshen and Yael S. Feldman. 1989.
Homer's Iliad *and* Odyssey. Ed. Kostas Myrsiades. 1987.
Ibsen's A Doll House. Ed. Yvonne Shafer. 1985.
Works of Samuel Johnson. Ed. David R. Anderson and Gwin J. Kolb. 1993.
Joyce's Ulysses. Ed. Kathleen McCormick and Erwin R. Steinberg. 1993.
Kafka's Short Fiction. Ed. Richard T. Gray. 1995.

Keats's Poetry. Ed. Walter H. Evert and Jack W. Rhodes. 1991.

Kingston's The Woman Warrior. Ed. Shirley Geok-lin Lim. 1991.

Lafayette's The Princess of Clèves. Ed. Faith E. Beasley and Katharine Ann
    Jensen. 1998.

Works of D. H. Lawrence. Ed. M. Elizabeth Sargent and Garry Watson. 2001.

Lessing's The Golden Notebook. Ed. Carey Kaplan and Ellen Cronan Rose. 1989.

Mann's Death in Venice *and Other Short Fiction*. Ed. Jeffrey B. Berlin. 1992.

Medieval English Drama. Ed. Richard K. Emmerson. 1990.

Melville's Moby-Dick. Ed. Martin Bickman. 1985.

Metaphysical Poets. Ed. Sidney Gottlieb. 1990.

Miller's Death of a Salesman. Ed. Matthew C. Roudané. 1995.

Milton's Paradise Lost. Ed. Galbraith M. Crump. 1986.

Molière's Tartuffe *and Other Plays*. Ed. James F. Gaines and
    Michael S. Koppisch. 1995.

Momaday's The Way to Rainy Mountain. Ed. Kenneth M. Roemer. 1988.

Montaigne's Essays. Ed. Patrick Henry. 1994.

Novels of Toni Morrison. Ed. Nellie Y. McKay and Kathryn Earle. 1997.

Murasaki Shikibu's The Tale of Genji. Ed. Edward Kamens. 1993.

Pope's Poetry. Ed. Wallace Jackson and R. Paul Yoder. 1993.

Shakespeare's King Lear. Ed. Robert H. Ray. 1986.

Shakespeare's Romeo and Juliet. Ed. Maurice Hunt. 2000.

Shakespeare's The Tempest *and Other Late Romances*. Ed. Maurice Hunt. 1992.

Shelley's Frankenstein. Ed. Stephen C. Behrendt. 1990.

Shelley's Poetry. Ed. Spencer Hall. 1990.

Shorter Elizabethan Poetry. Ed. Patrick Cheney and Anne Lake Prescott. 2000.

Sir Gawain and the Green Knight. Ed. Miriam Youngerman Miller and
    Jane Chance. 1986.

Spenser's Faerie Queene. Ed. David Lee Miller and Alexander Dunlop. 1994.

Stendhal's The Red and the Black. Ed. Dean de la Motte and Stirling Haig. 1999.

Sterne's Tristram Shandy. Ed. Melvyn New. 1989.

Stowe's Uncle Tom's Cabin. Ed. Elizabeth Ammons and Susan Belasco. 2000.

Swift's Gulliver's Travels. Ed. Edward J. Rielly. 1988.

Thoreau's Walden *and Other Works*. Ed. Richard J. Schneider. 1996.

Voltaire's Candide. Ed. Renée Waldinger. 1987.

Whitman's Leaves of Grass. Ed. Donald D. Kummings. 1990.

Woolf's To the Lighthouse. Ed. Beth Rigel Daugherty and Mary Beth Pringle. 2001.

Wordsworth's Poetry. Ed. Spencer Hall, with Jonathan Ramsey. 1986.

Wright's Native Son. Ed. James A. Miller. 1997.